# Assessing Policies for Retirement Income

## Needs for Data, Research, and Models

Constance F. Citro and Eric A. Hanushek, Editors

Panel on Retirement Income Modeling

Committee on National Statistics
Commission on Behavioral and Social Sciences and Education
National Research Council

NATIONAL ACADEMY PRESS
Washington, D.C.   1997

**NATIONAL ACADEMY PRESS • 2101 Constitution Avenue, NW • Washington, DC 20418**

NOTICE: The project that is the subject of this report was approved by the Governing Board of the National Research Council, whose members are drawn from the councils of the National Academy of Sciences, the National Academy of Engineering, and the Institute of Medicine. The members of the committee responsible for the report were chosen for their special competencies and with regard for appropriate balance.

This report has been reviewed by a group other than the authors according to procedures approved by a Report Review Committee consisting of members of the National Academy of Sciences, the National Academy of Engineering, and the Institute of Medicine.

The project that is the subject of this report is supported by funds from the Pension and Welfare Benefits Administration of the U.S. Department of Labor, the National Institute on Aging of the U.S. Department of Health and Human Services, the Pension Benefit Guaranty Corporation, the Social Security Administration, and TIAA-CREF.

**Library of Congress Cataloging-in-Publication Data**

Assessing policies for retirement income : needs for data, research,
    and models / Constance F. Citro and Eric A. Hanushek, editors ;
    Panel on Retirement Income Modeling, Committee on National
    Statistics, Commission on Behavioral and Social Sciences and
    Education, National Research Council.
       p.  cm.
    Includes bibliographical references and index.
    ISBN 0-309-05627-6
     1. Retirement income—Forecasting—Research—United States.
    2. Pensions—Forecasting—Research—United States. 3. Social
    security—Forecasting—Research—United States. 4. Insurance,
    Health—Forecasting—Research—United States. I. Citro, Constance
    F. (Constance Forbes), 1942- . II. Hanushek, Eric Alan, 1943- .
    III. National Research Council (U.S.). Panel on Retirement Income
    Modeling.
    HD7125.A78   1997
    331.25′2′072073—dc21
                                                96-51696
                                                CIP

Additional copies of this book are available from
National Academy Press
2101 Constitution Avenue, NW
Box 285
Washington, DC 20055
Call 800-624-6242 or 202-334-3313 (in the Washington Metropolitan Area).
http://www.nap.edu

Printed in the United States of America

# PANEL ON RETIREMENT INCOME MODELING

*v*

The National Academy of Sciences is a private, nonprofit, self-perpetuating society of distinguished scholars engaged in scientific and engineering research, dedicated to the furtherance of science and technology and to their use for the general welfare. Upon the authority of the charter granted to it by the Congress in 1863, the Academy has a mandate that requires it to advise the federal government on scientific and technical matters. Dr. Bruce Alberts is president of the National Academy of Sciences.

The National Academy of Engineering was established in 1964, under the charter of the National Academy of Sciences, as a parallel organization of outstanding engineers. It is autonomous in its administration and in the selection of its members, sharing with the National Academy of Sciences the responsibility for advising the federal government. The National Academy of Engineering also sponsors engineering programs aimed at meeting national needs, encourages education and research, and recognizes the superior achievements of engineers. Dr. William A. Wulf is interim president of the National Academy of Engineering.

The Institute of Medicine was established in 1970 by the National Academy of Sciences to secure the services of eminent members of appropriate professions in the examination of policy matters pertaining to the health of the public. The Institute acts under the responsibility given to the National Academy of Sciences by its congressional charter to be an adviser to the federal government and, upon its own initiative, to identify issues of medical care, research, and education. Dr. Kenneth I. Shine is president of the Institute of Medicine.

The National Research Council was organized by the National Academy of Sciences in 1916 to associate the broad community of science and technology with the Academy's purposes of furthering knowledge and advising the federal government. Functioning in accordance with general policies determined by the Academy, the Council has become the principal operating agency of both the National Academy of Sciences and the National Academy of Engineering in providing services to the government, the public, and the scientific and engineering communities. The Council is administered jointly by both Academies and the Institute of Medicine. Dr. Bruce Alberts and Dr. William A. Wulf are chairman and interim vice chairman, respectively, of the National Research Council.

# Contents

# Acknowledgments

At the outset, I wish to thank the members of the Panel on Retirement Income Modeling for their generous contributions of time and expert knowledge. Panel members took responsibility for summarizing the state of knowledge and identifying the needs for data, research, and modeling in particular subject areas. Several members also reviewed elements of existing retirement-income-related projection models. The members thought and worked hard to develop recommendations that would enhance the quality of data, research, and models and thereby the quality of national debate about retirement income security policy issues. The fruits of their labors will be evident in reading the report, but I feel it is necessary to go beyond that. This panel was unusual in the extraordinary knowledge, intelligence, and motivation it brought to our work. It has been a genuine pleasure to work with them.

At the same time, it is also evident that the best panel may not produce its best possible report unless it has the right study director. We did. Connie Citro, who has worked on many influential National Research Council reports, was the invaluable catalyst and driving force behind our work. She has the ability to decipher the real intent and conclusions of a panel when others see only chaotic discussion. She has the skill of keeping a panel directed toward producing results. And Job has nothing on her when it comes to dealing with the report review process. She is surely a model for what any chair would want in a study director.

The panel is greatly indebted to the people who presented and discussed papers at the panel's Conference on Modeling the Impact of Public and Private Policies on Retirement Behavior and Income: What Do We Know and What Do

We Need to Know? The six papers that were prepared for the conference represent comprehensive reviews of the literature in areas that are important to understand for retirement income policy analysis. They were subsequently revised on the basis of discussants' and panel members' comments and published in Hanushek and Maritato (1996; see Appendix A for contents). The panel also thanks Kevin Hollenbeck, W. E. Upjohn Institute for Employment Research, who prepared a background paper on existing retirement-income-related projection models, and Marilyn Moon, The Urban Institute, who prepared a background paper on factors in health care costs. Both were useful to the panel in its deliberations.

The panel thanks the staff of our sponsor agencies, the Pension and Welfare Benefits Administration in the U.S. Department of Labor, the National Institute on Aging in the U.S. Department of Health and Human Services, the Pension Benefit Guaranty Corporation, the Social Security Administration, and TIAA-CREF, for their help and guidance throughout the project. In particular, the panel is grateful to Richard Hinz and David McCarthy, Pension and Welfare Benefits Administration, and to Richard Suzman, National Institute on Aging. The panel also acknowledges the contributions of staff members of many federal agencies and private organizations who gave generously of their time to provide background information for the panel on data sources and models and to offer insightful comments at the panel's conference and other meetings.

The panel is grateful to Eugenia Grohman, Associate Director for Reports of the Commission on Behavioral and Social Sciences and Education (CBASSE), for her fine technical editorial work, which contributed greatly to the readability of this report.

Nancy Maritato, research associate with CBASSE, assisted the panel in some of its meetings and played an invaluable role in working with the authors to complete the volume of conference papers.

Candice Evans and Agnes Gaskin served ably as project assistants for the panel. Agnes made admirable logistical arrangements for the panel's first meeting and conference. Candice arranged the panel's third, fourth, and fifth meetings and coped cheerfully and competently with multiple rounds of revisions to this report, to the volume of conference papers, and to the panel's interim report (released in June 1995).

Overall, the panel was ably assisted in its endeavors at every stage of the process by many people, whom we are honored to thank.

Eric A. Hanushek, *Chair*
Panel on Retirement Income Modeling

# Assessing Policies for
# Retirement Income

# Executive Summary

When considering proposed legislation, government decision makers regularly call for estimates of the projected costs and other effects of current and alternative policies. The more complex and far-reaching a proposed change, the more needed are accurate estimates of its likely consequences but the more difficult it is to develop such estimates. The grueling debate in 1993-1994 over reforms to the nation's health care system was handicapped by highly uncertain estimates of the effects of alternative proposals.

Another major debate is pending over the retirement income security of older Americans and the costs to workers and the economy of providing that security. Questions such as the following are being raised: Can the U.S. Social Security system continue to provide an adequate level of benefits in view of demographic trends that imply a steadily increasing ratio of beneficiaries to contributors? With growing competitive pressures on employers to constrain employee compensation costs, will maintaining pension and retiree health care benefits (or extending them to uncovered workers) take lower priority than maintaining wages? Will most employees gain or lose from the increased opportunities to direct their own pension investments? Will income from personal savings and transfers from family members be adequate to help finance consumption in retirement and make up for any shortfalls in Social Security or employer benefits? Will the changing form of retirement benefits, particularly the increased use of lump-sum payouts at retirement that may not provide lifetime income, adversely affect certain groups of the elderly, such as widows? If more people decide to work to older ages in order to provide for their retirement, will jobs be available for them? Even if retirees have adequate incomes, will they still be secure if they are not adequately insured against rising costs of health care services?

The policy debate about retirement income security will likely consider a wide range of possible changes to the Social Security, Medicare, and Medicaid programs, as well as changes in tax provisions and regulations covering employer pensions and other forms of savings, such as Individual Retirement Accounts (IRAs). Anticipating the debate, the Pension and Welfare Benefits Administration in the U.S. Department of Labor asked the Committee on National Statistics to establish a Panel on Retirement Income Modeling. The National Institute on Aging, the Pension Benefit Guaranty Corporation, the Social Security Administration, and TIAA-CREF also provided support for the project. The panel was charged to answer the question: What do we need to know, and what kinds of models do we need to have, in order to estimate the short-run and long-run implications of current retirement-income-related policies and proposed changes to them?

## PRIMARY CONCLUSION:
## THE IMPORTANCE OF DATA AND RESEARCH

Assessing policy options requires the use of projection models, research, and data. Projection models, which take a variety of forms, are the tools that estimate the likely effects of current and alternative policies. They answer "what if" questions and project future outcomes by using data and research from a wide range of sources. Research findings, in turn, come from analytical models that seek to answer "why"—such as why people save or fail to save—and to estimate the strength of key relationships by applying theoretical constructs to empirical data. Data from panel surveys, which follow the same individuals over time, are particularly important to answer key research questions.

One impetus for the work of our panel was to give policy analysts working on retirement income security a head start on developing reliable broad-based projection models. The goal was to avoid the chaotic conditions of the 1993-1994 health care debate, in which policy modelers scrambled to keep up with the need for estimates and in which estimates developed by different models for the same proposal varied widely. On the basis of published reports and interviews with analysts, however, we determined that the problems with estimating the likely effects of proposed health care changes were due in only small part to the deficiencies of projection models as such: rather, models were significantly handicapped by the poor quality and lack of relevant data and behavioral research. For example, many proposals relied heavily on employer-based health insurance coverage, yet little information was available on employers' current health care costs or on their responses to changes in costs. Thus, it was hard to model the baseline situation, let alone develop widely shared estimates of employer behavior under alternative policy regimes.

As with health care, there are large gaps in needed data and research for retirement-income-related modeling, with regard both to individual behavior and the behavior of employers. It is critical that these data and knowledge gaps begin to be filled.

Generally speaking, it takes more time to collect new data and analyze them than it does to build a model to use data and research results. There are more than a few instances in the history of policy analysis when complex projection models were built in a span of weeks or months. It is rare that a critical unmet data or analysis need can be supplied in that short a time.

**We conclude that, given limited budget resources, the U.S. Department of Labor and other agencies should give priority to funding retirement-income-related data collection and behavioral research in preference to significant investments in large-scale projection models. It is particularly important for the federal government to take the lead in data collection, so that high-quality, comprehensive databases are available for policy analysis use in all sectors—government, private, and academic.**

## PRIMARY RECOMMENDATIONS

In keeping with our primary conclusion, our primary recommendations are for data and data-based analytical research. Much of the needed information about individual behavior can be obtained from continuing and analyzing existing panel surveys that are linked to selected administrative records. However, information with which to analyze the behavior of employers will require significant enhancement of existing databases and, possibly, new data collection as well. When relevant data and research insights are more complete, it will be important to develop improved large-scale models for projecting the likely effects of a variety of alternative policy proposals on employers, workers, and retirees. Until then, it makes little sense to allocate scarce resources for the development of complex new projection models, and we recommend against doing so. In the short term, agencies are best advised to address specific policy questions with limited, special-purpose projection models and the best available data and research findings.

### The Research Base

The long-run outcomes of retirement-income-related policies depend crucially on how workers and employers modify their behavior. For example, to understand the ramifications of pension simplification, one needs to understand the extent to which employers will set up new pension plans and the extent to which workers will elect to participate in them. One also needs answers to such questions as whether newly participating workers will save more or less on their own than they did previously and whether they will obtain retirement income from their pensions or take and use the benefits as lump sums.

Research is needed for retirement-income-related policy analysis in such areas as:

- factors that affect employers' demand for older workers and their decisions to adopt, modify, or terminate pension, disability, and retiree health care benefit plans;
- factors that affect people's decisions to consume or save and their choices of labor and leisure over the life cycle, including the decision to retire;
- the demographic processes of fertility, immigration, emigration, and particularly mortality, in order to project the numbers of people each year by age who form the population of potential workers or retirees at any given time;
- trends in marital status and family composition of older people, including interactions with trends in the form of retirement benefits (e.g., increased use of lump-sum payouts), and the implications for people's incomes; and
- trends in health status, health care costs, and health care financing arrangements of older people and the implications for income adequacy for other needs.

The knowledge base is deficient in many of these areas, largely due to deficiencies in data. In some instances, the data deficiencies have hampered the development of theory; in other instances, they have impeded the development of robust estimates of behavioral parameters. Data development and basic research need to go forward hand in hand.

## Data on Individuals

Fundamental understanding of the determinants of individual savings and consumption decisions is lacking. For example, there is considerable uncertainty about the reasons for the decline in personal savings rates over the past decade and for the wide disparity in savings levels across population groups. Thus, there is little basis on which to project the likely effects on savings decisions and, hence, on retirement income security, of changes in employer pensions and government policies.

Considerably more is known about labor supply and retirement behavior. However, the primary data source for analysis, the Retirement History Survey, is over 15 years out of date and does not provide adequate coverage of women in the work force.

New panel surveys sponsored by the National Institute on Aging, the Health and Retirement Survey (HRS) and its companion, Asset and Health Dynamics Among the Oldest Old (AHEAD) survey, are now beginning to provide appropriate longitudinal data for research on savings and for refinement of labor supply models—knowledge that is essential for the development of improved policy projection models. However, these surveys have not yet collected sufficient waves of data for analysis purposes; they must be continued.

Other panel surveys (e.g., the National Longitudinal Surveys of Labor Market Experience) can also support relevant analysis. They need to be continued and regularly reviewed, together with HRS and AHEAD, to determine ways to improve their usefulness for retirement-income-related research.

**Existing panel surveys of middle-aged and older people, particularly HRS and AHEAD, should receive continued government support. These surveys should be refreshed periodically with new cohorts in order to offer insight into how behavior changes over time.**

**Agencies and researchers involved in the major retirement-income-related panel surveys of individuals should collaborate regularly to identify ways to improve data quality and utility. The National Institute on Aging should facilitate such collaborative efforts.**

### Data on Employers

Important information on the characteristics and determinants of employer demand for older workers and employer benefit plan offerings is lacking, incomplete, or not provided in a usable manner. For example, no information is available on how many and what kinds of employers recently offered special incentive plans for early retirement—such as "window" plans—or intend to do so in the near future. Given the central role of employers in providing retirement income and health care benefits, the lack of an adequate database is a major handicap to evaluation of alternative policy proposals in these areas.

Collecting data for employers presents difficulties (e.g., low response rates) that can make it expensive to obtain high-quality results, but it is critical to do so. In order to make the best use of scarce resources, priority should be given to the development of creative ways to refine and extend existing data systems on employers, such as the Bureau of Labor Statistics Employee Benefits Survey, the Department of Labor Form 5500 data series, and the employer components of the HRS and AHEAD surveys. Consideration should also be given to the feasibility and cost-effectiveness of a panel survey (refreshed periodically) that collects detailed information on employers and their workers for behavioral analysis.

**The development of analytically useful databases on employers for retirement-income-related policy analysis and projection purposes should be an important government goal.**

**The U.S. Department of Labor should establish an interagency task force on employer data to specify an integrated data collection plan.**

**The employer data collection plan should include short-term and long-term goals for obtaining improved information on the distribution**

**across employers of benefit plan offerings (including pensions, health insurance, disability insurance, retiree health insurance, life insurance) and on labor demand for older workers and the factors that may affect that demand.**

### Expanded Use of Administrative Data

Some of the information that is essential for analysis of savings and retirement decisions and the effect of medical care use and expenditures on retirement income security is most cheaply and accurately obtained from existing administrative records. To be useful for estimation, this information (e.g., Social Security earnings histories, Medicare and Medicaid benefits) needs to be linked to the broad array of data for individuals that is available from such panel surveys as HRS and AHEAD. Similarly, linkage of employer survey data with administrative records could provide enhanced analysis and modeling capability at low marginal cost, although issues of confidentiality protection are more difficult for employer data.

**Matched files of survey responses and key administrative records should be regularly produced for retirement-income-related policy analysis and projection purposes. Agencies should vigorously explore creative solutions for providing research access to exact-match files that safeguard the confidentiality of individual responses.**

### Data Quality

Data collection efforts must include resources for evaluation of the quality of the information, both internally (e.g., by experimentation with alternate question wording) and in comparison with other data sources. For example, worker reports of pension and health care benefit coverage may differ from employer reports of such coverage, and the differences need to be understood in order to develop reliable analytical and projection models.

**Budgets for retirement-income-related surveys should include sufficient resources for regular evaluation of data quality.**

### Organizational Concerns

Responsibility for major retirement-income-related policy levers (e.g., employer pension regulation, Social Security, tax policy, health care programs) is spread among several agencies in different departments. Relevant data collection and research are also spread across these agencies and others. There are benefits of having many players involved in this complex policy area. However, in our observation, not enough attention has been given to the need for interagency coordination to identify data gaps and overlaps and to help establish priorities in light of resource constraints. We earlier recommended an interagency employer data collection task force and collaborative efforts to coordinate retirement-related panel surveys of individuals. Such efforts could usefully relate to the Interagency Forum on Aging-Related Statistics. Coordination mechanisms should recognize the need for flexibility and experimentation and not impose added bureaucratic requirements.

**Relevant agencies should establish coordination mechanisms to help improve the quality and utility of retirement-income-related data, reduce unnecessary duplication of effort, and identify priorities.**

Finally, closer collaboration between government agencies, private sector analysts and the academic research community is needed to spur advances in retirement-income-related knowledge and data that can support the development of improved projection models. Large numbers of researchers from several disciplines have worked effectively with agency people on the design, content, and analysis of the HRS and AHEAD surveys. This model should be extended to employer data collection systems, which should involve private sector representatives as well. Closer collaboration expands the community of people who can contribute to cost-effective, policy-relevant data collection and analytical research and to the development of projection models that appropriately use data and research results.

## GOALS FOR PROJECTION MODELS

Although data and research are the most important short-term priorities for government agencies that work on retirement income, it is important not to lose sight of the longer term need to use those data and research findings in projection models. Projection models are needed that can estimate the overall costs and other effects of specific policy options. More comprehensive models are also needed that can estimate such effects as:

- interactions among policies, such as how changes in Social Security or Medicare may affect coverage and benefits of employer pension plans and health insurance for retirees;
- heterogeneity or variability among workers, employers, and retirees—such as how a proposal may affect people of different income levels or couples in comparison with single people, and how fluctuations in markets and interest rates may produce winners and losers for retirement income from personal savings and pensions invested in IRA-type accounts; and
- long-term effects, such as the extent to which changes in the tax treatment of employee or employer contributions to pension plans may alter the behavior of

younger workers and employers, even if there is little immediate effect on people near retirement.

All of these needs pose formidable challenges. There is also the challenge of estimating the extent of uncertainty in model projections. Policy simulations are subject to errors and variability in data and research inputs and errors in model specifications. The longer the time period, the more complex a proposed policy change, and the more interactions it has with other policies and behaviors, the wider the margins of error are likely to be. Estimating the uncertainty of projections (even if very crudely) and conveying those estimates to decision makers is essential to informing the policy process.

Two important long-term goals for projection model development are the following:

• To develop employer-based models (using cell-based or microsimulation techniques) that can project the likely future distribution of benefit plan offerings and the demand for older workers. Such models are needed to answer questions about employer responses to policy changes and to interact with individual-level models to determine the consequences of employer decisions for workers and retirees. No such models currently exist.

• To develop a new large-scale individual-level microsimulation model to project the distributional effects of a range of policy proposals within a consistent framework. Existing models do not provide an adequate structure or database on which to build an improved model, although some of their components could contribute to such a model. Important capabilities for a new model are to estimate dynamically the effects of policy changes on individual behavior, to interact with employer-based models of worker demand and benefit offerings and with macro models of the economy, and to simulate random and cyclical shocks to employment and savings from such forces as market ups and downs. Considerable thought will be required to determine potentially useful approaches to implementing these capabilities—for example, how best to capture the heterogeneity of employer and worker behavior in linkages between individual and employer-based models.

These two goals should be kept in mind when determining priorities for data and research; however, no significant investments in development of large-scale projection models should be made until there is better understanding of key behaviors and better data with which to project trends in those behaviors and other factors.

Of course, the Department of Labor and other agencies cannot put off requests for analysis of retirement-income-related policy proposals because development of new large-scale models is being deferred. To respond to policy makers' legitimate information demands, agencies should use limited, special-purpose models together with the best available data and research findings to answer particular questions. Depending on the issue, a special-purpose model may already exist, or, more likely, it will be necessary to modify another model or construct a model on the spot. Agencies should seek opportunities for cost-effective improvements to special-purpose models and to make them known and available. Such models may not provide very accurate estimates. However, trying to develop complex new individual-level microsimulation or employer models in advance of improvements in data and research has little prospect of producing better results and will likely represent a misuse of scarce resources.

> **Relevant agencies should consider the development of employer models and a new integrated individual-level microsimulation model for retirement-income-related policy analysis as important long-term goals. Construction of such models would be premature until better data, research knowledge, and computational methods are available.**
>
> **To respond to immediate policy needs, agencies should use limited, special-purpose models with the best available data and research findings to answer specific policy questions.**

For the full text of these recommendations and for additional recommendations and suggestions on specific points, see Chapter 3 (research), Chapter 4 (data), Chapter 5 (projection models), and Chapter 6 (furthering collaborative arrangements among agencies and with the private sector and academia for data, research, and model development).

# 1

# Introduction

Many government policies and programs that affect the economic well-being of Americans are under scrutiny to assess their costs and benefits. In 1993-1994, the key public debate was on how to provide health care at a reasonable cost; in 1995-1996, the debate focused on the costs and benefits of federal and state programs to aid the poor. Although one cannot forecast with certainty what the next key public issues will be, it seems very likely that one of the major debates will be about the income security of current and future generations of retirees and the costs to workers and the economy to attain that security. Significant demographic changes—the aging of the baby boom generation and the relatively small size of the subsequent baby bust generation—coupled with fiscal pressures on the federal government are two factors that are raising concerns about the prospects for the U.S. Social Security system. Just as important are concerns about employer pensions and other benefits, personal savings rates, and the adequacy of retirement income in the face of rising health care costs.

As policy makers wrestle with the issues, they will need estimates or projections of the likely costs and other effects of continuing current retirement-income-related policies in comparison with one or more alternative policies. Anticipating these needs, the Pension and Welfare Benefits Administration (PWBA) in the U.S. Department of Labor asked the Committee on National Statistics at the National Research Council to establish a Panel on Retirement Income Modeling. The National Institute on Aging, Pension Benefit Guaranty Corporation, Social Security Administration, and TIAA-CREF also provided support for the project. The charge to the panel was to recommend improvements to retirement-income-related research, data, and models that analysts can use to help answer decision makers' questions and inform the policy debate.

Without reasonably good estimates from models of the short-run and long-run implications of current policies and alternatives to them, decision makers run the risk that the proposals they adopt may be ineffective or, worse, counterproductive. Yet the task of developing reliable estimates is far from easy, and it becomes even more challenging as any proposed set of policy changes becomes more complex and far reaching.

The experience of health care reform underscores the problems for decision making when estimates of the effects of alternative policy proposals are highly uncertain. During the course of the 1993-1994 debate, different projection models produced widely differing estimates of the effects of the same health care reform plan, and those estimates were often hard to reconcile. The lack of agreed-upon estimates was not the reason for the failure of Congress to enact any of the reform proposals, but it undoubtedly made the deliberative process more difficult (see Mann and Ornstein, 1995:Chs. 4,7,8).

Much of the uncertainty in the estimates of alternative health care reform proposals was because there was simply no experience with key provisions of the Clinton administration and other plans. Analysts could only guess at the likely effects of such changes as establishing statewide health insurance purchasing cooperatives or requiring employers to provide health insurance for their workers. Yet investments in relevant data and associated research and modeling efforts prior to 1993 could likely have reduced some of the uncertainty and, more generally, provided an improved capability for answering decision makers' questions. In particular, it appears that the lack of needed data and behavioral research handicapped the effort to develop useful models for health care policy projections (see Bilheimer and Reischauer, 1996).

In seeking advice about retirement-income-related data, research, and models, PWBA sought to learn from the health care reform experience. PWBA asked our panel to identify investments in research, data, and models that would better prepare analysts to respond to decision makers' likely information needs about retirement income.

## RETIREMENT INCOME SECURITY

To adequately assess the economic well-being of older Americans, it is important to consider all sources of income and wealth and the risks facing each source, as well as the overall risks to income security posed by increasing health care costs. It is also important to assess the associated costs—to workers, their families, and the economy—of policies that are designed to further retirees' well-being. A broader interpretation of retirement income security could include such issues as whether there are adequate labor market opportunities for retirement-age people who want to work on a full-time or part-time basis and whether there are adequate training and rehabilitation facilities for disabled older people.

Sources of retirement income include Social Security, employer-provided pensions, other transfer programs (e.g., public assistance, public and private disability payments, and workers' compensation), personal savings, inheritances and other transfers among family members, and post-retirement earnings (e.g., from part-time work). A major potential drain on retirement income is expenditures necessary to maintain or restore health; these costs, if they continue to grow as in the past, may significantly undercut the adequacy of income for other needs.

Public policies in many areas affect one or more components of retirement income security, both directly and indirectly through their effects on employer and employee behavior and on the general level of economic activity. These policy areas include:

- the Social Security system—both provisions of the payroll tax and the benefit structure, including retiree, survivor, and disability benefits;
- the federal personal and corporate income tax code—provisions that affect employer-provided pensions and health care benefits, such other forms of saving as housing and Individual Retirement Accounts (IRAs), and bequests;
- the Medicare and Medicaid systems and public assistance programs, such as Supplemental Security Income (SSI) for the poor elderly and disabled;
- government regulations that affect employer work force practices, such as laws prohibiting age discrimination in hiring and mandatory retirement and the Americans with Disabilities Act, and those that affect pension benefits, such as the Employee Retirement Income Security Act (ERISA);
- government agency (and employer) efforts to educate workers about their pension benefits and investment options; and
- overall macroeconomic policies that affect inflation, employment, and real wage growth, which, in turn, have major implications for retirement income security.

Many separate agencies are responsible for each of these policy areas: the U.S. Department of the Treasury; the Health Care Financing Administration in the U.S. Department of Health and Human Services (HHS); the Pension and Welfare Benefits Administration in the U.S. Department of Labor (DOL); the Pension Benefit Guaranty Corporation; and the Social Security Administration. In addition, other agencies are involved in retirement-income-related data collection and research: the Agency for Health Care Policy and Research, National Center for Health Statistics, and National Institute on Aging in HHS; the Bureau of Labor Statistics in DOL; the Bureau of the Census in the U.S. Department of Commerce; and the National Science Foundation.

The debate over retirement income security in the next few years will likely consider changes to many of the policies listed above. Areas of particular interest will be employer pension regulation, tax incentives for personal savings, and Social Security; health care policy will also be of continuing concern. Decision makers will likely want estimates for a wide range of questions about proposed changes in these areas, as illustrated below.

***Employer Pension Regulation*** There has been growing interest in pension simplification. Recent legislation simplified pension regulations for small businesses to encourage them to offer certain types of pension plans. In 1993, almost two-fifths of private full-time workers were employed by businesses with fewer than 100 full-time employees, and fewer than one-fourth of these workers participated in pension plans (Pension and Welfare Benefits Administration, 1994:Table B9). To evaluate the effects on retirement income security of the new legislation—and of future laws or rules to simplify pensions—one would like estimates of the number and proportion of small businesses that will respond by setting up particular types of plans; the number of workers in those businesses who will participate; and the amount of contributions, in dollar terms and as a proportion of earnings, that employers and workers will make. One would also like answers to such questions as: Will low-wage workers participate to the same extent as higher wage workers? Single workers as much as workers with dependents? Small businesses in certain industries as much as small businesses in other industries? Will there be any short- or long-term effects on total employment in small businesses? What will be the effects on workers' pension coverage during their working careers and on the income they receive in retirement?

***Tax Incentives for Personal Savings*** Proposals are often floated to induce more people to set up and contribute to IRAs. Recent legislation increased the limit on IRA contributions for spouses who do not earn income. Other proposals are to allow higher income people to defer taxes on contributions to IRAs and to allow IRA holders to use their funds for such purposes as medical care or college tuition, in addition to retirement. Important questions about such proposals include: Will they encourage an increase in total personal savings, or will people simply put money into their IRAs that they would have saved in other forms? Will people who are not now saving set up IRAs, or will most new accounts be set up by people who are already saving significant amounts in other ways? Will the amounts put into IRAs be available for retirement or will people spend them earlier? What will be the revenue losses (or gains) to the government of tax deferrals on IRA contributions or earnings?

***Social Security Reform*** Included in some proposals to resolve the Social Security financing problem for the long term is "privatization" of part or all of the old-age, survivors, and disability insurance contributions (some members of the Social Security Advisory Council recommended partial privatization; see Quinn and Mitchell, 1996). In this approach, all or a fraction of the current payroll tax contribution would be put into an individual retirement account for each worker. Key questions about privatization include: What are the implications for equity of Social Security taxes and benefits across generations? How can or will the social insurance components of the current system be funded (the provisions to support disabled workers and dependents of deceased workers and to provide disproportionately more benefits to workers with low contributions due to low earnings or interrupted work careers)? How will individual accounts be adminis- tered? What will be the administrative costs of such a system in comparison with the current system? What regulations will be needed to protect workers' invest- ments (particularly for proposals that allow worker choice)? How will the avail- ability of indexed Treasury bonds as an investment option affect the return on and security of workers' accounts? What restrictions, if any, will be placed on the use of workers' accounts when reaching retirement age, such as requiring single or joint life annuitization, possibly indexed for inflation? What will be the effects of those restrictions? How can a transition be made between the current and the new systems? What effects will there be on employer pension plan coverage and benefits, which, in many instances, are linked to Social Security provisions? What effects will there be on capital markets, and what will be the consequences for workers' retirement income security, overall and for workers with different characteristics?

## THE REPORT

The above examples illustrate the breadth and depth of questions that need to be addressed if choices among retirement-income-related policy options are to be made on an informed basis. The challenges of developing reliable estimates to respond to these and other questions about the likely effects of alternative poli- cies are major, and not all, or even many, of the questions may be answerable with currently available or foreseeable data and analysis. The purpose of our report is to identify improvements in data, research, and modeling that can better enable analysts to respond to decision makers' questions and information needs and that can reduce the uncertainty that is inevitable in projections.

Chapter 2 provides a framework for retirement income modeling. It briefly reviews concerns that have prompted increasing attention to policy issues in this area, policy options that are likely to be considered, outcomes on which to evalu- ate various options, and challenges to developing reliable projections of out- comes.

Chapter 3 summarizes the state of basic research knowledge in key areas, including employers' decisions about pension and health care benefits and their demand for older workers, people's choices about savings, consumption, and retirement, and factors that affect the size and composition of the older popula- tion and the health care needs and costs of older people. Drawing heavily on a set of commissioned papers in Hanushek and Maritato (1996; see Appendix A), the chapter identifies key questions that have not been satisfactorily addressed and lists priority topics for research and behavioral modeling.

Chapter 4 recommends improvements in data sources that are essential to understand key behaviors and to develop good projection models to answer policy makers' questions. Indeed, we argue that, in light of limited resources, agencies must give priority to investments in data and analytical research. Chapter 5 offers a vision for improved policy projection capabilities when better data and research knowledge become available.

Finally, Chapter 6 recommends ways to facilitate interagency coordination and the involvement of the private sector and academia in retirement-income-related data collection, research, and modeling. Appendices provide information on relevant data sets and projection models and on some of the problems with available models.

An important distinction that we make throughout the report is between *analytical* or *behavioral* models (which are the focus of Chapter 3) and *projection* models (which are the focus of Chapter 5). Very roughly, analytical models are research tools, and projection models are policy tools. Analytical models are intended to answer "why" and to determine the strength of key relationships. As an example, we include in the analytical category models that are used to estimate the probabilities of specific behavioral responses (e.g., increased savings, decreased work effort, increased employer contributions to benefit plans) as a function of characteristics of the individual or the employer, policy features, and other factors (e.g., interest rates). Projection models are intended to answer "what if" questions and to project future outcomes. We include in the projection category models that are used to estimate the likely costs and other effects over time of current and alternative policies. Projection models may use a variety of information, including estimated behavioral probabilities from analytical models. Both kinds of models are important to develop for retirement-income-related policy analysis purposes.

Analytical and projection models vary in scope, complexity, and modeling strategy, and, consequently, in their costs and benefits. For example, microsimulation is an approach to projection modeling that operates at the individual decision unit level. Microsimulation models can provide detailed information about the likely effects of policies for particular kinds of people or employers, but they have heavy data requirements and can be difficult to implement and understand. Other kinds of projection models, such as time-series models, cell-based models (e.g., population projection models), macroeconomic models, and computable general equilibrium models, have their own advantages and drawbacks. The same is true of different types of analytical models, such as reduced-form models and static and dynamic structural models.

To the extent possible, we endeavor to consider cost-benefit tradeoffs in our recommendations for models, data, and research. Decision makers need good policy analysis and projection capabilities, but resource constraints dictate that priorities be set and choices be made.

Finally, we consider decision makers to be not only officials of the federal government who are concerned with pension regulation, taxation, Social Security, and other relevant programs, but also federal, state, and local officials and private-sector executives in their capacity as employers. Pensions and other benefits and, more generally, hiring and compensation practices, are important factors in both retirement income security and employer costs. Improved data, research knowledge, and analytical and projection models can help employers, as well as policy makers, make more informed decisions.

# 2

# Considerations in
# Retirement Income Projections

## THE CONCERN FOR INCOME SECURITY

Historical data on economic well-being for retirees and their families show marked improvements over the post-World War II period. Yet more recent data and projections suggest that the average retiree in future years may face bleaker economic circumstances than the average retiree today. The data also suggest that disparities in income and wealth may widen, not lessen, among the elderly population.

The available data and indicators often pose difficult problems of interpretation. For example, there is considerable debate about the meaning of the recent leveling off in rates of pension coverage of the work force and, indeed, about the definition of "coverage;" see Box 2-1. There are also many areas of uncertainty, such as whether the marked postwar trend toward early retirement has ended and whether the recent cost reductions in health care achieved by the spread of managed care will prove long lasting or only temporary. Nonetheless, the weight of the evidence supports the conclusion that, with the aging of the population, it will be more difficult to sustain current levels of retirement income security at acceptable costs, and, consequently, that retirement-income-related policies will be the subject of increasing scrutiny and public debate.

### Current Status

On average, retired people and their families today enjoy a reasonable level of

---

**BOX 2-1**
**PENSION COVERAGE: DEFINITIONS AND TRENDS**

Trends in pension coverage can be difficult to interpret without clear definitions of terms. Pension "coverage" sometimes means that a worker's employer offers a pension plan and sometimes that the worker is participating in a plan; the Pension and Welfare Benefits Administration (PWBA) uses the latter definition in its reports. In contrast, the Employee Benefit Research Institute (EBRI) uses the following terminology for pensions, which we follow:

*Sponsorship*  Employer sponsors a plan for some or all workers
*Participation*  Worker participates in a plan
*Vesting*  Worker is entitled to receive some benefits from a plan at retirement age even if he or she has left the plan

The number of civilian workers aged 16 and over (including self-employed people) whose employers sponsor pension plans has increased over the period 1979-1993, although the sponsorship rate has remained flat at about 56-57 percent.

The participation rate for civilian workers aged 16 and over has remained flat at about 42-46 percent over the period 1979-1993; the participation rate among workers whose employers sponsor a pension plan has decreased from 81 to 76 percent.

The vesting rate for civilian workers aged 16 and over has increased from 24 to 38 percent over the period 1979-1993; the vesting rate among plan participants has increased from 52 to 86 percent.

Sponsorship of pension plans differs significantly by type of employer (self-employed, government, private wage and salary) and by employer size, so that trends in sponsorship rates may be affected by changes in the mix of employer types and sizes.

Both sponsorship and participation rates are significantly lower for new employees (less than 1 year on the job), part-time employees, and employees younger than age 21, so that changes in these characteristics of the labor force can affect trends.

(SOURCE: Data from Employee Benefit Research Institute, 1994:Tables 11, 12.)

---

economic security in the United States, particularly in comparison with earlier generations (although some elderly groups are much less secure). In 1959 the measured poverty rate for people aged 65 and older was 35.2 percent, well above the rate of 22.4 percent for the total population; in 1995 the poverty rate for the elderly was just 10.5 percent, below the rate of 13.8 percent for the total population (Bureau of the Census, 1996:Tables C-1, C-2).[1]

The expansion of the U.S. Social Security system, initially established some 60 years ago, played a major role in improving the economic circumstances of retired workers and their families. The system currently covers an estimated 96 percent of all jobs in the United States. From 1940 (when benefits were first paid) to 1972, Congress has increased benefit levels on 10 occasions, although recent legislative changes have curtailed benefits in several ways. Since 1975, benefits have been indexed annually for inflation.

Over the post-World War II period, U.S. workers also benefited from provisions of the federal income tax code that encouraged the expansion of employer-sponsored pension plans. In 1993, 47 percent of private nonagricultural wage and salary workers participated in a plan, up from 15 percent in 1940 (Employee Benefit Research Institute, 1994:Tables 9, 11). Most older people also have income from their own savings (although the amounts are usually small) or from other sources, including earnings from part-time and other jobs.

However, not all of today's retirees are in comfortable economic circumstances: 10.5 percent are poor and another 15 percent are categorized as near poor (with incomes between 100% and 150% of the poverty line). Among the poorest groups are elderly women not living with family members (including widows and others), with a poverty rate of 24 percent, and elderly blacks and Hispanics, with poverty rates of 25 percent and 24 percent, respectively (1995 data; Bureau of the Census, 1996:Table 2).

## Future Prospects

Looking to the future, there is concern that the economic situation of future retirees and their families will not improve, and may worsen, and that disparities in income and wealth levels among the elderly may widen. There are several factors that contribute to the concern, including trends in Social Security costs, employer pensions, personal savings, health care costs, and other demographic and socioeconomic factors. However, other factors, such as increased efforts by

---

[1]While the poverty rate is a useful measure of income adequacy, the arbitrariness of the poverty line should be acknowledged, and the official poverty measure is flawed in many respects. Implementing the recommendations of a National Research Council panel for an improved measure would somewhat alter the picture of who is poor. However, the elderly poverty rate would not differ markedly today from the total population rate (1 or 2 percentage points higher or lower depending on how the measure is altered), and the conclusion that the poverty rate fell disproportionately for the elderly over time would almost certainly not change (see Betson, Citro, and Michael, 1997; Citro and Michael, 1995).

employers and the government to educate workers about the need to save for retirement, may have countervailing effects.[2]

*Social Security*   The current level of Social Security benefits cannot be sustained indefinitely at the current tax rates.  One reason, which has been widely reported in the media, is the demographic transition:  because of the aging of the baby boom generation and the relatively small size of the baby bust generation, there will eventually be too few workers relative to the number of retirees to provide the needed level of contributions.  The 1996 annual report of the Old-Age, Survivors, and Disability Insurance (OASDI) trustees projects that the old-age and survivors insurance trust fund will start running a deficit by the year 2015 and will be increasingly unbalanced through the rest of the 75-year projection period (to 2070).  The disability insurance trust fund is projected to run a deficit as early as 2003, while the Medicare hospital insurance trust fund has already begun to run a deficit and is expected to be exhausted by 2001.

These figures are based on the "intermediate" projections of the Social Security actuary (Board of Trustees [OASDI], 1996:Table II.F13; see Board of Trustees [HI], 1996:Table II.D2 for Medicare).  The high-cost (pessimistic) projection shows the old-age and survivors insurance trust fund running a deficit as early as the year 2000 and markedly out of balance thereafter.  The low-cost (optimistic) scenario shows the trust fund only modestly out of balance for the period 2020-2070.

The expected Social Security trust fund imbalance must be corrected by some means, which could include reductions in benefits, increases in payroll tax rates, or both.  The problems with the Social Security system are particularly important because of pressures on other sources of retirement income and because a significant fraction of the elderly rely almost entirely on Social Security benefits for retirement income.  In 1992, 14 percent of Social Security beneficiaries aged 65 and older had no income from other sources, and another 21 percent had other income of less than $2,000 (U.S. House of Representatives, 1994:Table A-9).

*Pension Coverage*   Trends in employer-sponsored pensions are mixed.  The number of civilian workers aged 16 and over who report that they participated in an employer-sponsored pension plan increased from 53 million in 1979 to 67 million in 1993.  However, the *percentage* of all workers aged 16 and over who participated in a pension plan remained about the same over this period:  46 percent in 1979 and 44 percent in 1993, indicating that the expansion of em-

---

[2]Recent data indicate that education efforts by employers offering defined contribution pension plans can pay off in terms of the proportion of employees who choose to participate and the level of their contributions (Employee Benefit Research Institute, 1996b).

ployer-sponsored pension coverage in the post-World War II
reached a plateau (Employee Benefit Research Institute, 1994:Ta
Pension and Welfare Benefits Administration, 1994:Tables B16
positive side, the percentage of workers who were *vested* in a plar
entitled to receive benefits increased from 24 percent in 1979 to
1993. (The vesting rate increased more rapidly for women than men.)

Pension plan participation among workers is in large part a function of how many of them work for employers that sponsor plans. The sponsorship rate for civilian workers aged 16 and over has also leveled off (it was 56% in 1979 and 57% in 1993), due to such factors as the shift of employment from manufacturing to service companies, which are less likely to offer pension plans, and the declining influence of labor unions. In addition, the standards for pensions to qualify for favorable tax treatment may have led some companies to discontinue or scale back their plans, although recent legislation to simplify pension regulation may encourage more small companies to offer plans.

Pension plan participation is also affected by a plan's coverage provisions. The growth of part-time and temporary employment reduces participation because such workers often are not eligible to participate. Finally, participation for eligible workers is elective in some plans. Younger workers have shown a declining participation rate in recent years, which is partly due to the increasing propensity of employers to offer elective 401(k) plans that require employee contributions: younger workers are less likely than older workers to participate in such plans. Yet the fact that older workers have historically participated in pension plans at higher rates than younger workers suggests that participation rates will increase for today's younger workers as they age.[3]

In sum, the picture is mixed. However, should the flat pattern of sponsorship and participation rates continue, there will remain a significant number of workers who are not covered by employer pensions, which will only be partly reduced by a continued increase in the vesting rate.

***Types of Pension Plans*** Trends in the types of pensions offered to employees have raised questions about the likely contributions of employer pensions to retirement income security. There are two major categories of plans, each with many variants: defined benefit plans, which guarantee a specific retirement benefit, and defined contribution plans (401(k) plans, profit-sharing plans, and others), which provide for contributions by the employee, employer, or both, but do not guarantee a specific benefit. The number of defined contribution plans has grown from 67 percent of total plans in 1975 to 87 percent in 1992. Because many such plans are offered as a supplement to a defined benefit plan and be-

---

[3]Participation rates peak between ages 40 and 60 (60% in 1993), after which they fall, presumably because employees with vested benefits retire earlier.

_ause defined contribution plans are more prevalent among small employers, defined benefit plans are still the primary plan for the majority of active participants. However, the proportion of participants with a primary defined contribution plan is growing (Employee Benefit Research Institute, 1994:Table 14 and unpublished tables).[4]

There are arguments that the growing popularity of defined contribution plans is increasing the risks to retirement income security. However, much of the growth in defined contribution plans is among workers in small companies who would otherwise have no pension coverage at all (see Silverman, 1993). Moreover, it is not clear which type of plan ultimately provides more security. The benefits from defined contribution plans may be less predictable because of the greater flexibility that many such plans offer workers (e.g., to determine the level of contributions, to allocate contributions among investment vehicles, to make withdrawals for preretirement consumption, etc.), because workers who change jobs may spend their lump-sum distributions before retirement, and because market fluctuations may adversely affect workers' investment returns.

Yet workers covered by defined benefit plans face risks as well, even though their employers (backed up the Pension Benefit Guaranty Corporation) bear the risks from such factors as market downturns. For example, workers may not work long enough to be vested (vesting periods are typically longer for defined benefit than for defined contribution plans), and workers who are laid off in mid-career may receive significantly lower benefits because such plans typically link benefits to years of service and highest years of earnings (see Samwick and Skinner, 1993).[5] Also, because defined benefit plans increasingly offer partial lump-sum payment options, the risks that benefits will not last a lifetime may be increasing for the recipients (and their survivors) of these plans as well as the recipients of defined contribution plans. Indeed, what can perhaps be concluded is that the trend is toward greater flexibility of pension plan provisions generally. This trend may be beneficial (or not detrimental) to retirement income security in the aggregate, but it increases the likelihood of greater disparities in ultimate levels of retirement income.

---

[4]These figures are based on administrative data. In contrast, survey data suggest that defined contribution plans are already the primary plan for the majority of workers (Pension and Welfare Benefits Administration, 1994:Tables B13-B14).

[5]Moreover, workers who were vested in a defined benefit plan in a previous job may not be aware that they can apply for benefits (although there is a system of notification by the Social Security Administration). In general, the percentage of retirees who report that they receive benefits is smaller than the percentage of people nearing retirement who report that they participate in a plan. Reasons for the discrepancy may include survey reporting errors, failure to apply, failure to be vested, using lump-sum distributions for other purposes, etc. (Pension and Welfare Benefits Administration, 1995b:12).

*Personal Savings* It appears unlikely that personal savings will make up for any shortfalls that occur in Social Security and employer pension benefits. Survey data indicate that many people are approaching retirement with virtually no personal savings of any kind (except, perhaps, a home). For example, among people aged 51-61 in 1992, 25 percent of couples had less than $13,000 in financial assets (e.g., stocks, bonds, savings accounts), 25 percent of single men had less than $1,000 in financial assets, and 25 percent of single women had no financial assets. Adding the value of home equity, 25 percent of couples, single men, and single women aged 51-61 had, respectively, less than $56,000, less than $4,000, and less than $1,200 in such assets (Gustman and Juster, 1996:Table 2-A1). Aggravating the situation is that people with low asset levels are less likely to have employer pension benefits than are people with higher asset levels (Gustman and Juster, 1996:Table 2-5).

In fact, understanding people's motives for saving and why so many people save so little may be one of the key questions for policy makers, given that such motives influence not only personal savings but also elective pension plan contributions. Policy alternatives are likely to differ according to the reasons for lack of saving, such as an inability to save due to low earnings or to not understanding the levels of saving that are needed to maintain a comparable life-style in retirement. (In all likelihood, reasons differ across groups of the population.)

*Health Care Costs* Despite efforts to control rising health care costs, it is likely that they will continue to grow faster than incomes for the foreseeable future. Although virtually all elderly people have Medicare coverage and many of them have supplementary private insurance coverage or Medicaid coverage, they incur significantly higher out-of-pocket costs for medical care on average than younger people. In 1987 (the most recent data available), 89 percent of people aged 65 or older incurred out-of-pocket medical care costs, not counting insurance premiums or long-term care costs, and their mean expense was $1,005; the corresponding figures for younger people were 74 percent and $391 (Taylor and Banthin, 1994:Table 2). Also, the elderly on average spend a higher proportion of their income on medical care than do younger people: in 1987, 23 percent of elderly households—compared with only 7 percent of nonelderly households—had out-of-pocket medical expenses that exceeded 10 percent of their income (Taylor and Banthin, 1994:Table 8).

Among the reasons the elderly incur higher costs are that they have higher rates of medical care utilization and they face gaps in coverage (e.g., prescription drugs are not paid for by Medicare) and the requirement to pay insurance premiums, deductibles, and copayments. If medical care costs continue to increase, a retirement income stream that would previously have been adequate for living expenses, including health care, may no longer be adequate. Moreover, cutbacks in Medicare, Medicaid, and medical insurance provided to retirees by their former employers would exacerbate the situation, if elderly people cannot reduce their health care utilization or costs.

Such cutbacks may already be occurring. The proportion of all current wage and salary workers who were covered by employer-provided health insurance between 1988 and 1993 declined from 65 percent to 61 percent. The decline was concentrated among private-sector workers; it appeared to stem largely from lower rates of provision of health care plans by employers, rather than from higher rates of nonparticipation by workers at employers offering plans (Pension and Welfare Benefits Administration, 1994:4). Data on trends in retiree health insurance coverage are harder to obtain, but there are indications that a significant proportion of employers are curtailing health insurance coverage for current and future retirees or plan to do so in the near future (see, e.g., Buck Consultants, Inc., 1993; Lohse, 1993).

***Demographic and Socioeconomic Trends***  Several demographic and socioeconomic trends are contributing to the concern about future retirement income security. First, rising life expectancies mean that retirement income must be stretched out over a longer period—a particular concern when retirement income flows are not indexed for inflation. This is the case for employer pension plan payments for which there is no regular cost-of-living adjustment.

Second, lower ages at retirement mean that workers have fewer years in which to save for retirement (and fewer years to contribute to the financing of Social Security benefits for current retirees), while having more years of retirement consumption to support. The post-World War II period has seen a marked drop in labor force participation rates for older men. The rates for men aged 60 to 64 declined between 1955 and 1993 from 83 percent to 54 percent; the rates for men aged 65 and over declined from 40 percent to 16 percent (U.S. House of Representatives, 1994:856).[6] Recently, the trend toward earlier ages at retirement for men has leveled off, and the labor force participation rate for women aged 60 and over, which is significantly below that of men in the same age group, has increased somewhat.[7] Whether the 1983 Social Security amendments to gradually reduce initial benefits (sometimes referred to confusingly as an increase in the "normal" retirement age)—offset for workers older than ages 65 to 67 by an increase in the delayed retirement credit—will lead to later ages at retirement will not be known for some years.[8]

Third, an increasing rate of disabilities among workers lowers labor supply

---

[6]See Ransom, Sutch, and Streib (1988) for labor force participation rates for men aged 60 and over for 1870-1937; Lumsdaine and Wise (1994) continue the series through 1980.

[7]Burkhauser and Quinn (1994) argue that the decline in labor force participation rates has bottomed out, while Peracchi and Welch (1994) argue the opposite, particularly for low wage earners.

[8]For differing views on the likely effects of these provisions, see Gustman and Steinmeier (1991), Reimers and Honig (1993), and Rust and Phelan (1993).

and the opportunities to save and increases the need for income support over a longer period. Although surveys do not appear to show higher rates of disability in the elderly population (see, e.g., Freedman and Soldo, 1994; Waidmann, Bound, and Schoenbaum, 1995), higher proportions of workers have been applying for and receiving public and private disability benefits. Workers receiving Social Security disability benefits as a percentage of covered civilian workers increased between 1960 and 1975 from 0.8 percent to 3.2 percent. The number of beneficiaries declined to 2.7 percent of covered workers in 1985, largely due to a decline in the percentage of applications that were approved, but it increased to 3.1 percent in 1991 (calculated from U.S. House of Representatives, 1994:Tables 2-8, 3-5; see also Lewin-VHI, 1994). Also, there appears to be a trend among workers toward younger ages for first receipt of disability benefits (Rust, 1993).

All of these trends could result in a situation in which, absent changes in policy and behavior, future retirees as a group will be worse off than current retirees. It is even more likely that retirement income levels will vary widely: some people will be relatively well off (e.g., people who retained jobs in industries with good benefits), while many others will be badly off. Of course, the worst case may not develop because of countervailing factors. For example, higher immigration levels could mean increased revenues to the Social Security system; the spread of managed care could achieve significant, sustained reductions in the rate of increase in health care costs; and stepped-up efforts by the government, employers, and financial investment companies to educate workers about the need to increase pension plan contributions and other savings could have a positive effect.

Whether a worst-case or best-case situation will occur cannot be known, but policy adjustments (e.g., some changes in Social Security financing) will very likely be necessary to maintain future retirement income security even if such factors as low rates of personal saving show improvement. Moreover, to the extent that needed changes are delayed, they may have to be larger in magnitude.[9] The question is how to evaluate the range of policy alternatives that may be considered.

## NEAR-TERM POLICY OPTIONS

Debates about retirement income security in the United States are likely to focus on four broad policy areas: Social Security, employer-provided pensions, other personal savings and wealth, and health care needs and costs. The kinds of policy

---

[9]See 1994-95 Advisory Council on Social Security Technical Panel on Trends and Issues in Retirement Saving (1995) for an extensive discussion that reaches similar conclusions. For other reviews, see Congressional Budget Office (1993), Employee Benefit Research Institute (1994), and Reno (1993).

options in each of these areas for which decision makers are likely to want cost and other projections vary widely in scope and complexity and, hence, in the challenges they pose for projection models.

Below we identify many possible options in each area, but it is important to note that recent policy debates have shared several primary themes: a focus on containing costs (e.g., of employer pension and health care benefits, Medicare and Medicaid); a concern to maintain a mixed public-private system of benefits in which employers play an important role; and, perhaps most important, a focus on putting more responsibility on individuals to save for their own retirement and health care needs, through their employers and other means. Proposals to stimulate increased savings by individuals include simplifying pension regulations to encourage small businesses to set up certain kinds of defined contribution benefit plans for their workers, increasing incentives to contribute to Individual Retirement Accounts (IRAs), and providing for tax-advantaged medical savings accounts that encourage people to limit their health care spending. (Proposals to privatize part or all of Social Security payments would give individual workers choices about fund investments, but not about whether to participate in the program.)

These and similar options place a premium on understanding individual savings behavior, including how people react to perceived risks, and on the behavior of employers with regard to compensation policies—two areas in which data currently are very inadequate and research knowledge is weak. These kinds of options also call for capabilities to simulate the effects of random or cyclical shocks (recessions, bull or bear stock markets, etc.) that can be expected to affect employment and savings growth opportunities differently across time and population groups.

## Social Security

Social Security clearly needs and will receive attention to consider ways to restore a balance between costs and benefits. It seems likely that the policy debate will look first for incremental solutions that spread the costs broadly. Such a goal will likely require modeling the effects of a combination of several small changes in the system (instead of larger changes in one or two features). Such changes include the following, each of which is framed in terms of the direction that is needed to restore balance to the Social Security trust fund:

- raising the "early" retirement age (the age at which people can first collect benefits);
- increasing payroll tax rates for employers, employees, or both;
- increasing the payroll tax base, perhaps by removing the current cap on the amount of earnings that is subject to the old-age and survivors insurance

portion of the payroll tax and making all earnings subject to tax (as has already been done for the Medicare portion);
- decreasing benefits by changing the benefit formula;[10]
- adding a means test for benefits, so that retirees with other sources of income or assets receive smaller Social Security payments;
- increasing the amount of benefits that is subject to the income tax;
- repealing the recent law that increased the amount of earnings that beneficiaries can receive without a reduction in benefits;
- reducing the yearly cost-of-living adjustment; and
- investing some part of current trust fund surpluses in stocks instead of U.S. Treasury notes (as recommended by the Social Security Advisory Council; see Quinn and Mitchell, 1996).

Consideration of changes in Social Security benefit provisions in some instances will require consideration of whether the same changes should be made for other components of the system, such as disability insurance. For example, an increase in the Social Security early retirement age or a reduction in benefits will be less effective in restoring balance to the system if disability benefits—and the consequent incentives to apply for disability payments—are not also reduced.

There may also be policy interest in modeling yet more radical alternatives, such as partially privatizing the Social Security system, perhaps with the intent of restoring confidence in the system. (Some members of the Social Security Advisory Council recommended partial privatization.) At present, public opinion data indicate that younger workers doubt that they will receive Social Security benefits commensurate with the taxes they are paying into the system (see Burtless, 1996:244; see also Employee Benefit Research Institute, 1995). Privatizing some (or all) contributions could restore the confidence of younger workers that their taxes will in due course be returned to them as benefit streams from their "own" retirement accounts. Indeed, a problem with policy changes that tinker with the existing system, instead of attempting radical reform, is that they may increase the perception that the system is at risk and that workers cannot be confident that the rules will stay the same for any length of time.

## Employer Pensions

Social Security is not and was never intended to be the only source of retirement income security: historically, employer-provided pensions have also been ex-

---

[10]At present, the primary insurance (benefit) amount is calculated with two "bend points": for a worker reaching age 62 in 1996, it was 90 percent of the first $437 of the worker's average indexed monthly earnings (AIME), plus 32 percent of the next $2,198, plus 15 percent of the remaining amount above $2,635, if any (U.S. General Accounting Office, 1996b:52-53). (The AIME is based on covered earnings that are taxable for Social Security, for which the maximum amount in 1996 was $62,700.)

pected to make an important contribution. There is extensive legislation and government regulation of employer plans and, hence, a need to model the effects of changes to them. Policy changes could be made either to affect workers or employers (or both).[11] Examples of policy changes that could increase retirement income security by requiring workers to maintain their pension contributions for retirement purposes or by encouraging them to increase their contributions include the following:

• increasing the penalties for early withdrawals from 401(k) plans and other defined contribution pension plans and restricting loans against such accounts;
• allowing workers to contribute to 401(k) and similar plans immediately on employment, without a waiting period (employers can waive a waiting period, but most do not);
• requiring workers, when they change jobs, to roll over their pension plan contributions to some other plan (i.e., disallowing lump-sum payments that are not earmarked for retirement purposes);
• alternatively, allowing workers who change jobs to carry 401(k) or similar plans to which they and their new employers can contribute;
• mandating that workers draw retirement income from employer pensions in the form of regular payments or an annuity (i.e., disallowing any lump-sum benefits);
• raising the age (currently 70.5 years) at which workers must begin drawing from their defined contribution pension accounts;
• regulating pension investment options; and
• increasing tax incentives to contribute to defined contribution pension plans.

Perhaps even more important are policy changes that alter employer behavior. Examples of policy changes that could increase retirement income security by altering the behavior of employers include the following:

• raising the limits on the extent to which employers can prefund defined benefit pension plans;
• increasing protections for spousal benefits in pension plans;
• equalizing the tax treatment of employee contributions to defined benefit and defined contribution pension plans (contributions to defined benefit plans are

---

[11]Recent pension simplification legislation made changes in the direction of some of the policy options listed: for example, increasing the penalty for early withdrawals from a "simple" pension account within the first 2 years after the account is set up (the rules were not changed for 401(k) accounts); removing the requirement for currently employed workers (but not for former employees) that they must begin drawing benefits from their defined contribution pension accounts at age 70.5; and simplifying some administrative rules.

in after-tax dollars, but contributions to defined contribution plans can be tax deferred);

- changing nondiscrimination rules and other regulations so as to encourage employers to establish and expand pension plans;
- changing age-discrimination laws to encourage employers to retain older workers and provide benefits to them (e.g., giving employers flexibility to alter compensation for older workers);
- mandating additional pension plan design constraints for employers, such as indexation of pensions and altering the ability to offset employer pensions by Social Security benefits;
- allowing employers to opt out of Social Security (as is possible in the United Kingdom) and provide comparable or better benefits through pension plans; and
- mandating employer pensions.

Some of these policy proposals (e.g., a policy to require all employers to provide pensions) are radical steps that would require careful consideration of a wide range of effects, not only on retirement income security but on the economy more broadly (see "Outcome Criteria" below). In general, it is important to assess whether changes that are proposed to increase retirement security would actually have the desired effect or its opposite effect, for example, by inducing employers to opt out of pension plans. It is also important to consider the interactions of employer pensions with the corporate profits tax and other tax policy provisions and with the Social Security system. Many employer plans are designed to be integrated with Social Security (by paying different amounts of benefits for earnings below the Social Security payroll tax threshold), so that Social Security policy changes may affect these plans.

## Other Personal Savings and Wealth

Personal savings other than pension plan contributions are another potentially important source of retirement income support. IRAs are one type of personal savings that government policy has encouraged in order to increase retirees' income security. There is likely to be policy interest in modeling such options as raising the annual limit on the amount of tax-deferred contributions or allowing withdrawals for other purposes in order to increase incentives to contribute to IRAs, increasing (or decreasing) penalties for early withdrawals, and mandating that income be taken in the form of regular payments or an annuity and not as a lump sum.

Generally, it is important to address policy changes that affect people's ability to acquire wealth, broadly defined (including tax-deferred and non-tax-deferred financial investments, property, insurance), and save it for retirement, as well as to pass it on to the next generation. Given the pressures on Social

Security and the leveling off of growth in employer pension coverage, the baby boom generation may need to rely significantly on their own savings or bequests from their parents for retirement income.

The direction of policy with regard to parental assets is not clear. There may be reason to encourage older cohorts to hold assets for bequest purposes so as to enhance the retirement income security of their children. In this case, it would be important to model policy changes that protect assets against the risks of long-term health care costs—for example, subsidizing long-term-care insurance.[12] Alternatively, there may be reason to encourage current retirees to use their assets to reduce the taxpayer costs of providing health care and other benefits to them. In this case, it would be important to model such policy changes as raising estate tax rates; taxing capital gains on inherited assets; lowering asset limits for program eligibility (e.g., for Supplemental Security Income) or imposing asset tests (e.g., for Medicare or Social Security); and encouraging reverse-mortgage-type programs to allow the elderly to unlock housing equity.

If lack of understanding of needed savings levels is a factor in the low rate of personal savings for current workers, it would be important to model the effects of financial education programs. Such programs include direct education by government agencies (e.g., the Social Security Administration and Department of Labor) and programs to encourage or require employers to provide education to employees about pension plan contribution opportunities and investment strategies.

Finally, it could also be important to model the effects of changes in federal government fiscal policy on savings and wealth accumulation generally.

## Health Care Needs and Costs

Health care needs and costs are an important, as well as a highly uncertain, aspect of retirement income security and well-being. To the extent that medical care costs continue to rise, particularly for the elderly, no assessment of retirement income security is complete without consideration of health care needs and costs. In this report, we do not address models or modeling issues for the health care system as such. However, for completeness, we identify some of the kinds of policy changes for which there is likely to be interest in modeling. We also believe it is important to have links between projection models of retirement income security and health care costs and benefits.

There are a number of possible health care policy changes that relate specifically to retirees. Some of these changes are directed to making adequate health

---

[12]The Health Insurance Portability and Accountability Act of 1996 made an important change for current workers by allowing employers to sponsor tax-advantaged long-term-care accounts for their employees.

insurance coverage more widely available; others are directed to curtailing utilization of services and reducing costs:

- equalizing the tax treatment of employer-provided and individually purchased health insurance;
- mandating the provision of health insurance coverage for retirees by former employers;
- providing spousal protection in employer-sponsored health insurance plans;
- providing government insurance for long-term care (or providing tax incentives to purchase such insurance); and
- making one or a combination of changes to Medicare, such as: changing coinsurance rates and deductibles, changing the mix of benefits (e.g., providing prescription drug coverage but curtailing some other kinds of benefits), increasing Medicare payroll taxes, providing incentives for enrollees to move into managed care or to set up medical savings accounts, providing vouchers for enrollees to purchase lower cost private insurance, means-testing the receipt of Medicare benefits, improving the monitoring of Medicare claims to reduce unneeded services and fraudulent claims, or turning Medicare into a catastrophic insurance program with the expectation that private insurance will cover expenses up to the ceiling at which Medicare begins to provide benefits.

## OUTCOME CRITERIA

In order to evaluate the costs and benefits of alternative policy proposals, such as those just listed, decision makers need information on a range of outcomes. In consultation with members of a Social Security Advisory Council technical panel (cochaired by our panel member Olivia Mitchell), we developed a list of outcome criteria (see 1994-95 Advisory Council on Social Security Technical Panel on Trends and Issues in Retirement Saving, 1995).

*Retirement Income Adequacy* An important evaluation criterion is how a policy change affects the adequacy of retirement income. Measures of income adequacy include the poverty rate for the elderly, which focuses on the most vulnerable subgroup in the population, and the rate at which public or private pension income replaces earnings for all groups of elderly people. Information to apply this criterion requires a capability for disaggregation of projection model inputs and outputs (e.g., disaggregated data on earnings histories to estimate replacement rates for people with lower, average, and higher earnings).

*Insurance Against Income Fluctuations* Another criterion by which to evaluate the entire retirement income system, including Social Security and employer plans, is how well the system provides insurance against unforeseen events that cut off a worker's flow of income. Thus, Social Security and many employer pensions offer survivor and disability benefits and also permit early retirement for those without appealing job opportunities due to industry downsizing or obsolescence of skills, as well as for those who prefer leisure. (Another pension issue noted above that has an insurance aspect is whether to restrict lump-sum payments of pension benefits and thereby require individuals to insure against the risk of above-average longevity.)

A cost of providing such insurance is that its availability undoubtedly introduces labor market inefficiencies, such as encouraging early retirement or application for disability benefits. The question then is whether a proposed retirement income policy change achieves an appropriate balance between increasing insurance against unforeseen income shocks and increasing distortions in labor markets.

***Equity of Taxes and Benefits Within and Across Generations***   Current retirement income policies often involve transfers within and across generations. For example, in some employer pension plans, healthier people may, on average, receive more lifetime pension benefits than less healthy people with the same contributions because of their longer life expectancy (the same is true of Social Security). A comparison across generations shows that current retirees are the beneficiaries of large net transfers of Social Security benefits from current workers who are paying more in payroll taxes and will receive less in benefits relative to their contributions than current (and past) retirees. Assessments of proposed policy changes will often need to consider issues of within- and across-generational equity.

***Financial Soundness of the Retirement Income System***   Clearly, an important outcome criterion for any proposal to change the Social Security system concerns the implications for long-term actuarial balance of taxes and benefits. Reforms that do not provide for balance in the system over the standard 75-year projection period, or even longer, are not likely to be acceptable. Similarly, proposed changes in the rules under which employers maintain their pension plans, and under which individuals save for their retirement, should be considered from the perspective of their likely effects on the financial soundness of these plans. Two other issues are the extent to which government guarantees of pension benefits, such as are currently provided by the Pension Benefit Guaranty Corporation, should be provided as a back-up to private-sector guarantees and the appropriate price to charge for these guarantees.

***Avoidance of Market Inefficiencies***   Another important evaluation criterion is the extent to which a policy change avoids introducing or exacerbating market distortions with respect to individuals' choices of labor versus leisure and savings versus consumption.

Although research knowledge is not definitive about the magnitude of the effects on labor-leisure choices, it is clear that Social Security, employer pensions, the tax code, and other policy levers (e.g., disability benefits) influence people's choices, including their decisions on hours of work early and late in their careers and their decision about when to retire and whether to retire completely or only partially. It is important to know the extent to which a proposed policy change increases or reduces market distortions in terms of labor-leisure decisions.

Social Security, employer pensions, the tax code, and other policy levers (e.g., publicly provided health care benefits) also affect people's choices about how they allocate income between savings and consumption during their work years and during their retirement years. It is important to know the extent to which a proposed policy change increases or reduces market distortions with regard to pre-retirement savings in order to support post-retirement consumption. For example, Social Security could move toward ensuring adequate retirement accumulations by making retirement benefit payments depend more on the size of employer pension contributions. But such a policy would lower the value of any employee pension contributions or other personal savings, thus encouraging individuals to save less on their own during their working lives. Such distortions in the savings-consumption choices of individuals throughout their lives can have direct effects on the economy.

***Encouragement of National Savings*** It is widely believed that U.S. savings rates (including individual, corporate, and government savings) are too low, either to provide adequate income support to future retirees or to provide adequate investment levels with which to increase future economic output and the overall standard of living. Hence, one criterion for evaluating a proposed policy change is the extent to which it would increase national savings. For example, current restrictions on the extent to which employers can prefund defined benefit pension plans are designed to increase federal tax revenues in the short run, but these restrictions probably decrease corporate savings, certainly in the short run and perhaps in the long run as well, with the result that the net effect on national savings may be negative (see Schieber and Shoven, 1993; England, 1994). In this case, it is important to have estimates of the effects, not just on tax revenues, but on aggregate national savings.

***Encouragement of Overall Economic Efficiency, Competitiveness, and Growth*** For some kinds of policy changes, it is important to consider effects on the behavior of employers that, in turn, affects the overall efficiency of the national economy, the rate of economic growth, and the ability of the United States to remain competitive in world markets. For example, a policy change to require all or a large proportion of employers to provide health care benefits for their retirees or pensions for their workers could have macroeconomic effects.

Such mandates on employer behavior might affect the industrial structure of the economy or the rate of real economic growth.

*Cost-Effectiveness of Benefit Program Administration*  In evaluating the effects of retirement-income-related policy changes, policy makers should recognize the existence of important issues involving the efficiency and effectiveness of program administration. For example, "leakage" occurs in the Social Security system to the extent that benefits are paid in the name of deceased people or to disabled people who could return to work. However, minimizing leakage of benefits could entail increased costs for program administration. In the private sector, there is concern about the effects of government regulation of pension and health care benefit plans on employers' costs for plan administration and, in turn, the effects on employer decisions about whether and what kinds of plans to offer. If some or all of the Social Security system were privatized, it would clearly be important to evaluate the likely efficiency and effectiveness of schemes for administering workers' IRAs. Similarly, administrative costs are an important evaluation criterion for any major change in the health care benefit system, including changes to Medicare.

## CHALLENGES TO PROJECTION MODELING

### Outcomes

Evaluating one or more policy proposals on the range of outcome criteria listed above presents formidable challenges for projection models. Although few policy changes require information on every criterion, most changes will need to be evaluated on several criteria. There are often trade-offs to consider: for example, selecting the desired balance between benefit reductions and tax increases to restore actuarial balance to the Social Security system. Evaluating proposals on a range of outcome criteria is also important because policy changes can change behavior in ways that alter the original estimates of costs and benefits. For example, a policy change to maintain the adequacy of income for future retirees by, say, requiring increased contributions to employer pension plans or increased Social Security payroll taxes might induce workers to reduce work hours and thereby decrease their pension plan or payroll tax contributions.

### Program Interactions

Because there are many retirement-income-related policy areas and many different agencies handle different areas, it is difficult to carry out integrated analyses that consider interactions among components of retirement income security and the overall effects of policy changes. Typically, policy debates focus on only one component of retirement income, such as employer pensions or health insurance coverage. And decision makers often ask for answers to policy questions that are relatively narrow in scope: for example, how many small businesses will offer pension plans if certain kinds of regulations are relaxed or how the value of self-directed pension plan contributions will be affected by campaigns to educate workers about investment choices. At times, decision makers focus on entirely unrelated aspects of retirement-income-related policy proposals: for example, recent changes in tax laws on pension funding were evaluated for their potential to increase revenue in the short term without considering the possibly adverse effects for retirement income—such as leading employers to drop or scale back their pension plans (see, e.g., Lindeman and Utgoff, 1992).[13]

It will often be appropriate and cost-effective to have projection modeling tools that address specific policy levers and issues. Yet it is also critical to have broader based modeling tools (or ways to link issue-specific models) to consider the effects of policy changes on retirement income security overall. Even when the focus is on specific policies and narrow issues, it is important to consider such interactions among components of retirement income as the following:

• many employer pension plans are linked to the benefit structure of the Social Security system, so that plan provisions could be expected to change if Social Security changes;
• Social Security retirement and disability insurance benefits are competing sources of support for early retirees, so that changes in one program can be expected to affect the other; and
• newer forms of employer pension plans that allow workers to determine the level of their contributions and the choice of investment vehicles are very similar to other kinds of personal savings, so that there is a strong reason for analyzing them within the same framework.

## Heterogeneity

Retirement income and its components exhibit considerable heterogeneity among population groups. Almost all workers are covered by Social Security, but there is wide variation in the extent to which workers are covered by employer-provided pensions and in the provisions of such coverage. There is also variation in the amounts and form of pension benefits provided upon retirement: for example, whether benefits are taken as lump sums or annuities and whether annuity payments are indexed for inflation. Finally, there is wide variation in the population in personal savings behavior, earnings capacity, labor market opportunities,

---

[13]Sometimes, the broader implications of tax law changes are studied after their enactment (see, e.g., U.S. Treasury Department, 1991).

the availability of income support from other family members, and health care needs and resources.

Consequently, there are significant disparities in income and wealth—taking account of all sources—among retirees and workers, which means it is important to evaluate policy changes for their distributional as well as aggregate effects. Some models may usefully focus on constructing important overall estimates— for example, projections of the balance in the Social Security trust fund—by using aggregate, or relatively aggregate, inputs. However, there must also be projection models that can reflect the heterogeneity in the population and show, for example, whether a proposal helps some retirees but not others. These effects are as important to understand as the central tendencies. Indeed, much of the focus of government retirement policy is on ensuring some minimum living standard for the elderly people who may have been unlucky or unwise in preparing for their post-work years. Models are needed that can produce estimates of the likely numbers of such people, as well as estimates of the average experience.

In this regard, as the policy process increasingly looks to encourage people to assume more of the burden for their own retirement saving, models are needed that can simulate the effects of differential risk. Currently, promised benefits from Social Security come from the entire tax-paying population, while defined benefit pension plan entitlements come from employer resources, with backing from the Pension Benefit Guaranty Corporation. In other words, the risks to retirement income from such factors as downturns in markets, productivity declines, recessions, and poor business judgment are spread widely. In contrast, individual investments in defined contribution pension plans, IRAs, or privatized Social Security accounts are subject to risks that potentially vary widely. Some people, helped by good judgment and fortunate timing, may achieve windfall gains while others suffer large, unanticipated losses. Models need to be able to plausibly simulate variations in rates of return on investments across time and population groups in order to assess the distributional consequences for retirement income security within and across age groups and generations.

## Time Horizon

When assessing retirement income security overall and for population groups, it is critical to have models that can estimate the longer term as well as short-term effects of alternative policies. Many changes—for example, in the tax treatment of employee or employer contributions to pension plans—are not likely to alter the behavior of people who are near retirement, but such changes may well have significant behavioral effects on younger workers and their employers over the longer run. In turn, behavioral responses to policy changes may have yet further consequences for long-term outcomes.

The longer the time horizon for a policy projection, the more difficult it is to build in plausible assumptions about policy interactions, behavioral responses, and the like. For example, large, unanticipated changes in fertility behavior in the post-World War II period have periodically upset long-range population forecasts. Projecting over the long term can be more computationally taxing than projecting over the short term, but much retirement-income-related policy analysis, by its nature, requires long-term projections. Consequently, there is a premium on building models with capabilities for sensitivity analysis and other methods of estimating the much greater uncertainty in long-range forecasts.

## Knowledge About Behavior

Many behaviors and processes contribute to the retirement income security of current and future generations. The capability to address important questions about many retirement-income-related policy proposals, particularly over the longer term, requires a solid base of research knowledge—and ways to incorporate that knowledge effectively in projection models—in such areas as:

- employers' decisions about whether and what types of pension plans and other benefits (e.g., health insurance, disability benefits) to offer employees;
- employers' labor demand choices, particularly for older workers;
- performance of capital markets that determine the value of pension holdings and other forms of saving and of group and individual annuity markets;
- people's choices about how much of their income to devote to savings versus consumption at different stages of the life cycle and what kinds of investment decisions to make;
- people's labor supply choices at different stages of the life cycle, including job search and home production;
- basic demographic processes that affect the numbers of working-age and retirement-aged people, especially mortality, as well as net immigration, and—depending on the length of the projection period—fertility;
- people's marital histories and living arrangements, joint decisions with other family members about labor supply and savings, and the likelihood of financial and other support from relatives;
- interactions of trends in mortality and marital status with trends in retirement benefits (e.g., increased use of lump-sum payouts), which may affect retirement income security over the remaining lifetimes of retirees and their survivors;
- people's health status and disability, including trends over time and changes in status as people age;
- trends in health care costs and health care financing arrangements; and
- interactions between microlevel behavior (decisions of workers and employers) and the economy.

## Uncertainty

A final challenge for retirement income modeling is to provide estimates of the uncertainty in projection model outputs, which stem from errors and variability in data inputs, research parameters, and model specifications. The estimation of uncertainty has been much neglected in policy analysis work. When estimates have been done, the methods used—such as constructing "high," "intermediate," and "low" scenarios for long-range forecasts of the elderly population or the balance in the Social Security trust fund—have often had little scientific basis.

Admittedly, the task of estimating uncertainty is difficult. The difficulties are compounded when a projection model is asked to evaluate a complex policy change on several outcome criteria over a long time period and when the change interacts with other policies and behaviors in complex and varied ways for different groups. Yet it is precisely in these instances that decision makers most need to be aware of the likely wide range of uncertainty in the estimates.

The next three chapters address improvements in retirement-income-related research, data, and projection model capabilities. Research on methods to evaluate quality and estimate uncertainty should be a priority in all three areas, as should research on helpful ways to convey information about uncertainty to decision makers. Estimates of uncertainty are vital both to inform the policy process and to make possible continued improvements in research knowledge, data, and projection capabilities that can support informed policy debate.

# 3

# Key Research Issues

The economic security of retirees depends on their lifetime experiences of work, savings, and family ties and their health care and other consumption needs. Such experiences depend on individual choices; they also depend on decisions of employers that affect the provision of jobs, earnings, savings vehicles, and retirement and health care benefits. Government policies and programs constrain and shape all these individual and employer decisions. Consequently, projecting the implications for retirement income security of proposed changes in government policy requires basic research knowledge about the likely behavioral responses of people and employers and a capability for using it to estimate future outcomes.

Knowledge to project behavioral effects is not needed for every retirement-income-related policy question, but it is essential for many questions, particularly when projections are needed for the medium and long term. Contrast short-term versus long-term projections of the implications of reducing the annual cost-of-living adjustment (COLA) for Social Security benefits. In the short term, say for a 5-year period, the projection is straightforward: the Social Security benefits of current retirees and those expected to retire during the next 5 years are increased each year by a reduced COLA instead of by the full estimated amount of inflation as is currently done. If the 5 years are expected to be a period of low inflation, the effect of reduced benefits will not be great for many people, although some people will be moved below the poverty line. Over a longer projection period and particularly if the COLA is cut significantly, the real value of Social Security benefits will decline significantly over people's retirement years, with potentially severe effects on the income security of many retirees. Given this prospect, one would expect more and more people to change their behavior, for example, by delaying retirement or increasing savings. Employers may also change their pension plan provisions to compensate for workers' expected lower Social Security income. To the extent that such behavioral responses occur, projections need to take them into account to be useful for policy making.

Some policy proposals represent major, systemic changes for which there are no historical parallels and, hence, little possibility of obtaining appropriate behavioral parameters from available (or potentially available) data to use in projections. In these instances, it can still be useful to develop projections with a range of assumptions, reflecting expert judgment. Such estimates may indicate the extremes of possible outcomes, although they remain highly uncertain even then.

Many proposals, however, can be expected to influence behavior in ways that research can illuminate. In addition, for some major changes with which the United States has no experience, it may be possible to obtain useful data by analyzing the experience of other countries (such as the experience in several countries with various forms of privatization of social security systems; see World Bank, 1994). Although the cultural and social milieus are different, there may still be knowledge from comparative cross-national research that can contribute to U.S. projections.

In this chapter, we summarize what is known and not known about factors that influence key retirement-income-related behaviors of individuals and employers. For employers, we look at research about decisions on pensions and other benefits and demand for older workers. For individuals, we look at research about savings, consumption, and labor supply. Our reviews in the chapter text are quite brief, highlighting key knowledge gaps. They draw from extensive reviews of the literature and research issues in a set of papers we commissioned for our study (Hanushek and Maritato, 1996; see Appendix A for contents).[1]

For projecting the likely effects of retirement-income-related policy changes, particularly over the long term, it is also important to understand likely demographic and health-related trends. We thus look at research about factors and trends in basic demographic processes, particularly mortality, that will affect the size and makeup of the population of workers and retirees at future times; the health status of workers and retirees that will determine their needs for health care services and affect their decisions about work and savings; and health care costs and financing arrangements that will affect retirees' living standards. Our reviews of these areas are also brief.[2] Finally, we touch on factors and trends in

---

[1]The papers by Lumsdaine, Parsons, and Poterba review the literature on labor supply, employer behavior, and savings and consumption, respectively; the paper by Gustman and Juster looks at the distribution and sources of income and wealth of households with retired workers and reviews analytical models of labor supply, savings, and pension decisions that contribute to income and wealth at retirement.

[2]For more extensive discussion and literature reviews, see the paper by Lee and Skinner (in Hanushek and Maritato, 1996; see also Moon, 1995).

marriage and divorce, which can have important consequences for the economic well-being of the elderly.

Our discussion covers a large number of areas, but it is not comprehensive. For example, we do not consider factors that influence trends in worker productivity, even though such trends are key to growth in real earnings, which, in turn, affects Social Security and pension entitlements. Also, we do not discuss factors that influence the financial return to pension investments and personal savings, although the distribution of returns is of growing importance for retirement income security and will become even more important if such policy changes as privatizing all or part of Social Security contributions are implemented. Nonetheless, we cover most of the critical areas for which a strong research base is needed for retirement-income-related policy analysis. We identify important strengths and weaknesses in available knowledge and recommend improvements.

Our discussion of research topics is ordered by our assessment of which areas are most deficient in terms of basic knowledge that is relevant for retirement income security policy analysis. These deficiencies are largely due to deficiencies in data, which in some instances have hampered the development of theory and in other instances have impeded the development of robust estimates of behavioral parameters. Hence, improvements in data (discussed in Chapter 4) will be required to carry out much of the research agenda that we recommend. However, basic research should not stand still. Although some research cannot proceed very far without better data, other research can go forward with improved data that are or will shortly become available or with the use of methods (e.g., case studies) that require much less investment in new or better data.

Generally, research should proceed to refine and improve analytical models with the best available data. Indeed, data development and basic research go hand in hand: new findings from data suggest the need to rethink theories and models, and, in turn, analytical developments suggest further improvements to data. We stress in our report the need for investments in data *and* analytical modeling and research in areas that most need an improved base of knowledge with which to support retirement-income-related policy work. Given constrained resources, however, we recommend against major investments in complex, new projection models for policy purposes until investments in data and basic research bear fruit.

We begin our review with research on employer behavior. Employers play an important role in the provision of retirement income security through their decisions about personnel and benefits. Moreover, their behavior can change rapidly, as evidenced by the marked increase in recent years in the number of employers offering managed care health insurance plans. Yet very little is known about the strength of the factors that may influence employers' decisions. We next consider research on individuals' choices of savings and consumption, another area about which relatively little is known, and individuals' labor supply and retirement decisions. We then consider trends in relevant demographic characteristics.  Lastly, we comment briefly on key questions related to health care costs.

## EMPLOYER BEHAVIOR

Employer pensions represent a significant source of retirement income for many workers, and their availability and characteristics are important determinants of retirement decisions and other relevant behaviors.  The availability of other kinds of employer benefits (e.g., disability insurance and retiree health insurance) also plays a role in the retirement-related behavior of workers.  More generally, employers' demand for older workers affects retirement income security, both directly in terms of the labor market opportunities for older workers and indirectly in terms of the effects on employer decisions about benefits.

Employers' decisions to offer a pension plan or plans (or other benefits) and of what type(s) depend on several factors:

- expected benefits in terms of work force productivity, worker recruitment and retention, and retirement of older workers;
- federal tax law provisions, such as tax deductions for qualified plans, which are an incentive to provide benefits, and nondiscrimination rules for qualified plans, which are a disincentive;
- other government policies, including those for Social Security and Medicare, pension insurance laws and regulations, and antidiscrimination laws with respect to age and disability;
- employers' financial objectives and concerns, including tax liabilities, administrative costs, and costs of compliance with regulations;
- trends in benefit policies by similar employers; and
- the demand for benefits by employees.

There are a large number of competing theories about why employers offer pension plans, which differ in the importance accorded to the various factors listed above.  For example, some theories and models emphasize the importance of tax deferral, others stress the use of pension plans as a worker selection device or as a productivity enhancement mechanism, while others stress the importance of pension plans as incentives for workers to retire.  To date, there is no agreement on which of these theories best explains employers' behavior or on the extent to which different types of employers may have different mixes of motives.

In a literature review commissioned by the panel, Parsons (1996) emphasizes the importance of transaction costs in explaining the well-documented phenomenon that large, unionized employers are much more likely to offer pensions than are smaller employers:  large employers can benefit from economies of scale in administering pension plans that are not available to small employers.  He attributes the fact that small employers that do offer pension plans almost invariably offer a 401(k) or other type of defined contribution plan, rather than a defined benefit plan, to the same reason, namely, lower administrative costs. However, Parsons (1996:179) acknowledges that "alternative hypotheses . . . can explain many of the same observations." Moreover, such analysis cannot explain why some relatively large firms do not offer pensions and some relatively small firms do, nor the variety of pension plan provisions that characterize firms in the same size class. Nor does the research yet provide agreed-upon values of behavioral parameters that could be used to estimate the strength of employer responses to policy and other changes: for example, what degree of reduction in plan administrative costs or in regulatory burden would induce a specified percentage of small employers to set up pension plans of a particular type.

Employer demand for older workers is also affected by many factors, including:

- desired work force characteristics, in terms of retention, skill levels, productivity, and other attributes;
- employer perceptions of relative productivity of workers of different ages;
- employer financial objectives and concerns (such as the costs of providing benefits, costs of providing job training);
- employer personnel practices, such as flexibility in reassigning workers;
- government policies and regulations, including anti-age discrimination laws and restrictions on mandatory retirement; and
- older worker supply.

Again, a pervasive finding is that the larger the employer, the lower the share of older workers (age 55 and older) in an employer's work force. Moreover, when mandatory retirement rules were legally permitted in the United States, larger, unionized employers were more likely to have them. Considerable analysis has been conducted of differences among employers in mandatory retirement provisions, but there is no agreement on the underlying behavioral mechanisms. Theories to explain this phenomenon include:

- the propensity of large employers to have more formal rules of all types, reflecting their higher costs of making idiosyncratic decisions;
- the "representative worker" model, which posits that employers that engage in long-term contracting with workers (predominantly larger employers) pay workers more as they age than they are worth in terms of productivity and hence that these employers cap total compensation by mandating retirement by a specific age; and
- the desire of employers to limit the propensity of people who are hired later in life to work into their less productive older years in order to accumulate more generous pension rights.

Alternatively, workers' decisions could play a large role in the age profile of employers' work forces: that is, the smaller share of older workers at large employers could be attributed to the propensity of large employers to offer pensions, which, in turn, encourage retirement.

Untangling the mix of factors that influence personnel and benefit policies of different kinds of employers is critical for reliable projections of the likely effects of government policy changes, such as the effect of changes in Social Security and Medicare provisions on employer hiring and compensation policies and the consequences for workers' overall retirement income security. However, Parsons (1996:179-180) concludes that "we are not close to having the level of understanding that would permit us to make quantitative estimates on employer behavior."

There is yet another problem for estimating employer responses to policy changes in projection models, that of projecting trends in the mix of employer types. Given the association of pension offerings and fewer older workers with larger employers, a continued shift of employment from the large, highly unionized sector of the economy to the service sector, with many more small employers, may mean that older workers in the future have greater access to jobs but less access to pensions. Whether this trend will continue, and at what rate, and whether other significant shifts in employer mix will occur are difficult but important questions to answer, as is the question of whether observed relationships between employer type and pension and employment practices will continue to hold.

Even more than in the case of personal consumption and savings behavior (see below), data gaps and measurement problems greatly constrain researchers' ability to develop reasonable analytical models of employer behavior with regard to pension and other retirement-related benefits. Available cross-sectional data sets suffer from several limitations. The Form 5500 database of the U.S. Department of Labor, which characterizes employer benefit plans from annual filings to the Internal Revenue Service, does not cover public employers; it also does not provide information on the full range of private employer benefits, which include nonqualified as well as qualified pension plans, retirement window opportunities, retiree health insurance, disability insurance, and other relevant benefits. The Form 5500 database also contains limited information for analyzing differences in benefit packages as a function of employer or work force characteristics.

The Employee Benefits Survey (EBS) of the Bureau of Labor Statistics provides extensive information on types of public and private employer benefits for workers in broad occupational categories. However, the survey is based on small samples, has at present no data on benefit costs, and has very little information on employer characteristics. The National Employer Health Insurance Survey of the U.S. Department of Health and Human Services has large sample sizes, but it is limited to health care benefits and costs. Private sector surveys of pension and health care benefit offerings by consulting firms and others are generally limited to larger employers and often to the clients of the survey sponsor. Case studies by researchers with data from one or a few companies have supported innovative analysis,[3] but the results of such studies are not readily generalizable because of the heterogeneity of employers.

There are almost no panel data on employers that could be used to trace changes in benefit packages over time or to determine the factors that influence employer behavior in this regard. (The Form 5500 database can be used for only limited kinds of longitudinal analysis.) Similarly, there are no panel (or cross-sectional) data that could support analysis of interactions among employer and employee characteristics that in turn affect benefit plan decisions and, ultimately, retirement income security. Yet such analysis is critically important given the prominent role of employer pensions and other benefits in retirement income security and the evidence that employer behavior with regard to the extent and type of such benefits is dynamic and sensitive to public policies as well as broader economic factors.

Finally, there are almost no data with which to analyze employer demand for older workers. Repeated cross-sectional data from the decennial census and the Current Population Survey (CPS) have been used to study the employment of older workers by industrial sector, and panel data from the Retirement History Survey (RHS) have been used to study retirement paths of older workers (e.g., retiring from a career job versus moving from a career to a "bridge" job before exiting the labor force completely). However, no nationally representative data set exists that permits direct analysis of the factors that influence employers' hiring and retention decisions. A longitudinal employer database that the Census Bureau constructed from census and survey data is limited to manufacturing companies, and it contains no information on work force age structure except for a subsample of establishments with records matched to 1990 population census records for their workers. Researchers have made innovative use of personnel and other records of one or a few employers to study workers' compensation in relation to measures of productivity and other characteristics (e.g., Kotlikoff and Gokhale, 1992; Medoff and Abraham, 1981), but such studies are few and limited in generalizability.

In short, there are glaring gaps and deficiencies in data about employers (and their workers) with which to develop behavioral parameters for projecting employer responses to government policy changes and other factors that may affect personnel and benefit decisions. In Chapter 4, we describe in more detail the problems of existing data sets on employers and recommend improvements.

---

[3]An example is Mitchell and Luzadis (1988), who analyzed pension policies of 14 employers before and after legislation curtailing mandatory retirement.

## CHOICES OF FAMILIES AND INDIVIDUALS

### Savings and Consumption

People's decisions about allocating income between savings and consumption in their pre-retirement years have important implications for the level of consumption that they will be able to sustain after retirement. In this context, personal savings includes after-tax investments as well as tax-sheltered investments, including Individual Retirement Accounts (IRAs) and voluntary employee contributions to 401(k) and other pension vehicles.

The theoretical basis for savings and consumption choices has long been posited in terms of a life-cycle model, in which younger people, by borrowing, and older people, by spending down assets, exhibit high consumption-to-income ratios, while middle-aged people with the highest earnings potential exhibit relatively low consumption-to-income ratios. However, a "pure" life-cycle model does not explain observed macroeconomic and individual behavior, so the basic model has been elaborated in various ways (see Poterba, 1996). Three well-worked-out modifications include:

• a model that attributes precautionary savings motives to individuals (e.g., workers with pensions may save additional amounts to guard against possible future job loss);
• a model that attributes bequest motives (i.e., the desire to leave assets to descendants); and
• a model that imposes liquidity constraints (e.g., young people may not be able to obtain affordable loans).

All three types of analytical models fit reasonably well with cross-sectional data on the distribution of wealth at retirement, and there is no basis as yet to choose among them or to determine whether and what kind of mixed-motive model best explains savings behavior. Moreover, none of the existing models explains well the trends in personal savings rates over time.

Yet other types of models have been posited, in which behavioral or psychological elements play a significant role. One such model assumes that people hold different assets in distinct "mental accounts," which implies that changes in the level of one asset may have relatively small substitution effects on the holdings of other assets, contrary to the life-cycle model assumption. Other models posit that people use rules of thumb or other simple heuristics to make savings decisions (e.g., deciding to save a fixed percentage of earnings each year, regardless of the expected return on saving). These models are intriguing but, to date, have not been well specified or tested.

There are major unanswered questions in the area of consumption and savings behavior:

• Why have personal savings rates declined in recent years? As just noted, none of the existing models explains this trend. It may be that cohort factors—for example, the baby boom generation was not exposed to the Depression—are involved or that the development of a government safety net has had an effect.

• Why are so many middle-income people approaching retirement with very low wealth levels, when Social Security is not a sufficient income source to maintain their standard of living?

• To what extent does saving in IRAs and other voluntary pension plans offset other saving? There is continuing controversy about whether IRA-type investments are made with dollars that people would have invested in any case. A key policy question is whether making such accounts more substitutable with other saving (e.g., by permitting withdrawals) would increase or decrease net saving in the long run. (In the short run, the effect would most likely decrease net saving.)

• More broadly, how much is personal saving influenced by taxes, Social Security, and pension coverage?

• How much do behavioral elements, such as mental accounts and rules of thumb, influence saving behavior? As with retirement and pension acceptance decisions (see below), adding such factors to models would complicate analysis. Yet there is evidence from anomalous savings behavior (e.g., low rates of savings for middle-income families) that it may be important to take account of such factors.

• Relatedly, how much do families know about their future financial needs and potential sources of support, and would more knowledge influence their behavior?

The above questions refer to accumulation of savings until retirement age. Further questions arise about consumption and savings patterns after retirement:

• Looking at older people, does wealth decline in retirement as much as the life-cycle model would predict? There is conflicting evidence about the extent to which wealth, particularly housing equity, is spent down.

• What determines the demand for annuities of different types, and, specifically, how do couples decide between single and joint life annuities?

• What are the effects of changing the form of retirement benefits—lump sums as opposed to annuities, or nominal annuities as opposed to indexed annuities—on income security over retirees' life spans?

• What are the effects of inflation and nominal interest rates on real consumption patterns in retirement?

• What is the relationship between retirement income programs and support of the elderly by their families?

There is another problem in projecting the retirement income security implications of people's savings and consumption choices, namely, that of projecting rates of return on different assets. A major unanswered question is whether rates of return will be influenced by demographic changes. For example, will baby boomers' housing lose value, and what will be the likely effects on their post-retirement standard of living? Also, how much variation will there be in baby boomers' returns on housing and other assets and what will be the likely distributional effects on the adequacy of their retirement income?

Data gaps and measurement problems are a major impediment to addressing all of these questions. People's consumption, savings, and wealth are notoriously difficult to measure in surveys, although two relatively new surveys—the Health and Retirement Survey (HRS) and the Asset and Health Dynamics Among the Oldest Old (AHEAD) survey—have made significant progress in improving the measurement of sample members' financial holdings. To the extent that these surveys accurately measure income and change in net worth, then an estimate of consumption can be obtained by subtraction. Ideally, direct measures of consumption would be used in order to more accurately assess pre-retirement living standards, estimate the implications for post-retirement living standards of people's current savings rates, and help estimate likely future savings rates consistent with the life-cycle model. The third round of HRS and AHEAD includes a question on total expenditures that may prove useful for such analyses, although the data will require careful evaluation of their quality.

Better data are also needed on people's information about likely available sources of retirement income (e.g., their pension rights and anticipated savings) and their expectations about likely future events (e.g., their own life expectancy, the likelihood they will continue in good health, the likelihood they will receive Social Security or pension benefits or an inheritance). More detailed information on pension plan provisions of workers would also be helpful in determining factors that influence savings behavior. Linked family data would help determine the strength of the bequest motive and the factors influencing it. (Some analysis of savings behavior has been conducted with linked family data from the Panel Study of Income Dynamics.) This data need may be of lower priority if policy interest remains generally focused on people with low-to-middle levels of earnings for whom the prospects of significant bequests are relatively low. However, linked family data are important for other purposes, such as understanding care-giving responsibilities and intrafamilial sources of support.

HRS and AHEAD are designed to remedy these kinds of data gaps, and the two surveys will need to be continued if they are to make possible the development of a broadly accepted model of savings and consumption behavior with high explanatory power. Such a model will most likely retain a basic life-cycle approach; however, the evidence of substantial heterogeneity among the population with regard to savings behavior suggests that a satisfactory model will need to incorporate multiple savings motives or distinguish among motives for different kinds of people.

Retirement income projection models need to take account of personal savings, particularly given the possibility of cutbacks in Social Security and employer pension benefits. Although such cutbacks may not occur, they will very likely be considered, and, hence, policy makers will want estimates of their likely effects. The lack of agreement on the most appropriate analytical model constrains the ability of projection models to estimate the likely effects of policy changes on personal savings. In the absence of clear directions from research, it will be very important for projection models to provide sensitivity analyses under alternative behavioral assumptions.

## Labor and Leisure

A great deal has been learned about labor supply and retirement behavior in the last 20 years; indeed, more is known about labor supply and pension acceptance decisions than about almost any other aspect of retirement behavior (see Lumsdaine, 1996). One reason is that such behavior is easier to measure than, for example, consumption and savings. Another reason is the availability of rich longitudinal panel data sets for analysis of labor-leisure choices. Earlier panels, such as the Retirement History Survey (RHS), lacked detailed information about workers' pension and health care coverage, but this weakness has been corrected in the new HRS. Repeated cross-sectional surveys, such as the March Current Population Survey (CPS), have also provided valuable information on labor supply trends for population groups.[4]

What is known about men's retirement behavior underscores the extent of heterogeneity among workers.[5] A large fraction of men (40-50%) work full time at a career job until their early 60s and then remain out of the labor force for the rest of their lives. Typically, they apply for Social Security benefits and a pension, if they have one, at age 62 or at age 65. (Some apply for a pension even before they are eligible for Social Security at age 62.) Another large fraction (over 40%) never retire or have complicated in-and-out labor supply patterns.

---

[4]The availability of rich data sets in this area resulted from concerns with the trend toward early retirement in the 1960s that led to support for panel surveys, such as the RHS and the National Longitudinal Surveys of Labor Market Experience (NLS). Two decades later, HRS and AHEAD were initiated to update the picture on retirement and to respond to concerns about savings behavior and the health status of an aging population. We argue that a concern with changes in employer behavior should motivate support for employer-based surveys, in addition to the continuation of panel surveys of individuals.

[5]This summary description is based largely on the RHS. More recent studies support the general characterization, although some trends already evident in the RHS—such as the shift in the modal age of retirement from age 65 to age 62—are more pronounced in later data (see Buron, Haveman, and O'Donnell, 1995; Karoly and Rogowski, 1994; Peracchi and Welch, 1994). Less is known about women's retirement behavior because, historically, fewer data have been available.

Very few individuals (less than 5%) phase out of the labor market by gradually reducing their hours of work, probably because of employer constraints on work hours. Factors that influence age at retirement include the availability of employer pensions and retiree health insurance coverage, Social Security provisions, eligibility for Medicare, and the individual's health status.

There is general agreement among researchers that Social Security and Medicare provisions have important effects on retirement behavior, at least for the subset of workers who are not at the upper tail of the income and wealth distribution and whose Social Security benefits are not dwarfed by employer pensions. However, there is a large range of uncertainty about the exact magnitude of individual responses to various policies. Much of this uncertainty stems from disagreement about the appropriate strategy for modeling individual behavior—whether to use reduced-form statistical models or structural econometric models (see Lumsdaine, 1996:70-75).

Reduced-form models do not require the researcher to impose any underlying theory of individual behavior. Hence, they are much easier to formulate and estimate than are structural models, which are derived from an explicit theory of individual behavior and make strong, a priori assumptions. Reduced-form models allow for flexibility in the choice of functional form, which, in turn, makes it easier than in structural models to learn about the data. However, unless policies have changed a great deal in the past, reduced-form models cannot estimate the independent effect of policy parameters on behavior and hence have great difficulty in forecasting how behavior will change under alternative policy regimes.

Structural models can provide estimates of policy effects, even when there has been little historical variation, because they impose a priori identifying assumptions on the data, which typically involve strong restrictions on the nature of individual preferences. However, if the model's assumptions are incorrect, then its predictions are likely to be incorrect. Moreover, there will generally be several sets of assumptions about preferences that "explain" any given body of historical data. If each set gives different predictions about the likely effect of a policy change, there will be little objective basis to choose among them.

Despite these problems, the structural approach does appear to yield accurate predictions of the effects of policy changes on retirement behavior in the limited number of out-of-sample predictive tests that have been performed to date. For example, Lumsdaine, Stock, and Wise (1990) estimated a dynamic structural model of retirement decisions at a Fortune 500 firm by using data prior to the introduction of a temporary window plan that created substantial incentives for workers to leave the firm. The model did a reasonably good job of predicting the large increase in retirement rates for most people of the relevant ages after the introduction of the window plan, whereas a variety of reduced-form models performed poorly in this regard.

Questions about future directions for labor supply and pension acceptance research include in what ways to pursue the use of complex structural models.

Important issues to be addressed are whether such models should be static or dynamic, what kinds of uncertainties need to be modeled, and how comprehensive the overall model needs to be.

Another important question is whether structural models should continue to assume completely optimizing behavior (as defined by economic theory) on the part of individual workers. Such an assumption can be modified (e.g., by assuming that people use various rules of thumb, such as work until age 65 and then retire); however, doing so is likely to make the modeling task even more difficult. Moreover, it is not clear how to specify the ways in which people who are using rules of thumb or other psychologically influenced decision rules will respond to policy changes.[6]

Important aspects of retirement behavior that are not addressed in current analytical models include workers' decisions to retire or apply for disability benefits and joint retirement decisions of spouses. Another area for work is to integrate models of retirement and savings behavior. The usual approach is to ignore or drastically simplify the nature of consumption and savings choices as they relate to retirement behavior (e.g., assuming that consumption equals income). There is some theoretical and empirical justification for this approach (except for the very wealthy), and the practical difficulties of doing otherwise are formidable. Nonetheless, it may be increasingly important to tackle this problem in order to answer questions about future trade-offs among savings, consumption, and work: for example, the extent to which people will save more, consume less, or work longer if Social Security, employer pensions, or health care benefits become less generous or more costly.

Finally, it is important to determine the applicability of complex structural models for policy use. At present, it may not be feasible to incorporate a full-blown behavioral dynamic programming model of retirement into a microsimulation projection model for estimating the likely effects of alternative Social Security and employer pension policies on retirement income security. The question then becomes what kinds of simplifications are necessary in order to have a practical and usable projection model.

The ability to refine and extend behavioral models of labor supply and retirement depends on the continued availability of rich panel data sets. Data have been much more plentiful on these topics than on consumption and savings or employer behavior. Also, the new HRS promises to fill important data gaps in earlier retirement surveys. But HRS and related surveys must be continued and enhanced to permit the development of more robust estimates of behavioral parameters for use in projecting workers' labor supply responses to policy changes.

---

[6]Questions may be added to HRS and AHEAD to learn about this issue by asking people directly how they make decisions and what information they use.

## DEMOGRAPHIC VARIABLES

### Size and Composition of the Population

Projecting the likely costs and effects of current and alternative retirement-income-related policies requires estimating the number of people alive over the projection period and their distribution by age and other characteristics. In turn, to generate population projections requires estimating births, net immigration, and deaths.

For many retirement-income-related analyses, it is not necessary to estimate future fertility levels because the concern is with the number of retirees (for which projections can extend as long as 50-60 years on the basis of the population alive at year 1) or with the numbers of retirees and workers (for which projections can extend as long as 20 years on that basis). Net immigration is important, but it is heavily influenced by legislation, which means that immigration can be included in projection models as a parameter that can readily be given different values to reflect expected policies.[7]

Estimates of future mortality levels, on the other hand, are important determinants of Social Security trust fund balances in both the short and long term. They also affect the viability of employer pension plans. Simulations by the Social Security actuary show 75-year trust fund balance projections to be more sensitive to assumptions about the future course of mortality than to any other demographic or economic variable in the actuary's cost model (see Board of Trustees [OASDI], 1994:131-132). However, the projections do not allow for extreme assumptions, such as a return to the high birth rates of the 1950s, in which case mortality might not be the driving variable.

Reasonably good data are available on mortality rates by age and sex. The problem is what assumptions to apply to historical data to project mortality rates into the future and how to estimate the uncertainty in the projections, particularly over the long term. The Social Security Administration (SSA) essentially develops mortality projections by extrapolating rates of decline in age-specific death rates for specific causes of death over the previous 20 years. The results, which are inherent in the methodology, imply a sharp slowing of the rates of decline of mortality at all ages, relative both to the previous two decades and to longer run historical trends back to 1900. Lee and Carter (1992), in contrast, project the rates of decline in age-specific mortality rates observed over the twentieth century (not disaggregated by cause of death), which have been fairly steady despite periods of faster and slower progress. Hence, the Lee and Carter projections (and those developed by other researchers) imply a larger retirement-age population than do the SSA projections (or those developed by the Census Bureau).

---

[7]The task is somewhat more complicated than indicated in that net immigration must be distributed into immigration and emigration by such characteristics as age and sex.

A major advantage of the Lee and Carter approach is that it provides probability intervals describing the uncertainty in their extrapolative method. It does not, however, allow for the possibility of "structural breaks," such as the sharp decline in age-specific mortality rates that occurred between the nineteenth and twentieth centuries, and thus it probably underestimates the extent of uncertainty. Nonetheless, the stochastic models used by Lee and Carter and others to estimate the uncertainty in population forecasts represent a major step forward over the approach that is used by SSA and the Census Bureau to convey estimates of uncertainty to policy makers. In the SSA and Census Bureau approach, "high" and "low" scenarios are developed to bound the "intermediate" or expected forecast.

For many policy purposes, it would be highly useful to carry out research that could support projections of mortality rates for other characteristics on which mortality is known to vary, in addition to age and sex. In particular, in order to answer distributional questions, such as the retirement income security of widows relative to married couples or of low versus high earners, it is important to have mortality projections by such characteristics as marital status, income level and other indicators of socioeconomic status, and health or disability status. However, little work has been done to develop such projections.

Recent studies show that social class differentials in mortality (measured by educational levels) have widened sharply for men at all adult ages since 1960, somewhat less so for women (Preston and Elo, 1995). Data from Social Security administrative records could provide the basis for an authoritative study of mortality variation over time by earnings history for people of retirement age. It would also be valuable to use Social Security data to study mortality variation by marital status. However, at present, marital status is recorded only for people who are receiving benefits as a spouse or widow or widower; it is not recorded for people who are receiving benefits on the basis of their own earnings, who may be married or unmarried. SSA is currently appending information on Social Security benefits and mortality to several panels of the Survey of Income and Program Participation. These files could provide the basis for a study of the relationship of mortality to income and marital status for a limited sample.[8]

## Family History

Marital history can have important effects on the income and wealth of the elderly, particularly for women. Research has documented significant drops in economic well-being for women after the divorce or death of a spouse (see, e.g., Holden, 1991), and women are more at risk of being widowed and of not remarrying after either widowhood or divorce. The result, cross-sectionally, is a highly

---

[8]Another source of data on mortality differentials by marital status is the National Longitudinal Mortality Study, which Preston and Elo (1995) used. It has income data but only for the last year.

skewed distribution of income and wealth by marital status and sex among eld-erly people aged 65 and over. In 1995, the poverty rate for single elderly women was 5.6 times the rate for married elderly women; the corresponding ratio for elderly men was 3.0. At the same time, elderly women were more than twice as likely as elderly men to live without a spouse or other family member (Bureau of the Census, 1996:Table 2). Similar patterns are evident for wealth (see Gustman and Juster, 1996:Tables 2-A4, 2-A5). There are also differences in income and wealth by age: older subgroups of the elderly population are poorer and less wealthy than younger subgroups. It has not been determined how much these patterns reflect dissaving and outliving sources of income by people as they age and how much they reflect cohort differences in initial income and wealth levels.

Considerable research has been conducted on models of first marriage and divorce. Less work has been done on remarriage, and relatively little work has been done that is directly relevant for retirement income security policy analysis (see Caldwell, 1993, for a review of the literature; see also McLanahan and Casper, 1995). Needed work includes the development of models of marital behavior and projections of trends that explicitly account for the risks of mar-riage, divorce, widowhood, and remarriage for people as they approach retire-ment age and beyond. Such models and projections should take account of trends in mortality differences by sex and marital status. Work is also needed to draw out the economic consequences of marital histories for post-retirement income and wealth levels. Such work should take account of women's increased labor force participation, which may result in their accumulating higher levels of pen-sion and other wealth than in the past, and of trends in the form of retirement benefits (e.g., lump sums versus annuities), which may adversely affect the retire-ment income security of surviving spouses in particular. Data on former spouses' rights to pension and other benefits are also important to include in analyses that link marital histories and retirement income security.

Another way in which people's family histories affect retirement income security is through the effects on kinship networks. An important policy concern is whether the baby boom generation, which exhibited higher ages at first mar-riage and lower fertility rates than the previous generation, will be supported by as many kin (own children and other relatives). Work on the availability of kin to provide financial support and care-giving for older people has been hampered until recently by the design of household surveys, which historically have not asked about adult children or other relatives not living in the household (see Wolf, 1994, for a review of the literature in this field). Newer surveys, such as HRS, AHEAD, and the National Survey of Families and Households, have at-tempted to remedy this lack with detailed questions about kin networks and intrafamilial transfers.

## Health Status

An important factor to include in retirement-income-related policy projections is the health and disability status of workers and retirees and the likely trends over time. A decrease in mortality for older people has different implications for retirement income security if they suffer from disease or disability or if their additional years of life are active and healthy, with few expensive medical care needs and the opportunity to continue to earn income. Similarly, an increase or decrease in disability levels for workers as they approach retirement has implications for the extent to which they retire early or, when this is not possible, apply for benefits from public and private disability programs. Generally, income and wealth differ markedly by health and disability status. While the direction of causality is not established, it is clearly important to have indicators of health and disability status to understand the distributional consequences for retirement income security of many kinds of proposed policy changes.

Unfortunately, the identification of health and disability status, whether cross-sectionally or longitudinally, is beset with measurement problems and ambiguities of classification. Lee and Skinner (1996), in their review commissioned by the panel, consider the evidence on trends in disability status defined in several different ways: objective health measures, incidence of specific diseases, measures of functional ability, and self-reports. They find a mixed picture, although there appears to be a long-term trend toward lower overall disability levels among the elderly. Self-reported health assessments, however, show marked short-term fluctuations, which may be influenced by such factors as improvements in medical diagnosis. Also, there is a close match between increases and decreases in self-reported disability and changes in disability insurance programs, including changes in the intensity of administrative efforts to ascertain eligibility and to follow up cases once enrolled, as well as changes in eligibility requirements.

Panel data with improved measures of health and disability status are needed to model relationships with key behaviors, including decisions about savings, consumption, and retirement. (The HRS and the AHEAD survey are designed to serve this purpose.) Panel data are also needed to determine trends in disability levels over time and whether, as some researchers hypothesize, morbidity will be "compressed" into the last years of life. Such a compression could lead to significant reductions in the medical care needs and costs of the elderly, although this effect could be offset by such factors as an increase in the proportion of the "oldest old" in the population or a decrease in the availability of family caregivers.

For the purpose of establishing trends, panels need to follow large samples of people for long periods of time; large samples are required because relatively few people are disabled. Also, panels of new cohorts must be initiated periodically. Recent studies that find significant declines in the extent of disability among the elderly (e.g., Manton, Stallard, and Liu, 1993, who use a measure of functional status) are based on data spanning only 7 to 10 years. More years of data are required to confirm these results.

## HEALTH CARE COSTS

No assessment of retirement income security is complete without consideration of likely trends in the magnitude and distribution of health care costs. To the extent that older Americans face rising health care costs that they must finance through some combination of higher health insurance premiums, taxes, and direct out-of-pocket outlays, then a retirement income stream that would have been adequate in the past to cover other needed consumption in addition to medical care may no longer be adequate.

Projections of likely future trends in aggregate medical care costs and in the availability of medical care benefits are subject to extreme uncertainty, given the large number of actors whose behavior must be modeled—federal and state agencies, private health insurers, employers, medical care providers, medical care technology developers, and medical care consumers—and the complexities of the interactions among them. Economic incentives clearly play a role in medical care consumption. However, there is an argument that in the United States the development of new technologies and treatments coupled with a strong disinclination on the part of providers and consumers to forgo their use, once introduced, is a driving force for medical care cost increases. The shift to managed care has reduced the rise in costs, but it is not clear that this trend will continue once excess capacity is wrung out of the system (see Moon, 1995).

In short, determining the relative importance of various factors that influence medical care costs and benefit packages and the role of public or private sector policy changes in changing relevant behaviors presents an almost overwhelming research challenge. Research and models that are focused on retirement income security cannot hope to resolve these issues. What seems most fruitful for retirement-income-related research and modeling to address is the likely distributional consequences of alternative medical care cost and insurance coverage scenarios for the retirement income security of groups of the elderly population.

For this purpose, it is important to develop good estimates of the relationship of health and disability status, insurance coverage, and other individual-level variables (e.g., age, gender, ethnicity, employment status, income level) to medical care costs in a relative sense: that is proportionally how much more is spent on medical care in total and out-of-pocket by people in worse health than by people in better health. The National Medical Expenditure Survey (NMES) is an important data source for this purpose. However, it was last conducted in 1987 (see below), and key relationships may have changed since then as a consequence of major changes that have occurred in health care financing.

Panel data are also needed to determine differences in medical care spending patterns across the years of retirement, taking account of both acute and long-term care costs. The few available studies suggest that spending patterns are correlated across time (the small group of people who are high spenders in one year are high spenders in subsequent years), but that there is a considerable dropoff in the concentration of spending over a long period. There are plans to conduct NMES on a continuing basis, beginning in 1996 and renamed the National Medical Expenditure Panel Survey (MEPS), but individual sample members will only be followed for a 2-year period. The HRS and AHEAD surveys, when linked with Medicare and Medicaid records, may develop a capability to provide needed longitudinal data on the distribution of medical care costs across retirement.

## CONCLUSION

This discussion has touched on an array of important topics for understanding and projecting retirement income security and has identified many gaps in basic research knowledge. In some areas, such as employer benefit plan decisions, employer demand for older workers, and savings and consumption choices of individuals, there is no agreement on the underlying behavioral phenomena. The primary reason for the lack of agreement is lack of data: key data elements are missing or grossly inadequate in one or more respects for either cross-sectional or longitudinal analysis. In other areas, such as labor supply and retirement decisions, better data have been available and more is known. However, there is still disagreement about the strength of key relationships (e.g., to what extent Social Security or Medicare influences age at retirement), and there are still areas that are not fully explored (e.g., the retirement behavior of women and joint decisions of couples). New panel surveys, such as HRS and AHEAD, promise a rich set of information with which to refine labor supply models and also to unlock some of the puzzles in savings and consumption behavior. However, there has been little opportunity as yet to mine these surveys and determine their power or to identify enhancements that may be needed. In still other areas, such as mortality projections, the need is to develop more sophisticated projection models that exploit existing data and to develop methods for estimating uncertainty in the projections, which typically extrapolate past trends for long periods into the future.

We believe that little progress can be made in the development of improved projection modeling tools with which to estimate the likely effects of proposed changes in retirement-income-related government policies until improved analytical models are developed and key knowledge gaps are filled. Filling these gaps requires priority attention to the underlying data needs, the topic of Chapter 4. It also requires systematic research. We end this chapter with a list of priority topics for policy-relevant basic research that should move forward as new and improved data become available; see Box 3-1. Research in many of these areas should be extended to include the experience of other countries with policy initiatives that may be considered in the United States.

## BOX 3-1
## PRIORITIES FOR RESEARCH

### Employer Benefit Decisions and Demand for Older Workers

• Comprehensive descriptions of the distribution of employer benefit plan offerings by characteristics of employers and workers.
• Factors in employers' decisions about pension and other benefit offerings. An appropriate behavioral model could include a combination of such motives and factors as tax deferral considerations and the use of benefit plans as a device for worker selection, productivity enhancement, or to encourage workers to retire.
• The role of changes in government policies—such as anti-age-discrimination rules and other regulatory provisions, tax laws, Medicare, pension insurance—on employer decisions about pensions and other benefit offerings.
• Ways to measure worker productivity.
• Case studies of one or more employers to identify factors that explain employers' decisions about hiring and retention of older workers. Topics of interest include employers' health care costs for older and younger workers; worker productivity and total compensation profiles by age; formal and informal personnel rules; programs for retraining older workers and for allowing flexibility in compensation, hours, and types of jobs; the perceived substitutability of younger and older workers; and the effects of increased international competition, computerization, and the information revolution on the demand for older workers.

### Individual Savings-Consumption Decisions

• Modifications that are needed to the pure life-cycle model of savings and consumption behavior to best explain trends in personal savings. A modified model could include a combination of such motives and factors as precautionary savings, savings for bequests, the use of rules of thumb, different "mental accounts" for different forms of savings. A modified model should integrate consumption and savings with labor supply decisions (since working to older ages is one way to make up for lack of savings).
• Heterogeneity in savings behavior—including why many people approach retirement with very little savings—as a function of such factors as differences in preferences, differences in knowledge and expectations about sources of retirement income and likely future events, liquidity constraints.
• The substitutability of different forms of savings, specifically tax-deferred savings vehicles (e.g., IRAs and 401(k) pension plans) vis-à-vis non-tax-deferred savings vehicles.

- Patterns of savings and dissavings in the post-retirement years, including disposition of housing and pension assets, to determine differences in economic well-being at older ages.
- The effects of health status and expectations of future health status and expenditures on savings behavior and consumption levels after retirement.
- Lump-sum pension receipts, including how many and what kinds of workers are taking such benefits and the consequences for economic well-being after retirement.
- Reasons for the secular decline in personal savings, including such factors as the effects of government policies (expansion of Social Security, other safety net programs) and the extension of employer pension coverage.

### Individual Labor Supply Decisions

- The various paths to eventual retirement—such as spells of self-employment following a career job, retraining for a new job—and the consequences for economic well-being after retirement.
- The role of nonmonetary aspects of work, including the work environment as perceived by workers, on retirement decisions.
- Reestimation of dynamic structural models of labor supply and retirement decisions with panel data sets that provide detailed information on employer pension and health insurance plan rules; health status, disability, and illness; and Social Security benefits.
- Extension of existing analytical models to address simultaneous decisions to retire or apply for disability benefits.
- Extension of existing models to address joint retirement decisions of spouses.
- Extension of existing models to incorporate individual-specific information on subjective beliefs (e.g., one's own life expectancy or expected receipt of pension benefits), in order to relax the strong restrictions implied by the "rational expectations" approach that is typically used to estimate individuals' beliefs.

### Demographic Factors

- Use of Social Security Administration records and other data to estimate mortality rates by earnings and marital status, in order to improve projections of families' economic status after retirement.
- Better models of the determinants and consequences of marital changes, with explicit attention to marriage, divorce, and remarriage pat-

*continued on next page*

## BOX 3-1 *Continued*

terns for older people and the effects on retirement income and wealth of people with different marital experiences.

### Health, Health Care, and Care-Giving

- Trends in health status and disability over time and for people as they age, including acute and long-term care costs over the span of retirement. Address the question of whether, as life expectancy increases, morbidity and disability will likely "compress" into fewer years of life.
- The distribution of health care costs by age and for age groups by such factors as health status, gender, ethnicity, employment status, and income level.
- Trends in family living arrangements and the likely effects on care-giving patterns—including increased or decreased use of institutionalized care or home care—and retirement income security.

### Heterogeneity of Outcomes

- Comprehensive assessments of components of income and wealth for individuals and families to track the extent of heterogeneity in the retirement well-being of different cohorts and groups as they age.

# 4

# Data Needs

Within the next few years, policy debates about the retirement income security of current and future generations of Americans are likely to require a range of modeling capabilities with which to evaluate and project the likely effects of alternative policy proposals. However, as is clear from the preceding chapter, there are important gaps and uncertainties in what is known about the behaviors and processes that affect retirement income security. These gaps stem from deficiencies in available data, which hamper or preclude the development of robust analytical models and parameter estimates from them. In some cases, notably for employers, there are insufficient data with which to describe the distribution of relevant employer and employee characteristics, much less to support analysis of behavioral change over time.

These deficiencies need to be remedied and the knowledge base further developed before it will be possible to construct reasonably adequate projection models with broad capabilities. Moreover, existing retirement income related projection models and the associated databases have many limitations and do not generally provide an adequate platform on which to develop improved models once new data and research knowledge become available (see Chapter 5 and Appendix D; see also Hollenbeck, 1995).

Thus, there is a great deal of work to do to prepare for the policy debate. With very tight budget constraints, the question is one of priorities. We conclude that agencies should devote the bulk of their limited resources over the next few years to data collection and analysis rather than making significant investments in large-scale projection models. This conclusion is based on our assessment that some of the gaps in needed data and basic research are so critical that projection models, no matter how elaborate or elegant, cannot compensate for them. An example is the failure of existing research to adequately explain observed savings patterns in the population.

Moreover, past experience suggests that it takes more time to collect new data and analyze them than it does to build a projection model to use data and research in estimating the likely consequences of policy changes. There are more than a few instances in the history of policy analysis when models were built in a span of weeks or months. As an example, the prototype of the Carter administration's welfare reform projection model, KGB, was completed in a few weeks (see Citro and Hanushek, 1991:107-114). It is very rare that needed new data can be obtained and analyzed sufficiently in so short a time, particularly if the data set is rich enough to be useful. A small-scale, quick-response survey of employers' health care costs was completed for use in the recent health care reform debate within 10 months from initial design to final output (Ponikowski, Scheible, and Wiatrowski, 1994), but its scope was very limited. More detailed information on employers' health care plans and costs that would have been useful, from a large survey for which the design work had begun in spring 1993, was still not available by the end of 1996 (Hing et al., 1995).

## THE LESSON FROM HEALTH CARE REFORM

The experiences and reflections of policy analysts who provided estimates for the 1993-1994 health care reform debate underscore the panel's conclusion about giving priority to investments in data and research. Box 4-1 describes the major players in health care reform estimation and the models and databases they used.[1] More lead time and prior investment would have facilitated the development of usable projection models for estimating the likely effects of alternative health care reform plans. Indeed, some timely investments that were made in model building were helpful (e.g., the extension of the TRIM2 model to simulate employer-provided health care benefits). Conversely, inexperience with building health care projection models, particularly with a database not previously used for this purpose, was a handicap. That was the case, for example, for the Agency for Health Care Policy and Research (AHCPR), which based its new AHSIM model on the 1987 National Medical Expenditure Survey (NMES).

However, the model builders themselves pointed to major difficulties that stemmed from the absence of critical data and research; see Box 4-2.[2] Existing data were so inadequate that it was difficult to develop an agreed-upon "baseline" scenario—that is, a representation of the current distribution of health insurance coverage, utilization of services, costs, and other characteristics of consumers,

---

[1]Information for this discussion and Box 4-1 comes from Bandeian and Lewin (1994), Bilheimer and Reischauer (1996), Citro and Hanushek (1991, esp. Chap. 5), Nichols (1996), Office of Technology Assessment (1993, 1994), Sheils (1996), and interviews with analysts.

[2]See footnote 1.

providers, and insurers—let alone simulate the likely effects of alternative reforms relative to the baseline. Bilheimer and Reischauer (1996:149), speaking from the Congressional Budget Office (CBO) experience, flatly concluded: "To construct a comprehensive picture of the health care system is impossible with today's databases. What is known must be pieced together from several inadequate or dated surveys and sources."

Also lacking was up-to-date research with which to estimate behavioral responses to changes in the health care system. Bilheimer and Reischauer (1996:152) noted that "such studies can credibly illuminate only the effects of marginal changes in the current environment. The effects of large, systemic changes that major health care reform proposals would generate are far outside the boundaries of knowledge that can be gleaned from existing economic research or even from social experiments." Nonetheless, they identified several areas in which better data about the current system would have made it possible to develop more credible estimates of the effects of reform proposals (see Box 4-2; see also Bandeian and Lewin, 1994).

In the absence of key data and research, rough estimates based on very inadequate information or simply guesses were used for values of behavioral parameters, and no projection model, however complex or elegant, could compensate for the lacking information. Different models incorporated widely different assumptions in key areas, and consequently, there were significant differences in estimates of the likely effects for the same reform plan (see Office of Technology Assessment, 1993, 1994). Differences in databases—for example, between the March 1994 Current Population Survey (CPS) and the 1987 NMES aged to 1993-1994—also contributed to differences in estimates.

Moreover, in the heat of debate, it proved difficult, if not impossible, to develop new sources of needed information on a timely basis. Subsequently, and anticipating future health care policy debates, AHCPR and the National Center for Health Statistics (NCHS) are working to implement a major reorganization and expansion of health-related surveys that could meet many of the information requirements identified by participants in the 1993-1994 effort (Hunter and Arnett, 1996).

The picture is much the same for retirement-income-related policy analysis, namely, that key descriptive and analytical data with which to develop credible projections of the likely effects of current and alternative policies are missing or incomplete. As with health care reform, even the best data and analysis are unlikely to resolve the uncertainty associated with major policy changes, such as privatization of Social Security (which would resemble a system of universally mandated Individual Retirement Accounts), because there is no historical experience on which to base any models.[3] For example, an important issue about

---

[3]However, research on the experience of other countries with privatization schemes may help develop projections for a U.S. system.

---

**BOX 4-1
HEALTH CARE REFORM ESTIMATION:
MAJOR PLAYERS AND THEIR MODELS**

*The Congressional Budget Office (CBO)* was officially charged with "scoring" the administration's health care reform plan and alternatives that were introduced as legislation, that is, estimating the budgetary costs to the government. Originally, CBO tried to build a comprehensive micro-simulation model that could estimate medical care costs and premiums and the distribution of costs across taxpayers, consumers, and employers under each health care reform proposal. However, these efforts came to naught, and the agency fell back on ad hoc methods of developing estimates. (CBO budget analysts typically build their own spreadsheet models and make many "out-of-model" adjustments.)

*The U.S. Department of the Treasury* had official responsibility for estimating tax revenue gains or losses from the various plans. Treasury used its tax policy microsimulation model with estimates of medical care costs and premiums that were developed by the *Health Care Financing Administration (HCFA) in the U.S. Department of Health and Human Services (HHS)* by applying actuarial methods to aggregate data. Treasury also incorporated microdata from the 1987 National Medical Expenditure Survey (NMES) into its basic model, which uses a combination of Internal Revenue Service (IRS) tax returns and information from the March Current Population Survey (CPS). HCFA also had a March CPS-based model Special Policy Analysis Model (SPAM) to estimate distributions of aggregate premiums.

*The Assistant Secretary for Planning and Evaluation (ASPE) in HHS* obtained estimates of costs and financing for various reform scenar-

---

privatization is whether it will increase or decrease personal saving. One can argue that privatization will educate people about saving and what it can do for them and thereby lead millions of people who now save little or nothing to save much more, in addition to their mandatory privatized accounts. But one can also plausibly argue that people will be more confident of actually obtaining payments from their dedicated personal accounts than they are of receiving Social Security benefits and thus will curtail other forms of saving (see Mitchell and Zeldes, 1996).

Nonetheless, as with health care reform, filling key gaps in data and research knowledge can go a long way to make it possible to develop credible projections of the likely effects of many retirement-income-related policy alternatives. We urge that priority be given to strengthening the base of data and research for ios from the March CPS-based TRIM2 microsimulation model. TRIM2 is maintained by the *Urban Institute* under contract to ASPE and has been used for many years for welfare program policy projections. Recently, the *U.S. Department of Labor* funded an extension of the model to simulate employer-provided health insurance benefits with data from the 1987 NMES and other sources. TRIM2 employed HCFA's aggregate estimates of medical care costs and premiums in projecting the likely effects of various reform plans. (HCFA's methods assumed that medical care providers and consumers would not change their behaviors in ways that would affect the case mix under alternative proposals.)

*The Agency for Health Care Policy and Research (AHCPR)* developed its own model (AHSIM) from scratch on the basis of the 1987 NMES. Beginning in summer 1992, AHCPR devoted substantial resources (money, agency staff, and subcontractor programming staff) to model development, and ultimately the agency was able to provide large numbers of estimates to the *Office of Management and Budget (OMB)*. However, development of the model was delayed by such factors as its scope (AHSIM simulated premiums under health care reform and included some behavioral response) and the decision to use the 1987 NMES as a primary model database in contrast to adding selected data elements and parameter estimates derived from NMES to another database, as was done in the case of TRIM2 and the Treasury tax model. Delays in producing estimates from all the models stemmed from attempts to resolve key differences, such as between premium estimates.

*Lewin-VHI,* a private consulting firm, had developed a Health Benefits Simulation Model in the late 1980s with data from the 1980 National Medical Care Utilization and Expenditure Survey (NMCUES). Lewin/VHI updated its model with data from the 1987 NMES and prepared estimates for a number of private sector clients.

retirement income modeling—through improvement of existing data sets whenever possible and through new data collection when necessary, and including appropriate levels of funding for analytical research and validation.

The remainder of this chapter addresses: the dimensions of databases that should be considered in designing and evaluating cost-effective retirement-income-related data collection systems, whether new or modified; issues in continuing existing panel surveys of middle-aged and older people in order to provide sufficient longitudinal observations for analysis of consumption, savings, and retirement behavior of individuals; issues in developing new and improved cross-sectional and panel data for employers and their workers in order to understand labor demand and employer decisions about pensions and other benefits; issues in linking administrative and survey data, which can be a cost-effective

## BOX 4-2
## MAJOR DATA GAPS FOR HEALTH CARE
## REFORM ESTIMATION

*No household survey provided a complete set of needed information for constructing a baseline.* The March Current Population Survey provides data on type of insurance coverage (employer-provided, Medicare, etc.); whether the employer paid all, part, or none of the premium; and demographic and socioeconomic characteristics. It does not cover household members' health status or health care utilization; the type or generosity of their health care plans; how much the household paid in premiums or out of pocket; the fraction of the premium paid by the employer; whether people without insurance could have obtained it but chose not to; or whether workers with individual coverage could have obtained family coverage. The National Health Interview Survey provides data on type of coverage, reasons people lack coverage, health status, and use of health services, but its information on income and employment is limited, and it provides no data on premiums or cost-sharing requirements or the exact share paid by employers. Finally, NMES provides much of the needed information for households, but, to date, it has been conducted sporadically: for health care reform estimation, the 1987 NMES had to be "aged" forward to 1993-1994.

*Even fewer baseline data were available for employers.* County Business Patterns provides basic information on employer size and payroll from Census Bureau sources, but the public-use version provides data for types of establishments, not employers. The employment data do not distinguish full-time from part-time employees, and there is no information on employer wage distributions or benefits or on the age or family status of employees. An employer survey conducted by the Health Insurance Association of America provided some of the needed information but suffered from high levels of nonresponse. The Employee Benefits Survey describes health care coverage that is available to employees in broad occupation categories in small and medium and large-sized companies and governments, but the information is not available by characteristics of employers, and there is no information on employer costs. The 1994 National Health Employer Insurance Survey was designed to fill this lack but was not completed in time for use in the reform debate.

*No state or substate estimates of medical care costs were available.* The Health Care Financing Administration prepares annual estimates of aggregate medical care spending in total and for various services. However, such information is not available for states or substate regions, which were the relevant market areas in most of the proposed health care reforms.

*Up-to-date research was lacking on which to develop assumptions about behavioral responses to health care reform.* Kinds of information that would have improved the estimation include the following:

• Information on how much employers currently pay for premiums, as a function of various characteristics, would have made it easier to estimate how many and which kinds of employers would have paid more than the minimum required by the employer mandates in some of the reform plans. In turn, such estimates were needed to estimate the likely behavior of two-worker families who were eligible for coverage in both a community-rated and an experience-rated insurance pool, which was used for large employers. These estimates were also needed to estimate the costs of subsidies and tax expenditures associated with employment-based health insurance.

• Information on the health status of workers and their families for different types of employers and the variation among large employers would have been helpful in estimating the proportion of large employers who would have chosen to participate in the community pool, an option under the administration's plan.

• Information on individuals' risk aversion, inertia, and other noneconomic factors that affect choice of policies would have been useful in estimating how many people would drop out of the community pool because the premium exceeded their expected benefit, adjusted for risk. Such estimates were needed under plans that did not require people to obtain health insurance.

• More recent information than the 1987 NMES on the size of population groups not currently covered by health insurance and their employment status and health care utilization would have made it easier to estimate participation in the community-rated versus experience-rated pools and the effects on premiums. These groups are people who have been denied coverage because of preexisting conditions, those who want to but cannot afford to obtain insurance, and those who could afford coverage but have other priorities, such as healthy young adults who assume they have low risk.

• Information for employers on wage distributions, workers' family types, and other linked employer-employee characteristics would have been helpful for estimating subsidy amounts for employers under various proposals. The 1987 NMES linked characteristics of employers and health insurance plan provisions with characteristics of employees in the NMES household sample, but the information was out of date.

---

**BOX 4-3**
**DIMENSIONS OF DATABASES**

*Source* Databases may derive from sample surveys or censuses or from administrative records systems that are primarily intended for such nonresearch purposes as program operations or regulation. Some databases are hybrids that link survey or census data and administrative records.

*Reporting Unit and Universe* Typical reporting units include members of such universes as adults in households, workers covered by Social Security, people in certain age ranges, employers of certain types or sizes.

*Type and Frequency* Databases may represent a single cross-section, in which data are collected for a set of reporting units for one time (e.g., a month, year); a set of repeated cross-sections, in which the same data are collected for new sets of reporting units at regular intervals (e.g., every year or 5 years); a single panel, in which data are collected at regular intervals for the same set of reporting units over time; or a set of repeated panels, in which a new panel is introduced periodically. Panels are the primary source of longitudinal data; however, repeated cross-sections may include some panel features, such as retaining part of the previous time period's sample for a subsequent reporting period or ascertaining historical information on a retrospective basis.

*Scope* Included in the scope of a database are the subject areas covered, the detail provided on each covered topic, and the geographic identification available for each reporting unit.

---

means of obtaining high-quality measures of key variables with minimal added expenditure; and issues of data validation, internally and in comparison with other sources.

## DIMENSIONS OF DATABASES

Databases differ on a number of dimensions, including source, reporting unit and universe, type and frequency, scope, size, data collection method(s), accuracy or validity, uncertainty, ease of use, level of aggregation, and cost; see Box 4-3. There are trade-offs to consider among these dimensions. For example, the level of uncertainty in survey responses can be reduced by increasing the sample size; however, such a decision will increase costs. Similarly, an expansion of the number and detail of survey questions will make a survey more useful for a wider

*Size* As distinguished from the scope of a database, size refers to the number of reporting units, both in numerical terms and as a fraction of the universe.

*Data Collection Method(s)* Data may be collected by mail, telephone, or personal interview, using paper-and-pencil or computerized questionnaires or administrative reporting forms.

*Accuracy or Validity* Data accuracy is influenced by many factors, such as the wording of questions, recall and other response errors on the part of reporting units, and the extent of missing or refused responses.

*Uncertainty* The degree of uncertainty in the estimates from a survey is a function of sample size and design. (Censuses and administrative records that cover an entire universe are not subject to sampling variability.)

*Ease of Use* The ease with which the data can be used for analytical or projection modeling purposes is influenced by the complexity of the underlying information, the file formats and coding schemes that are used to represent the information, and the data file documentation.

*Level of Aggregation* Data are generally collected on a microlevel basis, that is, for individual people or employers; however some databases provide information only for aggregates, such as all large employers or all elderly people as a group.

*Cost* The costs of collecting, processing, and analyzing the information in a database are affected by many factors, including scope, size, type and frequency, data collection methods, and others. Another cost is the burden on respondents to provide the information.

range of purposes, but increase its cost and the burden it places on respondents. Such an expansion may also make the data more difficult for analysts to use.

There are also trade-offs with regard to the use of administrative records instead of survey data. Administrative records are usually thought to be more accurate than survey responses. They are also relatively inexpensive to use for analysis because the costs of data collection and processing have already been incurred for administrative purposes. However, such records usually lack detailed content, and their content may change from year to year to reflect changes in program data requirements. Also, administrative records are not without errors (e.g., Social Security and Medicare records may have inaccurate information on whether individuals are still alive). Indeed, when comparing information for the same variable in an administrative records data set with a survey estimate, it is important to take account of likely errors in both sources and of differences in definitions and other features that could affect the comparison. Finally, administrative records are often inaccessible to researchers because of concerns about maintaining confidentiality for individuals and other reporting units.

Data sources are rarely satisfactory for both analytical and projection modeling purposes on every dimension. In fact, analytical and projection models often use different types of data. For example, analytical models of individual behavior generally require rich longitudinal data from panel surveys, but models that project individual outcomes rarely use panel surveys as their primary database because of small sample sizes and restricted universes.[4] Yet if the projection model database does not contain a similarly rich set of variables as were used to estimate key behavioral relationships in an analytical model, it will not be possible to take advantage of the most advanced behavioral models. Instead, the behavioral relationships will have to be reestimated with a reduced variable set, or such procedures as statistical matching (see Cohen, 1991b) will have to be used to impute needed variables to the primary database. (We discuss this issue further in Chapter 5.)

## PANEL DATA ON INDIVIDUALS

An underlying theme throughout our report and the papers we commissioned (Hanushek and Maritato, 1996) is the need to understand how people reach their retirement years. What enters into decisions about working as people age? What are the implications of different employment paths for pension plan participation and the level of benefits received in retirement? How do government and employer policies affect personal savings behavior and the ultimate wealth accumulations that influence both retirement decisions and well-being in retirement?

Questions such as these emphasize two key issues that have implications for data collection and analysis. First, many of the antecedents of retirement outcomes are present long before any actual retirement decisions. Second, behavior that is related to policy often has a long time horizon, with individuals looking many years into the future as they make decisions. To obtain suitable data for analysis, it is essential to follow individuals over many years in order to understand their retirement behavior and outcomes.

This central fact leads us to emphasize the development of panel surveys that obtain longitudinal data by interviewing the same individuals over time. Panel surveys, which have become increasingly common to study individual behavior, permit investigation of behavior that evolves and that has implications over long periods. Moreover, panel surveys provide a variety of ways for dealing with the heterogeneity across individuals that can complicate analyses based

---

[4]An exception is a recently developed public assistance model—STEWARD (Simulation of Trends in Employment, Welfare, and Related Dynamics)—which directly uses data from the National Longitudinal Survey of Youth (NLSY) to simulate the effects of welfare reform proposals on program participation (Jacobson and Czajka, 1994).

solely on a cross-section of individuals. Finally, panel surveys can often permit corrections for measurement and observational errors because consistency checks for individuals over time can aid in separating errors from true changes for individuals.

Of course, the need to follow the same individuals over long periods implies that a panel survey is likely to be expensive—certainly more expensive than a one-time cross-sectional survey of equivalent size and perhaps more expensive than a repeated cross-sectional survey.[5] Also, for cost reasons, it may be difficult in a panel survey to refresh the sample frequently enough to address such questions as whether patterns of behavior remain the same for newer cohorts or to maintain representation of a changing population (e.g., to represent immigrants).

The trade-offs often suggest the need for cross-sectional data collection. For example, we argue below for collecting data to understand employer behavior that is relevant for retirement income security, but we believe that the first step is to improve cross-sectional data. Although a panel may later be appropriate, the initial efforts—which include learning about what data to collect and how and what the sampling frame should be—would most appropriately be thought of as a cross-sectional effort. Also, there is a need for regularly updated descriptive information on trends in the characteristics of employers, work forces, and benefits that more efficiently comes from repeated cross-sections than from panels.[6]

Similarly, repeated, nationally representative cross-sectional surveys are needed to provide important data on trends in the population that are relevant to tracking and understanding retirement outcomes (e.g., trends in ages at retirement). Nonetheless, the central longitudinal data with which to analyze individual behavior and individual decisions should almost certainly be gathered through panels of individuals. Although cross-sectional surveys can use retrospective questions to collect longitudinal information, such as employment and earnings histories (and in some cases this is done), the quality of retrospective information is much less, compared with panel surveys, because of recall and other errors, which may be large (see, e.g., Kennickell and Starr-McCluer, 1995). Also, cross-sectional surveys are limited in the amount of retrospective information that they can collect due to considerations of respondent burden. Panel surveys, in contrast, can obtain a wealth of information with which to understand different life courses and retirement outcomes.

---

[5]Whether a panel survey is more or less expensive than a repeated cross-sectional survey with the same number of sample members is affected by many factors, such as frequency of interviews, costs of obtaining an interview (a panel survey may have higher costs to locate sample members but lower costs to obtain an interview once the sample member is located), and others.

[6]Panel surveys will provide consistent time series for a population as well if a new panel is introduced on a frequent basis, such as every year; however, costs will be prohibitive unless the size or length (or both) of each panel is reduced, which will, in turn, reduce the usefulness of each panel for longitudinal analysis.

## Features of Long-Term Panel Surveys

Several completed and ongoing panel surveys sponsored by government agencies have made possible a wide range of retirement-income-related analyses. Table 4-1 presents the basic features of major retirement-income-related panel surveys, which have followed or are intended to follow samples of individuals over long periods; see also Figure 4-1. (Appendix B provides more detailed descriptions for these and other relevant panel surveys of individuals.)

In particular, the Retirement History Survey (RHS), sponsored by the Social Security Administration (SSA), and the National Longitudinal Surveys of Labor Market Experience (NLS), sponsored by the Bureau of Labor Statistics (BLS), have supported extensive research on labor supply behavior and the retirement decision. As of 1988, over 200 articles and reports were identified that drew on the 1969-1979 RHS (Smith, 1988). An annotated bibliography of research conducted with the various NLS cohort panels over the period 1968-1995 fills a 2-inch volume and numbers 2,540 entries (Fahy, 1995).

However, surveys like the RHS that were initiated several decades ago do not contain the richness of data needed for research on retirement and savings decisions. Thus, the RHS, which followed a cohort of single men and women and married men (aged 58-63 in 1969) and their spouses over 10 years, lacks questions on respondents' expectations about such factors as their own life span. The RHS also lacks detailed information on pension plan coverage and health status and health care benefit coverage. It contains a fair amount of information about assets and expenditures, but no direct measure of total consumption. The NLS cohorts that began in the late 1960s (mature women, older men, young men, and young women) and the cohort of youth (young men and women) that began in 1979 (NLSY) also lack the full set of information that researchers would like. Boxes 4-4, 4-5, 4-6, and 4-7 show, respectively, the information in major retirement-income-related panel surveys about expectations, pension coverage, health status and health insurance coverage, and assets and expenditures.

The older panel surveys also vary in the length of time with which they followed, or are continuing to follow, sample members. For example, the National Longitudinal Survey of Young Women has followed for over 25 years a sample of women who were aged 14-24 when first interviewed in 1968; they are now in their 40s. However, the companion National Longitudinal Survey of Young Men stopped following a sample of men who were aged 14-24 when first interviewed in 1966 after only 15 years.

Hence, there are gaps in the extent of longitudinal data that are available across cohorts of men and women; see Table 4-1 and Figure 4-1 (below). Specifically, there are no NLS surveys that cover men who are currently in their 40s, 50s, or 60s or that cover women who are currently in their 50s or 70s. A new

*Text continued on page 88.*

TABLE 4-1  Features of Major Retirement-Income-Related Panel Surveys

| Survey | Ages of Sample Members and Date at Initial Interview | Initial Sample Size | Frequency of Interviews | Links with Administrative Records Performed or Planned |
|---|---|---|---|---|
| Asset and Health Dynamics Among the Oldest Old (AHEAD)[a] | Men and women aged 70+ in 1993-94; spouses also interviewed | 8,223 (oversample of blacks, Hispanics, and Florida residents) | Every 2 years; ongoing | Medicare, SSA earnings, SSA benefits, Medicaid, NDI |
| Health and Retirement Survey (HRS) | Men and women aged 51-61 in 1992; spouses also interviewed | 12,654 (oversample of blacks, Hispanics, and Florida residents) | Every 2 years; ongoing | Medicare, SSA earnings, NDI, employer health plans, employer pension plans (Summary Plan Description) |
| AHEAD/HRS New Cohorts[a] | Men and women aged 51-56 and 69-75 in 1998-99; spouses also to be interviewed | About 7,000 | Every 2 years | Same as original cohorts |
| National Longitudinal Survey of Mature Women (NLS-MW) | Women aged 30-44 in 1967; some data collected also for spouses | 5,000 (oversample of blacks) | Every 1 to 3 years; ongoing | Employer pension plans (Summary Plan Description) for 1989 |

continued on next page

TABLE 4-1  Continued

| Survey | Ages of Sample Members and Date at Initial Interview | Initial Sample Size | Frequency of Interviews | Links with Administrative Records Performed or Planned |
|---|---|---|---|---|
| National Longitudinal Survey of Older Men (NLS-OM) | Men aged 45-60 in 1966; some data collected also for spouses | 5,000 (oversample of blacks) | Every 1 to 2 years until 1983; reinterview in 1990 with surviving sample members and widows | None |
| National Longitudinal Survey of Young Women (NLS-YW) | Women aged 14-24 in 1968; some data collected also for spouses | 5,000 (oversample of blacks) | Every 1 to 3 years; ongoing | None |
| National Longitudinal Survey of Young Men (NLS-YM) | Men aged 14-24 in 1966; some data collected also for spouses | 5,000 (oversample of blacks) | Every 1 to 2 years until 1981 | None |
| National Longitudinal Survey of Youth (Young Men and Women) (NLSY) | Men and women aged 14-21 in 1979; some data collected also for spouses | 13,000 (oversample of blacks and Hispanics; oversample of economically disadvantaged | Every year until 1994; then every 2 years beginning in 1996; ongoing | None |

| Survey | Sample | Sample size | Frequency | Administrative data |
|---|---|---|---|---|
| Retirement History Survey (RHS) | Men and single women aged 58-63 in 1969; data collected also for spouses of married men | whites dropped after 1990; oversample of people in military dropped after 1984) 11,150 | Every 2 years until 1979 | SSA earnings |
| Panel Study of Income Dynamics (PSID) | Households headed by people of all ages in 1968; household head interviewed; detailed information collected also about spouse or cohabitor since 1976 | 5,000 original families; new families formed from them; sample of Hispanic families added in 1990; sample of immigrant families to be added in 1997; as of 1993, sample included 2,250 people aged 65+ | Every year until 1995; then every 2 years beginning in 1997; ongoing | Medicare data beginning in 1984 for sample members giving permission in 1990 |

NOTES: SSA, Social Security Administration; NDI, National Death Index. For more information about each survey and references, see Appendix B; data collected for spouses are useful for analysis of sample members but are not themselves a representative sample of any particular age group.

[a]When the HRS/AHEAD new cohorts are introduced in 1998-1999, HRS/AHEAD will be representative of the entire population aged 51 and older and will be conducted as one survey with a combined questionnaire. If planned funding continues, new cohorts will be added every 5 years as they reach ages 51-56.

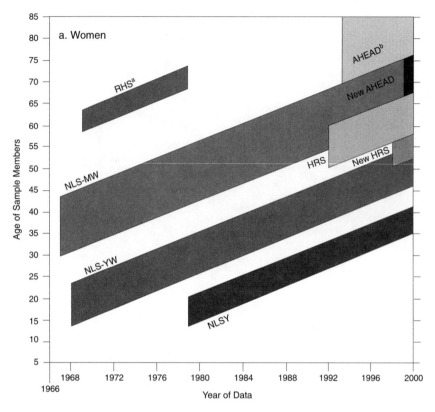

FIGURE 4-1   Ages of participants in retirement-income-related panel surveys.

NOTES:  AHEAD, Asset and Health Dynamics Among the Oldest Old; HRS, Health and Retirement Survey; NLS-MW, National Longitudinal Survey of Mature Women; NLS-OM, National Longitudinal Survey of Older Men; NLS-YM, National Longitudinal Survey of Young Men; NLS-YW, National Longitudinal Survey of Young Women; NLSY, National Longitudinal Survey of Youth (Young Men and Women); RHS, Retirement History Survey.  See Table 4-1 for frequency of data collection for each survey; interviews after 1996 are subject to provision of funding.

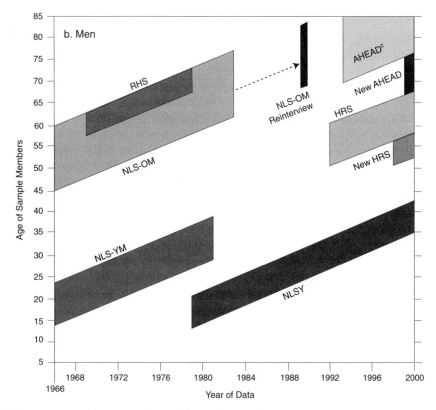

[a]Single women and spouses of married men in age cohort.

[b]No upper age limit; 4.5 percent of female respondents in the initial AHEAD interview in 1993-1994 were aged 90 or older (Hurd et al., 1994:Table 5).

[c]No upper age limit; 2.6 percent of male respondents in the initial AHEAD interview in 1993-1994 were aged 90 or older (Hurd et al., 1994:Table 5).

## BOX 4-4
## DATA ON RETIREMENT-RELATED EXPECTATIONS:
## SELECTED PANEL SURVEYS

### HEALTH AND RETIREMENT SURVEY (HRS)
#### People Working for an Employer

Probability of being laid off in next year (scale of 0-10)
Probability of finding an equally good job if laid off
Whether would accept move to another state or a layoff
Probability of working full-time after age 62, after age 65
Probability that health will limit activity during next 10 years
Expect real earnings to go up, down, or stay the same in next few years
Retirement plans: whether expect to retire completely, never stop work,
    work fewer hours, change kind of work, work for oneself, haven't
    thought about it
How much personal savings expect to have accumulated by time retire
Whether and how much expect living standards to change after
    retirement

#### Other Probabilities, Expectations

Whether expect to have to give major financial help to family members in
    next 10 years (scale of 0-10)
Whether will live to age 75 or more, age 85 or more
Whether housing prices in neighborhood will go up faster than prices in
    general  over next 10 years
Whether Congress will make Social Security more or less generous
Whether U.S. will experience major depression in next 10 years
Whether U.S. will experience double-digit inflation in next 10 years
When expect to receive Social Security, how much in today's dollars,
    ever had SSA calculate expected benefits
Looking 2 years ahead, whether expect to be better or worse off
    financially

#### Risk Aversion, Time Preference

Whether would take another job with 50-50 chance that it would double
    family  income or cut by a third, with 50-50 chance that it would double
    family income or cut in half, with 50-50 chance that it would double
    family income or cut by 20 percent

In deciding how much to spend or save, which time period is most important: next few months, next year, next few years, next 5-10 years, longer than 10 years

### Attitudes Toward Bequests

Importance of leaving a bequest
Whether expect to leave a sizable bequest

## NATIONAL LONGITUDINAL SURVEY OF MATURE WOMEN (NLS-MW)

When expect to retire from regular job
Three largest sources of income expect to have during retirement

## RETIREMENT HISTORY SURVEY (RHS)

### People Not Yet Retired

When expect to retire and for what reasons
Whether expect to continue to work after retirement
Whether expect to get along financially
Whether expect to spend more or less money than now
How much expect to need per month in retirement
Whether expect to receive a private pension
Whether expect to receive Social Security and how much
How much expect to receive from various income sources after
    retirement or 5 years from now (1971 interview)
Attitudes and expectations about types of work would do (1971 interview)

### Other Expectations

Whether expect health status to be better or worse in 5 years (1971 interview)

NOTES: AHEAD provides data similar to that from HRS. Questions are not necessarily asked in every interview of a survey.

## BOX 4-5
## DATA ON PENSION COVERAGE AND BENEFITS:
## SELECTED PANEL SURVEYS

### SELF-REPORTED PENSION COVERAGE ON CURRENT JOB

#### Health and Retirement Survey (HRS)

(Similar questions for previous job if not working and for each job in job history section; questions include disposition of lump sums)

If participating, for each plan, whether defined benefit or defined contribution or combination

For each defined contribution, type of plan, how much accumulated, how much employer contributes, how much respondent contributes, how many years in plan in total, whether can choose how money is invested and whether mostly stock or interest-earning assets or evenly split, whether can receive lump sum or installments, youngest age when could start receiving benefits, what age expect to receive benefits and in what form

For each defined benefit, age for full benefits and how much, expected earnings at full retirement age with this employer, age for reduced benefits and how much benefits would be reduced, whether plan benefits depend on Social Security benefits, whether can take lump sum

If not participating, whether employer offers pension plans, whether respondent eligible and intends to participate in future and whether employer contributes

#### National Longitudinal Survey of Mature Women (NLS-MW)

**1989 interview**

(Questions refer to "most important pension;" similar questions for previous job if not working)

If eligible, how much respondent knows about pension plan

Youngest age at which could receive full benefits and how much would receive per month

Youngest age at which could receive reduced benefits and how much

Type of plan: defined benefit, defined contribution

Whether vested and how many more years to be vested

**1992 interview**

Much more extensive set of questions for self and spouse for each plan with current and former employers (e.g., employer and self contributions for defined contribution plans, linkage of defined benefit plans to Social Security)

### National Longitudinal Survey of Young Women (NLS-YW)

(First asked in 1991 interview; similar questions for previous job if not working)
Whether employer provides pension plan and whether enrolled
Whether defined benefit or defined contribution or both
Whether vested and how many more years to be vested
If were to leave, what would happen to money in pension account

### National Longitudinal Survey of Youth (NLSY)

Whether employer offers pension plan and respondent participates (first asked in 1994 interview)

### Retirement History Survey (RHS)

(Similar questions for previous job if not working and for longest job)
Whether covered by private plan and type (employer, union, etc.) (assumption is that all plans are defined benefit)
Age when eligible for full benefits
Age when eligible for reduced benefits
If left, could respondent draw benefits and at what age
Whether employer has mandatory retirement age

### SELF-REPORTED EARLY RETIREMENT WINDOW OFFERS

### Health and Retirement Survey (HRS)

Whether and how often offered, which employer, type of incentive (cash bonus, improved benefits, other), how much was incentive, whether accepted, whether would have left anyway, whether would have accepted if twice the amount

### INFORMATION FROM EMPLOYERS

### Health and Retirement Survey (HRS)

Summary Plan Description obtained for each pension for respondents who provided address of current or former employer in first interview (addresses also sought for employer for whom worked 5 or more years prior to current or former employer)

### National Longitudinal Survey of Mature Women (NLS-MW)

Summary Plan Description and Form 5500 obtained for each pension for respondents who provided address of current or former employer for self and spouse (or ex-spouse) in 1989 interview

---

NOTES: AHEAD provides data similar to that from HRS. Questions are not necessarily asked in every interview of a survey. See Box 4-4 for questions on expectations of receipt of Social Security benefits.

**BOX 4-6**
**DATA ON HEALTH STATUS, HEALTH CARE**
**INSURANCE, USE, AND COSTS:**
**SELECTED PANEL SURVEYS**

**HEALTH STATUS**

**Health and Retirement Survey (HRS)**

Self-reported health status now and compared with a year ago
Self-reported emotional health status
Difficulty with activities of daily living, including instrumental activities
Self-reported medical conditions indicated to the respondent by a doctor
(high blood pressure, diabetes, cancer, chronic lung disease, strokes,
emotional problems, arthritis, other problems, broken bones, pain,
poor eyesight, hearing problems)
Self reports of smoking, drinking, exercise
Cognition battery and mood assessment and clinical depression battery
Self-reported work disabilities and employer accommodations

**National Longitudinal Survey of Mature Women (NLS-MW)**

Whether have a work disability, conditions, how long been limited
Difficulty performing various job-related activities (e.g., lifting weights,
reaching, seeing, dealing with people, standing)
Bothersome conditions (e.g., pain, aches, fainting spells)
Job situations that would be a problem because of health (e.g., working in
hot or cold or damp places)
Whether had accident that affected health
Whether health is better, worse, or same compared to several years ago
Difficulty with activities of daily living
Smoking, drinking, depression indicators

**National Longitudinal Survey of Young Women (NLS-YW)**

Whether have a work disability, conditions, how long been limited
Difficulty performing various job-related activities (e.g., lifting weights,
reaching, seeing, dealing with people, standing)
Bothersome conditions (e.g., pain, aches, fainting spells)
Job situations that would be a problem because of health (e.g., working in
hot or cold or damp places)
Smoking, drinking
Medical problems have or have ever had (about 40 conditions in all, in-
cluding asthma, heart trouble, high or low blood pressure, allergies,
gastrointestinal trouble, depression, arthritis, paralysis, dizziness, eye
trouble, high cholesterol)
Weight, height

Ever need help with personal care, able to use public transportation
Whether health is better, worse, or same compared to 5 years ago

### National Longitudinal Survey of Youth (NLSY)

Whether have a work disability, conditions
Whether any work-related injuries
Smoking during pregnancy, drinking, drug use, depression indicators
Weight, height

### Retirement History Survey (RHS)

Whether a work disability, how long limited
Whether bedridden, able to use public transportation

## HEALTH INSURANCE COVERAGE

### Health and Retirement Survey (HRS)

Type of coverage: government, employer, individual, other
If employer coverage, whether employer pays part or all of premium,
    whether available to retirees and whether employer pays part or all,
    whether retirees pay the same as other employees, whether spouses
    can be covered and whether retirees pay the same for spouse cover-
    age as other employees
If individual coverage, type and cost
Whether ever turned down for coverage and why

### National Longitudinal Survey of Mature Women (NLS-MW)

Type of coverage and who covered in household
Reason not currently covered and how long
Ever had a change in coverage and whether and how long uncovered
Whether expect to have employer health insurance coverage after retire-
    ment

### National Longitudinal Survey of Young Women (NLS-YW)

Whether covered by current or former employer health insurance, others
    in household covered, whether plan pays for hospital and doctors' bills,
    whether employer pays all, part, or none of premium, amount paid by
    employee, whether plan has a deductible, whether a health mainte-
    nance organization (HMO)
Whether covered by employer dental or vision care insurance, types of
    servicescovered, whether a deductible, whether extra deduction from
    paycheck
Whether covered by employer insurance for prescription drugs, whether
    a deductible, whether extra deduction from paycheck
Type of health insurance coverage and who covered in household

*continued on next page*

## BOX 4-6 Continued

### National Longitudinal Survey of Youth (NLSY)

Type of health insurance coverage and who covered in household

### Retirement History Survey (RHS)

Type, annual premium, whether others pay part of premium
Types of services covered, who in household covered
Whether will have employer, private, or Medicare insurance after age 65

### HEALTH CARE USE AND COSTS

### Health and Retirement Survey (HRS)

Stays in hospital or nursing home last 12 months
Doctor visits last 12 months
Home health care last 12 months
Itemized medical care deductions
Cost of individual insurance
Total and out-of-pocket medical care expenditures (asked in second
    wave); expanded to several categories of medical care services in
    third wave

### National Longitudinal Survey of Young Women (NLS-YW)

Stays in hospital in last 12 months
Consulted doctor for other than minor illness in last 5 years

### Retirement History Survey (RHS)

Annual doctor bills: total, amount paid out-of-pocket, amount paid by
    insurance, whether free care provided and by whom
Annual hospital bills per stay (same information as doctor bills)
Annual dentist bills (same information as doctor bills)
Annual prescription drug costs (same information as doctor bills)
Annual nonprescription medicine costs
Annual costs for medical services and supplies (same information as
    doctor bills)

### INFORMATION FROM EMPLOYERS

### Health and Retirement Survey (HRS)

Employer survey of health insurance plan provisions and costs (for em-
    ployers for whom respondents provided addresses)

---

NOTES: AHEAD provides data similar to that from HRS. Questions are not necessarily asked in every interview of a survey. See Box 4-4 for questions on expectations about future health status and health care needs.

## BOX 4-7
## DATA ON SAVINGS AND EXPENDITURES:
## SELECTED PANEL SURVEYS

### ASSETS AND DEBTS
### (other than pension and Social Security wealth)

### Health and Retirement Survey (HRS)

Value of house, mobile home and site, farm, ranch
Amount of mortgage, second mortgage, home equity loan
Value of second home, time-share; amount of mortgage
Net value of motor home or recreational vehicle
Net value of other real estate
Net value of other vehicles
Net value of business
Amounts in Individual Retirement Accounts (IRAs) or Keogh accounts
Net value of stocks, mutual funds
Money in checking, saving, and money market accounts
Money in certificates of deposit (CDs), government savings bonds,
    Treasury bills
Money in corporate bonds
Net value of other savings/assets
Amount of other debts
Inheritances, when and from whom received, worth at the time
Value of other transfers of $10,000 or more from relatives
Life insurance settlements, when received, worth at the time, who was
    insured
Large, unexpected expenses over last 20 years that made it difficult to
    meet financial goals
Cash value of life insurance
Capital gains component of asset value increases after first interview

### National Longitudinal Survey of Mature Women (NLS-MW)

Value of home, amount of mortgage
Money in checking, savings, CDs, money market funds, credit unions
Value of U.S. savings bonds
Value of stocks, bonds, or mutual fund shares
Value of loans or mortgages held
Value of IRA, Keogh, or 401(k) accounts
Cash value of life insurance
Value of farm, amount of mortgage
Value of business, amount of liabilities
Value of other property, amount of debt
Value of vehicles, amount of debt
Other debts (e.g., to doctors or banks)

*continued on next page*

## Box 4-7 Continued

Value of estate or investment trust
Amount received from estates, inheritances, gifts from relatives

### National Longitudinal Survey of Young Women (NLS-YW)

Value of home, amount of mortgage
Value of farm, amount of debt
Value of business, amount of debt
Money in checking, savings, credit unions
Value of U.S. savings bonds
Value of stocks, bonds, or mutual funds
Value of loans owed by others
Value of other property, amount of debt
Value of automobiles, amount of debt
Value of estate or investment trust
Amount received from estates, inheritances, gifts from relatives
Amount of other debts

### National Longitudinal Survey of Youth (NLSY)

Net value of real estate
Net value of farm
Net value of business
Net value of vehicles
Money in savings accounts
Total debts, including mortgages, back taxes, and debts over $500

### Retirement History Survey (RHS)

Value of home, amount of mortgage
Value of farm, amount of mortgage and other debt
Value of business assets and liabilities
Value of other property, amount of mortgage and other debt
Value of U.S. savings bonds
Value of stocks, bonds, or mutual fund shares
Value of loans owed by others
Money in checking accounts
Money in savings accounts or credit unions
Face value of life insurance, annuities
Debt on vehicles
Debt to stores, medical care providers, banks, other lenders
Value of lump-sum payments (e.g., from inheritance)

### EXPENDITURES

### Health and Retirement Survey (HRS)

Mortgage, rent, taxes, utilities, condominium fees

Financial assistance of $500 or more in past 12 months to children or
   parents
Food per week or month (including value of food stamps) in stores and
   delivered
Meals eaten out (not counting at work or school)
Itemized medical care deductions
Charitable contributions (if $500 or more)
Support to others outside household
Medical care expenditures (see Box 4-6)
Total expenditures in third wave

### National Longitudinal Survey of Mature Women (NLS-MW)

Commuting costs
Cost of child care while working

### National Longitudinal Survey of Young Women (NLS-YW)

Commuting costs
Cost of child care while working

### National Longitudinal Survey of Youth (NLSY)

Cost of child care while working

### Retirement History Survey (RHS)

Food expenditures last week (with some detail on type)
Meals eaten at work
Dinners outside the home
Charitable/political contributions
Professional and social organization dues
Entertainment
Gifts
Magazines and newspapers bought
Beauty shop visits
Gasoline costs
Commuting expenses
Personal travel costs
Mortgage or rent, taxes, and utilities
Home help expenses
Medical care expenses (see Box 4-6)

---

NOTES: AHEAD provides data similar to that from HRS. Questions are not necessarily asked in every interview of a survey. See Boxes 4-5 and 4-6 for questions
on contributions to pension plans and health insurance premiums, respectively.

NLS cohort will begin in 1997, but it will be limited to young people aged 12-17. These kinds of gaps are important, given the economic changes that are affecting middle-aged workers, such as layoffs and employer incentives for early retirement. Analysis is needed of whether and to what extent middle-aged people respond differently to economic and policy changes than either older or younger people.

For almost 30 years the Panel Study of Income Dynamics (PSID), sponsored by the National Science Foundation and other agencies, has followed a sample of the entire population that includes all age groups (Table 4-1). However, the sample for middle-aged and older men and women is not as large as in the NLS panels or in the Health and Retirement Survey (HRS) or the Asset and Health Dynamics Among the Oldest Old (AHEAD) survey, discussed below. Also, the focus of the PSID is on income and program participation. Supplemental modules have covered such retirement-income-related topics as savings behavior, net worth, extended family ties, financial situation and health of parents, disability and illness, and retirement plans and experiences, but they are not regular parts of the survey.

HRS and AHEAD, sponsored by the National Institute on Aging, are specifically designed to provide the kinds of comprehensive, high-quality, multivariate data that are needed to develop improved analytical models of retirement-income-related behaviors of individuals. (Features of these surveys are shown in Table 4-1 and Boxes 4-4 to 4-7.) HRS covers men and women who were aged 51-61 in 1992, and AHEAD includes people who were aged 70 and older in 1993. The two surveys include married as well as single women and men in their samples. In contrast, the RHS included only single women in the sample, along with married and single men. (Married men's spouses were also interviewed, but they were not necessarily the same age cohort.) HRS and AHEAD also obtain extensive information about spouses of sample members.

HRS and AHEAD obtain a wide range of information for sample members on employment, income, savings, assets, family status and kinship networks, health status and health care arrangements, and retirement-related expectations. From analysis of the initial waves, the surveys appear to be making important improvements in data quality; for example, they obtain more complete reporting of wealth than most other household surveys.

Further enriching the HRS and AHEAD databases are descriptions of pension and health care plans for sample members obtained at the first interview from their current and former employers. Information about health care plan provisions is obtained directly from the employer; information about pension plan provisions is abstracted from Summary Plan Descriptions provided by the employer (which employers are required to have on file). The NLS-Mature Women survey also obtained Summary Plan Descriptions from the current or prior employer of sample members in 1989, when they were aged 52-66. Also planned for HRS and AHEAD is the addition of data from Social Security and

Medicare administrative records. Having a rich array of data in the same survey is important for at least two reasons: researchers can explore behavioral models of joint decision making (i.e., joint labor supply and savings decisions), and comparisons among different researchers' analyses of the data are facilitated by the use of common concepts and variables.

## Features of Other Surveys

We stress the importance of long-term panel surveys of individuals and their families, but there are also repeated cross-sectional and short-term panel surveys of the entire population that provide needed data for retirement analysis.

The Survey of Consumer Finances (SCF), sponsored by the Federal Reserve Board, has been conducted every 3 years since 1983 under its current design (predecessor surveys were conducted as early as 1963). The survey is a source of detailed information about household wealth in the United States that is frequently used as a benchmark with which to evaluate the quality of wealth reporting in other surveys. The SCF obtains information on pension wealth by obtaining descriptions of pension plan provisions from sample members' employers. Features of the survey that contribute to the high quality of the wealth data include its sample design and detailed editing and imputation procedures. The sample design combines an area-frame household sample with a list-frame sample of high-income households drawn from Internal Revenue Service (IRS) records.[7]

The SCF originally included a panel component: the 1986 SCF was a reinterview of the 1983 sample, and the 1989 SCF included a subset of the 1983 sample in addition to a new cross-sectional sample. However, the 1986 survey data were not used because of quality problems, and, for cost reasons, the 1992 and 1995 surveys have not repeated the panel feature of the 1989 survey. Other limitations of the SCF are its small sample size (about 3,000-4,000 households) and limited or no information on some topics, such as health status and health care use. Nonetheless, the SCF is important for its periodic reporting of trends in household wealth.

The Survey of Income and Program Participation (SIPP), conducted by the Census Bureau, is a repeated, short-term panel survey of individuals that began in 1983. From 1983 to 1993, a new panel was introduced every year that followed members of about 12,000 to 24,000 households for 2-1/2 years, with interviews every 4 months. The survey collects detailed monthly information on employment, income, and program participation. Periodically, it asks about a wide range of other topics, including assets, health status and health care utilization, pension plan participation, and retrospective information on employment and family history. Beginning in 1996, the SIPP design will have larger panels (37,000 house-

---

[7]Households selected from the IRS list frame must give written permission in advance to be included in the survey.

holds for the 1996 panel), whose members will be interviewed every 4 months for 4 years, with a new panel introduced every 4 years.[8]

SIPP has been used extensively for analysis of trends and transitions in income receipt, program participation, health insurance coverage, and other topics. The survey supports cross-sectional analysis by combining panels. Its usefulness for retirement-income-related behavioral analysis is limited by the short panel length.[9] SIPP may gain added relevance for analysis of retirement-income related trends in the future; for example, it may replace supplements to the Current Population Survey, not only as the source of official poverty statistics, but also as the source of information on pension plan participation.

The Current Population Survey (CPS) is a monthly survey of about 50,000 households (previously 60,000), which is sponsored by BLS and has been conducted by the Census Bureau since the 1940s. It collects information on labor force participation each month to use in calculating the monthly unemployment rate; the March income supplement collects information on sources and amounts of income for the preceding calendar year; a supplement conducted every 5 years has provided information on employer-provided pension and health care plan coverage. The CPS has been used to follow employment and earnings trends for many years. The CPS supports limited kinds of longitudinal analysis: there is overlap in the sample across pairs of months and years;[10] but the overlap is limited, and the sample households may not contain the same individuals (the interviewers return to the same address and do not follow household members who move).

The Consumer Expenditure Survey (CEX), which is sponsored by BLS, has been conducted on a continuing basis since 1980 (predecessor surveys were conducted as early as 1901). Its major uses are to provide the market basket for the Consumer Price Index and to provide data for analysis of expenditures in relation to demographic and other characteristics. The CEX includes two components: the Interview Survey and the Diary Survey. The Interview Survey collects detailed information for most expenditures from about 5,000 consumer units that are interviewed every quarter for 5 quarters. (In the CEX rotation group design, each month one-fifth of the sample is new and one-fifth is completing its fifth and

---

[8]The design may change if the survey becomes the source of official annual poverty statistics as recommended by a National Research Council panel and if additional funding can be obtained. Under consideration is a design of 3-year panels, with a new panel introduced each year. One of the panels in the field each year would have a sample size of about 37,000 households; the other two panels would include about 11,500 households each.

[9]The 1992 and 1993 panels will be extended with annual interviews from 1997 through 2002 to collect data for tracking the effects of recently legislated changes in social welfare programs. The focus of this Survey of Program Dynamics will be on families with children.

[10]In order to reduce the variability of estimates of month-to-month change in unemployment, household addresses are retained in the sample for 4 months, dropped for 8 months, and brought back into the sample for another 4 months.

final interview.) The Diary Survey collects records of daily expenditures for 2-week periods from about 6,000 consumer units; interviews are spread over the year. BLS makes use of data from both surveys to develop a total picture of consumer expenditures.

Each of these surveys serves as a benchmark in its area and provides information on trends that are important to monitor for purposes of retirement-income-related analysis and projections: trends in wealth (SCF), income (SIPP), labor force participation (CPS), and expenditures (CEX). Each is also well established; we assume that they will—and certainly support that they should—continue. Our recommendations pertain to long-term panel surveys that are critical for retirement-income-related behavioral research and whose benefits may be less apparent than the benefits of these other surveys.

We discuss below the advantages of coordinating aspects of the questionnaire design and content of long-term panel surveys with the SCF and SIPP, both of which provide (or have provided) relevant data for longitudinal analysis over short periods in addition to key cross-sectional estimates. In that regard, it could be useful for future rounds of the SCF to include a panel component to help measure change in savings. We discuss the contributions that such surveys as the SCF and SIPP can make to data validation and (in Chapter 5) the possible role for SIPP as a microsimulation model database.

### Directions for the Future

#### HRS and AHEAD

HRS and AHEAD promise to make possible important new and refined analyses that can add materially to understanding savings and retirement decisions and other topics that are relevant to Americans' retirement income security. However, both surveys are very new—HRS began in 1992 and has completed three waves of interviews; AHEAD began in 1993 and has completed two interviews. To achieve their full potential, the original HRS sample must be continued until its members are well past retirement. The original AHEAD sample must also be continued for a significant length of time in order to understand patterns of saving and dissaving, health care utilization, and mortality among the very old. In addition, new cohorts need to be introduced periodically in HRS to make it possible to analyze differences in behavior across cohorts in response to socio-economic and policy changes.

At present, funding is in place for HRS to introduce in 1998 a new cohort of people aged 51-56 and to continue the original cohort for another interview (for a total of four interviews). Funding is also in place to conduct two more interviews with the AHEAD sample and to introduce a cohort that fills the age gap between HRS and AHEAD. The sample size of the new and filler cohorts will be smaller than the current cohorts in order to contain overall costs (see Table 4-1 and Figure 4-1, above).

When the new and filler cohorts are added in 1998-1999, HRS and AHEAD will be fully integrated and will use the same questionnaire with appropriate skip patterns (e.g., younger sample members will be asked fewer questions than older sample members about health care use, while older sample members will be asked fewer questions than younger sample members about employment). The intent for HRS/AHEAD is to continue to introduce new cohorts of people aged 51-56 every 5 years, so that the combined survey is both continuously representative of the population 51 years or older and follows each new cohort until its sample size is no longer useful because of mortality. We support the implementation of this plan, which will likely require a modest increase in future funding until the system reaches a steady state and then continuation of funding levels in real terms.

**Other Long-Term Panel Surveys**

HRS/AHEAD is not the only useful panel survey of individuals. As indicated above, several cohorts of the NLS are continuing to provide valuable data, as is the PSID. We support the continuation of these surveys at their current funding levels. In particular, the NLSY, if the questionnaire is appropriately modified (see below), can play an important role in explaining the substantial heterogeneity in savings and net worth levels that is already evident by the time people reach age 50. (NLSY covers people who are now aged 31-38.) Similarly, the NLS-Young Women cohort (women who are now aged 42-52) and NLS-Mature Women cohort (women who are now aged 59-73) can provide useful data for cohorts of women who are not yet covered by HRS/AHEAD. Unfortunately, there are no equivalent surveys for male cohorts in these age ranges. In the future, HRS/AHEAD may obviate the need to continue NLS-Young Women or NLS-Mature Women.

**Content Enhancements**

Some content additions to existing panel surveys would be very desirable for analysis purposes, although the marginal costs of each proposed enhancement need to be carefully evaluated against the expected benefits. In the case of the younger NLS cohorts, it may be that, as they age, some existing modules that are more appropriate for younger people could be cut back to make room for new modules that are more relevant for retirement-income-related behavior.

For analysis of consumption and savings behavior, it would be very useful to have direct measures of total consumption in all of the major panel surveys. It would also be useful to have direct measures of housing and medical care expenditures, which are two important elements for assessing retirement income security. Although it is possible to estimate total consumption as a residual by subtracting change in net worth from income, direct measures are useful for at least two reasons: first, changes in asset values will reflect not only realized capital income, but also unrealized gains and losses; second, there is a considerable amount of "noise" in the measurement of asset values and change in net worth over a time period.

Typically, in surveys, most people are willing to indicate the types of assets (and liabilities) they hold, but they are not always willing or able to specify the value of each asset, or they may underestimate the value of their assets. Because of substantial imputation for nonresponse (which does not usually capture all of the missing information) and underreporting, most surveys underestimate the value of families' asset holdings. Curtin, Juster, and Morgan (1989) found that estimates of wealth from the 1984 SIPP panel and the 1984 round of the PSID were only 61 percent and 79 percent, respectively, of the estimates from the 1983 SCF. Juster and Kuester (1991) similarly found that estimates of wealth from the 1979 round of the RHS and the 1981 round of the NLS-Older Men survey fell short of those from the 1983 SCF.[11]

In HRS/AHEAD, range cards permit holders of an asset to select a category (e.g., $1,000 to $5,000) if they do not know or do not wish to state the exact amount. "Unfolding" or "bracketing" techniques are also used to increase response. In the bracketing technique, holders of an asset who don't know or refuse to provide an exact value or a range are asked if the value is above a certain amount; if yes, whether it is above another (higher) amount, and so on.[12] HRS/ AHEAD obtains high rates of response to the asset value questions by this method; however, the response categories are very broad—for example, less than $1,000, $1,000 to $10,000, $10,000 to $50,000, $50,000 or more. The resulting wealth estimates appear reasonably robust; Smith (1993:13) estimates that HRS obtains 88 percent of the wealth aggregates in the SCF. However, it is difficult to obtain a precise estimate of consumption by subtracting change in net worth from income, given the broad categories for so many of the asset value responses. HRS/ AHEAD plans to separate out the capital gains and losses component of change in net worth from the component of savings per se. This step will be helpful for estimating consumption, but the calculation will still be hampered by the inherent imprecision in estimating the two components.

The NLS surveys do not include questions on expenditures, except for child care and commuting costs (see Box 4-7). The PSID obtains information about

---

[11]The SCF is taken as the standard for asset valuation in household surveys. Its wealth aggregates compare very favorably with aggregate figures on household balance sheets from the Federal Reserve flow of funds accounts, when proper adjustments are made to achieve conceptual compatibility (Antoniewicz, 1994).

[12]The SCF pioneered the use of range cards and also uses bracketing, which was initially developed for the PSID; see Kennickell (1996).

housing and food expenditures but not about other expenditures. HRS/AHEAD has questions similar to those on the PSID, as well as questions on medical care expenses that use the bracketing approach; Wave 3 of HRS/AHEAD includes a one-question assessment of total expenditures.

There are obvious problems in attempting to measure consumption directly in surveys that cannot afford to include the detailed questions used in the CEX: people may not be able to provide accurate information on their aggregate expenditures, and the lack of detail can cause problems for such issues as how to treat durable goods expenditures in deriving conceptually appropriate estimates of total consumption. Despite the problems, we encourage work on measuring consumption in such surveys as HRS/AHEAD and NLS, including careful evaluation of the information obtained from the new HRS/AHEAD questions and further experimentation with question detail and wording. (HRS/AHEAD has a subsample explicitly for experimenting with new content and alternative question wording.)

Another desirable content enhancement would be to add retirement-income-related questions to the NLS surveys for younger cohorts—NLSY and NLS-Young Women—whose sample members are in their 30s and 40s. As noted above, by the time people are in their 50s, significant disparities in income and wealth are evident. To understand how these disparities arise, it would be very useful for the younger NLS cohorts to include modules for pension coverage, savings and net worth, health status, and retirement- and savings-related expectations, similar to the modules in HRS/AHEAD (see Boxes 4-4 to 4-7). NLSY and NLS-Young Women include members of the baby boom cohort, and it would be particularly useful to have information about their savings behavior as they approach their pre-retirement years. (The baby boom generation will ultimately be picked up in successive new cohorts of HRS/AHEAD, but only on reaching age 51.) Retirement-related modules could be included in NLSY and NLS-Young Women without necessarily increasing questionnaire length, given that modules related to education and training may be less relevant as these cohorts age and likely could be curtailed without loss of important analytical information.

Finally, it could be useful to expand the content in HRS (and in the retirement-related modules that are added to the NLS) that is intended to help explain savings behavior, in particular, why so many people appear to be saving so little. HRS already includes a large number of relevant questions (see Box 4-4), but it could consider adding a few more. For example, in addition to the question on how much personal savings respondents expect to have accumulated by the time they retire, there could be a question on how much they think they will need (in today's dollars) to finance their retirement. Also useful would be questions on respondents' awareness of and participation in employer financial education programs, in order to analyze the effectiveness of such programs in increasing employee pension contributions and personal savings.

## Cross-Survey Reviews

We urge collaborative efforts among NLS, PSID, and HRS/AHEAD to review their questionnaires and data collection procedures on a regular basis to determine ways to improve the quality, utility, and comparability of the data. It would also be useful to include the SCF and SIPP in these reviews so that analysis and validation of key questions can be carried out across surveys in a comparable manner both cross-sectionally and longitudinally.

Each of these panel surveys has its own orientation and user community, and each tends to consider content or procedural changes from its own perspective. However, the return to the investment in all of the surveys would be increased to the extent that each includes some common modules on key topics that permit comparable analyses across surveys or with data pooled from two or more surveys to increase sample size. Furthermore, with common modules on key retirement-income-related topics, it would be possible to combine the samples from several panel surveys into a rich and broadly representative database for projection models (see discussion in Chapter 5).

In this regard, plans for the newest NLS cohort are to include such questions as expectations that HRS/AHEAD has pioneered (e.g., of one's own life expectancy). This development is very welcome, although the newest NLS cohort, which includes people in their teens, will not be relevant for retirement-income-related research for several decades to come.

Finally, when one panel survey pioneers techniques that demonstrably improve data quality—such as the bracketing or unfolding technique in HRS/AHEAD, which is used for medical and total expenditures as well as assets—it seems highly desirable for other surveys to adopt them. Such techniques should also be adopted in other household surveys, such as SIPP, that are a resource for tracking assets and other retirement-relevant variables in the general population.[13]

Mechanisms to provide for regular cross-cutting reviews could include joint meetings of major panel surveys' advisory groups and principal investigators and commissioning papers on specific areas of possible interchange and congruence in questions and data collection techniques. We recommend that the National Institute on Aging organize an interagency working group of survey sponsors and investigators and facilitate means to bring together and learn from the experiences of the major retirement-income-related panel surveys of individuals. (See discussion in Chapter 6 of issues of interagency coordination to support improved data and models for analysis of retirement income security.)

---

[13]The 1996 SIPP panel uses bracketing for measurement of asset values and interest income.

## Recommendations

**1. Existing panel surveys of middle-aged and older people should receive continued government support.** Longitudinal data from these surveys are essential to analyze retirement and savings decisions and determine behavioral responses to changes in public and private sector policies. Such analyses in turn are essential to develop better models for projecting the likely effects of alternative policy proposals on retirement income security. In particular, the HRS and AHEAD surveys should receive continued support. These surveys should be refreshed periodically with new cohorts in order to offer insight into how behavior changes over time.

**2. Panel surveys of middle-aged and older people should experiment with methods to develop measures of families' total expenditures and expenditures on housing and medical care.** Such consumption measures are important for projections of economic well-being in retirement.

**3. Panel surveys of younger people, such as the National Longitudinal Survey of Youth (NLSY), should include detailed questionnaire modules on pension coverage, wealth, health status, and retirement- and savings-related expectations.** Such information is needed to understand more fully life-cycle behavior and to track the disparities in income and wealth that are evident by middle age.

**4. Agencies and researchers involved in retirement-income-related panel surveys of individuals, and other surveys as appropriate (such as the SCF and SIPP), should collaborate regularly in reviewing questionnaire content and data collection practices to identify ways to improve data quality and utility.** For example, the bracketing technique used in HRS and AHEAD that has been demonstrated to reduce nonresponse to important items should be adopted in other surveys. Also, such surveys might include a common core of questions on specific topics. The National Institute on Aging should facilitate such collaborative efforts.

## DATA ON EMPLOYERS

The discussion in Parsons (1996) and in Chapter 3 makes it clear that there are major gaps in understanding employer demand for older workers and what causes employers to adopt, modify, or drop pension and health care benefit coverage for current and retired employees. There has also been little systematic study of the consequences for workers and retirees of changes in the mix of employers with different hiring and compensation preferences.

These gaps in understanding cripple the ability to develop useful projection models of retirement income security, given the prominent role of employers in generating earnings and benefits for so much of the population. The gaps in research knowledge about employers in turn stem from deficiencies in available data: relevant cross-sectional data are not adequate, and relevant longitudinal data are almost entirely lacking.

We would have discussed the needs for improved employer data before the needs for improved panel data on individuals except for the cost implications. The first priority, we believe, is to continue and improve existing panel surveys of individuals for which budgets are already largely in place. To improve employer data to the extent that is needed is likely to entail costs for new data collection as well as modification of existing data systems. New data collection is not undertaken lightly in a time of constrained budgets. There must be careful planning to evaluate existing databases and what can be done relatively inexpensively to improve them and then to evaluate and choose among alternative strategies for obtaining needed new data in the most cost-effective manner.

## Government Sources

Federal agencies collect substantial amounts of information about business enterprises and other employers in the United States (e.g., payrolls, sales), but relatively little information is directly relevant for retirement-income-related descriptive and behavioral analysis. Moreover, the relevant data sources all have important deficiencies. Table 4-2 summarizes features of these databases (see also Appendix B).

***Employee Benefits Survey (EBS)*** The EBS of the Department of Labor's Bureau of Labor Statistics (BLS) began in 1979 as part of an effort to develop information on the comparability of wages and benefits between the federal government and other employers. The focus of the survey design and published tabulations is on benefits available to workers in several broad occupational categories—for example, professional, technical and related; clerical and sales. From surveys of large private employers in one year and smaller private employers and state and local governments in alternating years, the EBS obtains extensive information on features of pensions, health insurance, and other benefit plans. However, the data are limited for analytical purposes for several reasons, some more important than others:

• The sample of about 6,000 establishments excludes agricultural enterprises, private household employers, and the federal government, so that it covers most but not all of the employer universe.
• The sample design, which is based on unemployment insurance records, is in terms of establishments, not employers (or enterprises). Linkages to the

TABLE 4-2  Features of Federal Databases on Employers

| Database | Source of Data | Sample Size and Frequency | Longitudinal Potential | Comment |
|---|---|---|---|---|
| BLS Employee Benefits Survey (EBS) | Establishment survey; sample drawn from state unemployment insurance records; first conducted in 1979 | 6,000 nonfarm private sector establishments and state and local governments; private establishments with 100 or more employees surveyed one year, smaller establishments and state and local governments the next year | Limited; one-half of sample is same over 2 years; none is the same over 4 years | Extensive data on types and features of benefits for employees in broad occupational categories; no tabulations by employers |
| BLS Employment Cost Trends Survey (source of Employer Cost Index) | Same source as EBS | Same sample as EBS; surveyed quarterly | More than in EBS because employers are interviewed quarterly | Quarterly index of wage and benefit costs by occupation and industry |
| HHS National Employer Health Insurance Survey (NEHIS) | Establishment survey; sample drawn from Dun and Bradstreet file of private establishments, Census of Governments, and self-employed people in NHIS; first done in 1994 | 39,000 establishments in 1994; survey will be annual beginning in 1997, with sample size of about 25,000 establishments | Will probably include a longitudinal component, but specific design not yet decided | Detailed information on health benefit plans and costs; includes self-employed people; state estimates possible |

| | | | | |
|---|---|---|---|---|
| Survey from SBA U.S. Establishment and Enterprise Microdata (USEEM) File | 1991 survey of private for-profit establishments; sample drawn from Dun and Bradstreet file | | No potential; one-time survey | Distribution by age of total employees and new hires; benefit plan features; low response rate (29%) |
| PWBA/DOL Form 5500 Database | Constructed from Form 5500/5500-C/R filed with IRS by private employers (excludes Form 5500EZ filed by self-employed people with one plan participant) | Annual data from 1977 for all employers with 100+ employees in a pension plan (55,000 plans) and for all or 5 percent sample of smaller employers (645,000 plans) | Significant; employers and plans are linked by EINs and plan numbers from year to year | Limited to private sector; primarily financial aspects of pension plans; Summary Plan Descriptions with more information available but often out-dated |
| Census Bureau Longitudinal Research Database (LRD) | Constructed from quinquennial Census of Manufactures (350,000 establishments) and Annual Survey of Manufactures (55,000 establishments) | Data every 5 years from 1963 for all manufacturing establishments; data every year from 1972 for large manufacturing establishments | Significant; establishments are linked by EINs from year to year | Limited at present to manufacturing establishments; no benefits data; partial link to worker data from 1990 census |

SOURCES: See Appendix B.

NOTES: BLS, Bureau of Labor Statistics; DOL, U.S. Department of Labor; EIN, Employer Identification Number; HHS, U.S. Department of Health and Human Services; IRS, Internal Revenue Service; NHIS, National Health Interview Survey; PWBA, Pension and Welfare Benefits Administration.

unemployment insurance records system would be necessary to identify and appropriately characterize establishments that are part of larger enterprises.

• The survey publishes estimates of how many employees in various categories are covered by certain kinds of benefits, but not estimates of how many *employers* are providing these benefits; the latter estimates are needed to help understand employer benefit behavior.

• The survey microdata could be a source of employer-based estimates, but very few characteristics of employers are available for cross-classification purposes (these include whether public or small or large private employer, standard industrial classification, and geographic region), and sample sizes are small for analysis of specific employer types.

• The survey obtains detailed information on benefit plan characteristics (e.g., vesting period and type of pension plan) but not on employer (or employee) costs. (The EBS sample was queried on a one-time basis in 1993 about employer health care plan costs to provide information for the health care reform debate; a related BLS survey on Employment Cost Trends (ECT) obtains information about wages and benefit costs in a form that pertains to types of jobs and not employers.)

• Microdata files that can be obtained for analysis purposes only upon request cannot be linked with other data sources, such as the Form 5500 database (described below).

**Form 5500 Database**  Private employers have been required since 1975 to file information annually with the IRS about pension, welfare, and fringe benefit plans. More detailed information is filed for large pension or welfare plans (those with 100 or more participants) than for smaller plans; more detailed information is also filed for defined benefit plans than for other pension plans.

The IRS transmits the Form 5500 data to the Pension and Welfare Benefits Administration (PWBA) in the U.S. Department of Labor (DOL), which edits the information and makes available a research database of all large pension plans and a 5 percent sample of smaller pension plans. PWBA also publishes summary information from the database twice a year (see, e.g., Pension and Welfare Benefits Administration, 1995a). The information for each plan includes various financial characteristics, number and type of plan participants, and total employees and those excluded from the plan for various reasons. Researchers have used employer identification number (EIN) and plan number to link the Form 5500 database records for longitudinal studies; in many of these same studies, they have also linked the Form 5500 data to financial information for publicly owned, for-profit employers abstracted in the Standard and Poor Compustat database from annual reports filed with the Securities and Exchange Commission (see, e.g., Bajtelsmit, 1996; Ghilarducci, 1996; Kruse, 1991).

While an increasingly important resource for researchers (see, e.g., Clark and McDermed, 1990; Employee Benefit Research Institute, 1996b; Papke, 1995;

studies cited in the preceding paragraph), the PWBA/DOL Form 5500 database is limited in many respects:

• The database pertains to pension plans of private employers, but information that is filed for health insurance and other welfare benefit plans (e.g., life insurance, disability insurance) is not included because of inconsistencies in reporting, and there are no reports for public employers.

• Within the universe of private employer pension plans, the database excludes some plan types: for example, employers are not required to file reports for "model simplified pension plans" or for plans that do not qualify for tax-exempt status, and reports filed by self-employed people whose plan covers the person and his or her spouse (Form 5500EZ) are not picked up. Also, special "window" offers are not documented in the database.

• The database has limited information about employers per se, although researchers have obtained some added information for publicly owned, for-profit employers by linkage with the Compustat database. Because the reporting unit is the plan, the linkage to the employer is not always accurate (e.g., when subsidiaries do not indicate that they are part of a holding company).[14]

• The database has limited information about an employer's work force. Beginning in 1992, defined benefit pension plans—but not defined contribution plans—are asked to report the number of participants and average compensation by 5-year age and service groupings (average compensation is not to be reported for any grouping that contains fewer than 20 participants). However, these data are not being keyed or provided to PWBA.

• Summary Plan Descriptions that provide additional information about features of both pension and welfare benefit plans are available as paper copies only and are often out of date: the filing requirement is once every 5 years or every 10 years if there has been no change. (For defined benefit pension plans, there is an added requirement to file annually a brief description of features that are used in calculating funding requirements.)

As part of an effort to reduce regulatory burden, beginning in 1996 IRS and DOL curtailed some of the information required of smaller employers on the Form 5500.

***Census Bureau Longitudinal Research Database (LRD)*** The Census Bureau maintains a longitudinal database on U.S. manufacturing establishments that derives from the quinquennial Census of Manufactures (with data back to 1963)

---

[14]Longitudinal matching of employees and plans is hampered by similar problems; achieving a satisfactory match rate over several years requires the use of other information besides EIN and plan number.

and the Annual Survey of Manufactures (with data back to 1972). The database has been used for a growing number of innovative studies about such topics as the relationship of business investment and technology use to productivity (see Center for Economic Studies, 1995). LRD data on establishments were recently matched to data from the 1990 census long-form sample on their workers, including demographic characteristics, occupation, and income (see Troske, 1995).

The LRD is limited to manufacturing establishments. The Census Bureau is working to develop a Longitudinal Business Database (LBD) that will include comparable data on establishments in other industrial sectors (e.g., services). If both the LRD and LBD were linked to census data on workers, they could be a resource for studies of employer demand for older workers, although neither database has or will have information on employer benefits. To protect confidentiality, research with these databases is restricted to on-site use, although the Census Bureau recently set up secure offices for research use at two locations outside the Washington, D.C., area (see discussion below in "Expanded Use of Administrative Data").

**National Employer Health Insurance Survey (NEHIS)** The NEHIS was first conducted by the National Center for Health Statistics in 1994 of a large sample of public and private employers, including self-employed people, in order to provide needed data for the health care reform policy debate (although data were still not available as of the end of 1996).[15] As part of the plan of the U.S. Department of Health and Human Services (HHS) to redesign and integrate the department's health surveys, the NEHIS will become an annual survey, beginning in 1997, with a sample size of about 25,000 employers and a design that permits state estimates.[16] The survey covers the universe of employers and has extensive information on health care benefit plan provisions and costs, but it lacks detailed employee characteristics or any information on pension plans and other nonmedical benefits. A longitudinal component, as yet unspecified, will likely be built into the NEHIS sample design.

*U.S. Establishment and Enterprise Microdata (USEEM) File* The Small Business Administration (SBA) maintains a file of basic information about private for-profit businesses that derives from the Dun and Bradstreet Market Identifier File (which NEHIS also used in drawing the largest part of its sample). The

---

[15]Prior to the NEHIS, the Health Care Financing Agency (HCFA) in HHS conducted a Survey of Private Health Insurance Plans (SHIP) in 1989, which covered about 4,000 private employers, 1,000 state and local governments, 700 labor unions, and 800 membership associations (see Garfinkel, 1995).

[16]Administration of the NEHIS will be integrated with the health insurance provider survey component of the Medical Expenditure Panel Survey (MEPS). This component obtains health insurance plan information from employers of household respondents included in MEPS.

SBA USEEM File (see description in Jack Faucett Associates, 1990) has occasionally been used for one-time special surveys of employer benefits and work force characteristics. Scott, Berger, and Garen (1995), with financial support from SBA and the National Science Foundation, conducted such a survey in 1991 of about 2,250 employers. Results from the survey indicate that employers with health care plans are less likely to hire people aged 55-64 than are other employers, but that whether the employer offers a defined benefit or defined contribution plan has no effect on hiring of older workers. However, the response rate for the survey was very low (29%), so that the resulting analysis sample is small and very likely biased.

## Private Sources

Private benefit consulting and actuarial companies and professional and trade associations collect significant amounts of information about employer benefits; see Table 4-3 for features of selected private sources. Some of these sources have the potential to fill important gaps in government databases: for example, the Public Pension Coordinating Council provides information on features of public employer pension plans that is not otherwise available from federal sources (which include surveys of governments by the Census Bureau). On the whole, however, private sources tend to be even more limited in focus than federal sources of employer data: many cover only defined benefit pension plans, or health care plans, or large employers. Information in these sources on employer and employee characteristics (other than plan features) tends to be very limited. Also, many private data sources rely on convenience samples of their clients, which may not be representative of all employers or even large employers (see Mitchell, 1991, for reviews of several private data sources).

In addition to the databases developed by benefit consulting companies and associations, individual researchers and research groups have carried out original data collection. Some researchers have conducted special-purpose, one-time surveys of employers; others have obtained detailed information from one or a handful of companies to use in case studies of employer hiring and compensation policies and their effects on workers; see Box 4-8 for examples. These data sets have supported some very innovative research, including the few attempts to measure and relate worker productivity by age to compensation patterns (Kotlikoff and Gokhale, 1992; see also Medoff and Abraham, 1981). However, the results of special surveys—and, even more so, case studies of one or a few employers—are inherently limited in their generalizability, although if they are focused on certain groups, such as large employers, they may yield some generally-applicable results for those groups.

TABLE 4-3  Features of Selected Private Databases on Employers

| Database | Data Source and Frequency | Universe and Sample | Comment |
|---|---|---|---|
| Buck Consultants (1995a, 1995b): The Health of America's Pension Plans; Other Retirement Benefits | Reports to shareholders as required by the Financial Accounting Standards Board (FASB); new requirements instituted in 1993 to accrue expected costs of nonpension as well as pension retirement benefits; annual | Single-employer defined benefit pension plans and other nonpension retirement benefits (e.g., health care) of Fortune 500 industrial and 500 service companies; analysis sample is one-half total (489 companies) | Analyses of funding status and assumptions (e.g., discount rate, salary increase rate) for defined benefit plans; similar report begun in 1995 for other postretirement benefits; no employer or employee characteristics |
| Buck Consultants (1993): Postretirement Nonpension Benefit Design | Survey; conducted in 1991 and 1993; no plans to repeat on a regular basis | Private employers; sample of 2,859 companies drawn from mailing list of clients and other employers; 330 (11.5%) responded | Characteristics of retiree nonpension benefits, particularly health care (e.g., Medicare coordination, coverage of spouses, plan to change benefits) |
| A. Foster Higgins (personal communication): National Survey of Employer-Sponsored Health Plans | Annual beginning in 1993; conducted by mail with telephone follow-up | Private employers and governments with 10 or more employees; sample drawn from Dun & Bradstreet database and Census of Governments; 1995 database includes 1,771 respondents; supplemented by a convenience sample of 993 Foster Higgins clients (latter have zero weights, but are included in database) | Covers all types of health care benefit plans (e.g., fee-for-service, HMO, dental, long-term care, retiree); data for each plan type include percent of employees enrolled, annual per employee cost, employee contributions, funding, etc.; limited employer and employee characteristics |

| | | | |
|---|---|---|---|
| Hay/Huggins (personal communication; see also HayGroup, 1993) | Survey; annual for 10 years | Private medium- and large-sized employers and some state and local agencies; about 1,100 employers in all, representing those that buy into the data system (not all respond each year) | Detailed information on benefit plan provisions; analytical reports also published |
| Hewitt Associates (personal communication; see also Hewitt Associates, 1995): Plan Descriptions Database, published in *Specbook* | Survey; annual for 20 years | Benefits provided to salaried employees of major employers; convenience sample of about 1,000 clients (mostly large private employers) | Detailed plan specifications for each employer in sample; no employer or employee characteristics; analytical reports also published |
| KPMG Peat Marwick (1995) | Survey; annual since 1993; conducted by telephone | Private and state and local government employers with 200 or more workers; stratified sample of about 1,200 employers originally drawn from Dun & Bradstreet database; sample for 1995 survey used participants from prior surveys with randomly selected replacements from the same industry, region, and employer size category for employers declining to participate | Detailed information on characteristics of employer's defined benefit plans, 401(k) plans, profit-sharing plans, and 403(b) plans for nonprofits; information on employer's philosophy of retirement planning and changes in plan offerings (9% of sampled employers did not offer retirement benefits) |

*continued on next page*

TABLE 4-3 Continued

| Database | Data Source and Frequency | Universe and Sample | Comment |
|---|---|---|---|
| Public Pension Coordinating Council (PPCC)[a], (U.S. General Accounting Office, 1996a) | Survey; conducted in 1991, 1993, and 1995 | All members of two PPCC member associations and sample of members of other two associations (extent of follow-up for nonresponse differed across associations); the 451 respondents to the 1993 survey represented 83% of assets of all state and local government plans and 76% of active plan members | Information on plan provisions, funding status, and contribution ratios |
| Society of Actuaries: (personal communication) Survey of Large Companies of Employee Turnover and Retirement | Survey; first conducted in 1995; plan to conduct every 3 or 4 years; data to be obtained for each plan year in the interval from the previous to the current wave | Defined benefit plans of private employers with over 5,000 employees; sample selected by asking major actuarial consulting firms to obtain data for 5 clients each and by directly surveying 30 large companies that employ actuaries | For each plan year, census at beginning and end of number of employees, total salary, and accumulated benefits by sex, single years of age, and years of service; eligibility conditions for participation and retirement, early retirement windows, and plan changes |

[a]PPCC members are the Government Finance Officers Association, National Association of State Retirement Administrators, National Conference on Public Employee Retirement Systems, and National Council on Teacher Retirement.

## Problems with Employer Surveys

Academic and private and public sector analysts have made imaginative use of a variety of data sources about employers. However, the available data are fragmented and greatly deficient for comprehensive analysis of trends and behavior with respect to employer demand for older workers and benefit offerings and their effects on workers. A reason for the lack of much analytically useful data for employers and their workers, in contrast to the relative richness of data for households and people, is the greater difficulty of surveying employers (see Cox et al., 1995; Federal Committee on Statistical Methodology, 1988). The problems involve every step of the process.

*Developing and Maintaining a Comprehensive List of Employers as a Sampling Frame* Business organization in the private sector is complex and dynamic: mergers, splits, liquidations, relocations, and, especially, start-ups make it difficult to keep a list complete and up to date and to identify which employers are the same over time. The same phenomena also make it hard to characterize employers by size, number and location of establishments, and industry, variables that are important stratifiers for cost-effective sample designs. In the public sector, incorporations, annexations, and other jurisdictional changes complicate maintenance of an accurate employer list. A growing trend toward self-employment requires a method of sampling these people (e.g., selecting them from a household survey, as was done for the 1994 NEHIS).

*Identifying Appropriate Sampling and Reporting Units* Enterprises with multiple establishments (i.e., separate business locations) complicate decisions about survey design—whether to have an establishment-based sample (as is common) or an enterprise-based sample, each of which has advantages and disadvantages. There are also issues of the appropriate reporting unit and how to minimize respondent burden. For example, information about benefit plans may be maintained at the establishment level, or it may be maintained at headquarters for all establishments, even when the benefit plans differ among establishments for such reasons as state regulation (see discussion in Chapman, Moriarity, and Sommers, 1996). Simply characterizing the enterprise-establishment structure can be difficult in many situations (e.g., holding companies, conglomerates, multinational companies). Nonetheless, it is vital to understand the enterprise-establishment distinction in comparing survey results; distributions of workers by size of employer, for example, will likely differ between the two kinds of surveys (see discussion in Zarkin et al., 1995).

*Identifying Appropriate Respondents* Finding the right respondent(s) in an enterprise or establishment can be difficult: for example, to understand the

---

**BOX 4-8**
**SELECTED EMPLOYER STUDIES USING**
**RESEARCHER-OBTAINED DATA**


*Barringer and Mitchell (1993)* Analyzed health insurance plan selection behavior in a large firm in which employees could choose among six health insurance options. Found that older and more highly paid workers are more likely to select a traditional fee-for-service plan; older workers respond to changes in health plan premium costs and deductible amounts to the same extent as younger workers.

*Employee Benefit Research Institute (1996a, 1996c)* Analyzed worker investment decisions and contribution rates for 401(k) plans of three large employers. Data included plan features, education programs offered to workers, and worker contributions, asset allocations, and other characteristics (age, race, sex, marital status, tenure, and salary). Found that plan features (e.g., employer matching rate) and legal limits affect workers' contribution rates (the effects differ by age and earnings). Also found heterogeneity in workers' allocation decisions (e.g., many younger workers have large equity holdings while many others have no equity holdings).

*Kotlikoff and Gokhale (1992)* Estimated age-productivity profiles using the present value of workers' compensation (wages and pension entitlement) for employees of a Fortune 1000 firm with over 300,000 employees in 1969-1983. Data included earnings histories for workers by age of hire, sex, and broad job category (office, sales, management). Found that productivity declines with age and that workers are paid more

---

reasons for changes in benefit plans, the chief financial officer may be a more relevant respondent than the chief personnel officer.

*Obtaining Information* It can be difficult to obtain comparable information across employers: for example, definitions of fiscal year differ, as do definitions for other characteristics. More important, it is often difficult to obtain any response to surveys (or administrative records systems) that have many or very detailed data items. One reason is that the more complex the data request, the more burden it likely imposes on employers to consult more than one set of records in multiple locations and departments. Another reason is employers' concerns about revealing information that might affect their competitive position.

than they produce when old to offset being paid less than they produce when young.

**Kruse (1993)** Studied the effects of profit sharing (one-sixth to one-fourth of employers and employees participate in such plans), based on a telephone survey of 500 public companies drawn from the 1990 Standard and Poor Compustat database. The survey had a response rate of 62 percent (500 of 812 companies). Data included profit-sharing coverage, types, and formulas, company unionization and personnel policies, and financial performance (from Compustat). Found no clear answers as to why companies adopt profit sharing—only unionization and increases in profit margins and stock prices seem to play a role, suggesting that profit sharing is an effect rather than a cause of better company performance. Profit sharing initially appears to increase productivity by 3-5 percent, particularly for smaller companies. The evidence is not clear on whether profit sharing increases employment stability.

**Medoff and Abraham (1981)** Analyzed performance, length of service, and earnings of managers and professionals in a large U.S. manufacturing company for 1972-1977. Data included employee characteristics (education, length of service, age, job grade, salary history), annual performance evaluations, and annual assessments of employees' potential for advancement. Found that higher earnings are associated with length of service but not with higher performance ratings.

**Mitchell and Luzadis (1988)** Analyzed the pension policies of 14 employers over three decades. Found marked enhancement of pension plan early retirement incentives, particularly for employers that had mandatory retirement provisions before legislation circumscribed the practice.

More generally, many employers have "gatekeepers" to steer away inquiries, particularly those directed to management.

As a consequence, even when limited information is requested, response rates to voluntary business surveys tend to be lower than response rates to household surveys. Rates are particularly low for surveys conducted by mail and by private organizations and researchers, compared with those conducted by government agencies (see Christianson and Tortora, 1995; Paxson, Dillman, and Tarnai, 1995). With intensive efforts, the BLS Employee Benefits Survey obtains quite high response rates for medium and large private establishments (85% in 1989) and for governments (94% in 1990), but its rate for small private establishments is significantly lower (72% in 1990). Also, 21 percent of the original sample of small private establishments was determined to be out-of-business or out-of-scope (see Bureau of Labor Statistics, 1992a). In comparison, the household response rate to the BLS-sponsored Current Population Survey averages about 95 percent each month.

***Providing Anonymous Data***   Many employers are concerned that they could be identified in survey data releases. Because of the relatively small numbers of establishments and enterprises and their skewed distribution by size, it is in fact difficult to provide analytically rich microdata for employers that protects the confidentiality of individual replies. Confidentiality concerns also affect the maintenance of a government-wide employer list: the Census Bureau Standard Statistical Establishment List is not shared with other agencies. Agencies like BLS maintain their own lists, and there is evidence of discrepancies in completeness of coverage and industry categorization among lists (see, e.g., Federal Committee on Statistical Methodology, 1990).

## Directions for the Future

Clearly, the development of analytically useful databases on employers is a necessity for retirement-income-related research and projections, and we believe it should be an important government goal. Below, we identify priority areas and strategies to move toward that goal. However, recommendations like ours that are developed primarily from a data user perspective need careful consideration in a broad context. The gaps in available data on employers are sufficiently large and the problems of employer data collection sufficiently formidable that a measured and comprehensive approach is needed to determine feasible and cost-effective goals for improvement, both in the near term and the longer run.

To this end, we urge the Department of Labor to establish an interagency task force on retirement-income-related employer data. The charge to the task force should be to develop and implement an integrated, multiyear plan for providing the data needed to understand and project employer demand for older workers and the causes and consequences for workers of changes in benefit offerings.

We suggest that BLS and PWBA jointly lead the task force: PWBA has responsibility for oversight of pension and other benefit plans and hence has the most policy interest in improving employer data; BLS brings extensive statistical experience and expertise. The task force should also involve other agencies with relevant analytical interests and expertise, such as the Pension Benefit Guaranty Corporation, relevant HHS agencies, and the Census Bureau. In addition, the task force should involve people in the research and modeling communities—including the principal investigators of panel surveys of individuals, such as HRS/AHEAD, that collect employer data—along with private benefit consultants and representatives of public and private sector employers. Involving data users is essential to focus the work of the task force on priority research and projection modeling issues. Involving employers and benefit consultants, who are often both users and providers, is essential to develop cost-effective methods for collecting and providing analytically useful information. The task force needs to get information about useful and feasible data collection from large and small employers in various sectors of business and with different benefit structures: sponsors of private single-employer pension plans, private multi-employer plans, and public plans are subject to different regulatory regimes with possibly differing data implications.

## Benefits: Descriptive Information

A critically important area for the task force to consider is how to improve data on employer benefits. At present, there is no comprehensive series with which to characterize and track benefit offerings for the entire universe of employers. The Employee Benefits Survey comes closest, but it is designed to describe benefits available to categories of employees and not benefits offered by types of employers; also, at present, it lacks important information, such as benefit costs, and has other limitations.

The recommended DOL task force needs to consider how best to develop a baseline picture for public and private employers and the self-employed and update it on a regular basis with information on benefit features and costs (including pension, health care, disability, and life insurance plans), employer characteristics (e.g., number of employees, financial characteristics, wage structure), and work force characteristics (e.g., age structure). Frequent updating is critical because benefit plans are dynamic, changing frequently. For reasons of cost and feasibility, the task force should give priority to modifying and coordinating existing data systems as far as possible toward the goal of a comprehensive database. Involvement of public and private sector employer representatives is critical in determining modifications to enhance data quality and utility that are feasible to implement. Given the overlap in existing surveys, it may be possible to reduce reporting burdens or, at least, to identify some information that can be dropped or curtailed to make room for needed new items.

Data systems to consider for modification include the Employee Benefits Survey, the Form 5500 database, and the National Employer Health Insurance Survey. In addition, data collected by the Public Pension Coordinating Council, if coverage were improved, could serve as an important resource with which to augment federal agency sources on state and local government employer benefits at little or no added cost. Although the federal government does not regulate state and local government benefit plans, retirement-income-related research and policy analysis needs to consider the full range of employers.

***Employee Benefits Survey*** Improvements to the EBS and the companion Employment Cost Trends survey (which includes the data published as the Employment Cost Index) were recently discussed in a meeting of researchers convened by BLS (MacDonald, 1995). Suggestions included adding questions on health care and other benefits for retirees, providing more data for establishments, facilitating the construction of estimates for establishments, and providing microdata for research purposes that could be linked with other sources of employer data. Currently, BLS is working to integrate the EBS more closely with the Employment Cost Trends survey and with local-area occupational compensation surveys. Such an integrated system could potentially bring together information on benefit plan provisions, employee participation in benefit plans, and employer costs. The task force should review these and other suggestions and goals for the EBS in the context of developing an overall plan for comprehensive employer benefit information.

***The Form 5500 PWBA Database*** This database has many limitations for research use, but it offers information not otherwise available on pension plan costs and coverage for all large employers and a large sample of small employers. Efforts to reduce government regulation may curtail the reporting requirements for the system. We urge the recommended task force to determine the usefulness of the system, both as it exists now and if it were improved, in the context of an overall plan for obtaining comprehensive benefits data. The use of the system for this purpose should be a factor in decisions about reporting requirements.

Relatively low-cost improvements for this database include:

- linking Form 5500 records over time to provide panel data;
- merging Form 5500 records with employer financial characteristics such as those in the Compustat database for publicly owned, for-profit companies;
- making the data more timely and accessible, perhaps by providing the data files on the Internet.

With regard to linking and merging, researchers have carried out linkages on their own, but it would be useful for PWBA to develop standard linking procedures that handle such problems as business mergers and splits. It would also be useful for PWBA to perform linkages on a regular basis and to determine if there are ways to fill gaps in Compustat and other information.[17] If staff resources are a constraint, consideration could be given to contracting for these activities.

We also suggest exploring ways to improve the consistency of reporting of welfare benefit plans, particularly health care and disability plans. Form 5500

---

[17]In the future, the EDGAR database of the Securities and Exchange Commission may provide more complete financial coverage than Compustat.

data for these plans are not currently provided in the PWBA database. Similarly, consideration could be given to including in the database the newly required information on demographic characteristics of participants in defined benefit pension plans and to obtaining such information from defined contribution pension plans and other benefit programs.

A more difficult question is how to obtain useful information at reasonable cost from the narrative Summary Plan Descriptions that are filed with the Form 5500, which does not itself describe plan features. An information-rich but costly procedure would be to require more frequent filing of the descriptions (which are often out of date) and to regularly abstract and code analytically useful information from them. Many private benefit consulting firms categorize features of a large variety of plans, and their categories could be the basis for a coding scheme, as could the categories used in the EBS. A less costly and less information-rich procedure would be to develop a limited set of categories of plan features to add to the Form 5500 itself and to drop the requirement to file Summary Plan Descriptions. If this option were adopted, it could still be possible to obtain detailed plan feature information and the cost and coverage data in the Form 5500 database for a sample of employers by providing the applicable Form 5500 records to BLS to merge with the EBS data and prepare a file that could be tabulated at researchers' request.

Finally, to reduce regulatory burden and costs but provide information for monitoring and research purposes, consideration could be given to conducting the Form 5500 data collection program on a sample basis. If it is necessary to have complete reporting in order to monitor compliance with pension law, then consideration could be given to asking a sample of employers information that would be useful for research purposes but is not necessarily needed for compliance. The sample design should consider the need for information from employers of different types and sizes. The design should also build in a longitudinal component, so that changes in benefit provisions can be analyzed behaviorally as well as on a time-series basis. Finally, the design should consider the degree of integration that is feasible with the sample design for the Employee Benefits Survey; without some degree of integration, it will not be possible to relate the data from the two systems.

***National Employer Health Insurance Survey*** The U.S. Department of Health and Human Services plans to conduct NEHIS annually to obtain detailed information on employer health care benefit plan features and costs. NEHIS will play an important role in an integrated system of health status and health care surveys. In this context, it is probably not practical to turn NEHIS into a full-scale employer benefit plan survey, including pensions and other benefits. However, it might be useful to broaden the survey on a periodic basis. If this were done, there would be less need to find ways to improve reporting of health care and disability plans in the Form 5500 series.

Determining the set of possible options for improved data on employer benefits and then determining which options appear more cost-effective is a challenging task. Is it preferable, for example, to enhance the Form 5500 system and rely less on such surveys as EBS or NEHIS? Alternatively, is it preferable to take advantage of the large sample size of NEHIS by periodically expanding the NEHIS questionnaire to cover pension as well as health care benefits? The recommended task force will need to address such questions in order to find cost-effective ways to provide needed information while minimizing duplication among data collection systems.

## Labor Demand: Case Studies

Another important but difficult area for the task force to consider is how to obtain data for analyzing and projecting employer demand for older workers. For this purpose, detailed information is needed for employers with which to relate work force composition by age with compensation, benefit costs, and worker productivity by age. Obtaining such information presents formidable problems, including not only employer reluctance to furnish the level of detail required, but also the fact that some of the information may not be readily available. For example, employers may not know the details of their health care benefit costs by employees' (and dependents') ages.

Estimating productivity differences by age presents particularly difficult conceptual and measurement problems. Pioneering work by Kotlikoff (1988) and Kotlikoff and Gokhale (1992) determined age-productivity differences among employees of a large company by comparing the expected values of total compensation, including wages and pension benefits, across age cohorts. This method is indirect and involves some strong assumptions (for commentary, see Lazear, 1988). Medoff and Abraham (1981) related performance evaluation and salary data for white collar employees of a large company, not to age per se, but to length of service. However, the suitability of performance evaluations (where they exist) for measuring age-productivity differentials has not been established.

While case studies, such as those conducted by Kotlikoff and Gokhale and Medoff and Abraham (see Box 4-8 for other examples), are not readily generalizable, they offer a feasible and cost-effective way to begin to address the data collection problems in the area of employer demand for older workers. We suggest that the recommended DOL task force, with the cooperation of private and public employer representatives, arrange to sponsor a series of employer case studies. The studies should be chosen to include a variety of employers confronting a variety of situations. They should focus not only on substantive issues of the factors that affect labor demand, but also on ways of obtaining needed data that could be feasible for more structured, representative surveys. They can do so by exploring a wide range of potentially useful information—for example, attitudes and perceptions of operating, financial, and personnel officers and of employees—and by investigating cost-effective methods and sources of data collection that could be implemented on a larger scale.

Medoff and Abraham (1981) support such an approach. They comment (p. 215) on the need for richer data with which to empirically test theories of experience-earnings differentials:

> It is our belief that major steps [to obtain needed data] can be taken through interaction with those who formulate company compensation policies and with those affected by these policies. In particular, interviews with the members of top management who are responsible for the outlines of a company's pay practices should be conducted; discussions with supervisors about how they determine the proper salaries for their subordinates should be initiated; and the attitudes of employees toward different compensation schemes should be assessed. ... Moreover, we should seek data that would permit analysis of the impact of changes in the nature of firms' compensation practices on things such as productivity, quits, discharges, ability to attract new hires, absenteeism, and job satisfaction.

**Panel Data for Behavioral Analysis**

Improvements in such data systems as the EBS, Form 5500 series, and NEHIS can provide valuable information for tracking trends in employer benefit offerings and analyzing some of the factors involved. However, such systems are not likely to provide the richness of detail that is needed for in-depth behavioral analysis of employer compensation policies and their effects on workers. Case studies will also not suffice to establish the underlying mechanisms in employer decisions about recruitment and retention of older workers.

What is needed, ideally, is an employer-employee panel survey that provides detailed information on characteristics of a sample of employers linked with characteristics of a sample of their workers.[18] Alternatively, given that confidentiality concerns could prove a barrier to implementing such a survey, an employer panel survey that provides aggregate information about the work force characteristics of sampled employers would be useful. In either case, the employer sample would need to be refreshed periodically to include new businesses. The survey should include data on the financial and other characteristics of employers and skills, earnings, benefit plan participation, and demographic and family characteristics of employees. Similarly to HRS/AHEAD for individuals, the survey ideally should also include data on attitudes and perceptions of corporate officers, supervisors, and workers, although confidentiality concerns may make it difficult to obtain such information.

The recommended employer data task force should carefully consider the

---

[18]See Gustman and Mitchell (1992) and Parsons (1996) on the need for such a survey.

feasibility of an employer-employee (or employer) panel survey and its costs and benefits. Such a survey would undoubtedly be expensive. It could also encounter more than the usual problems of employer cooperation and response (given the level of detail and possible sensitivity of the information required), but the data provided would be very valuable for needed research on factors in employer behavior and its consequences for workers.

There is little experience with this type of survey in the United States. In the 1970s, BLS sponsored several Quality of Employment Surveys of small samples of workers that included a panel component. Information was collected in these surveys on many aspects of the employment situation (e.g., work-related problems, work attitudes and behaviors, job/task characteristics, earnings, fringe benefits, and noneconomic forms of compensation), but no questions were asked of the sample members' employers or about benefit costs. An advisory group recommended expanding the program to include a survey of employees that also obtained limited information from their employers, together with a survey of employers that also interviewed samples of their employees (Kalleberg, 1986); however, no further surveys were conducted.

The Census Bureau recently matched 1990 census data on workers with employer data from its Longitudinal Research Database. Future matches may be possible if plans are approved for a very large continuing household survey with census-type content (the American Community Survey). However, the LRD is limited to manufacturing establishments, which include only 20 percent of the work force, and census data for workers are very limited in scope. (A longitudinal database for nonmanufacturing establishments is under development.)

Of possibly more relevance, Statistics Canada (the national government agency) is launching an employer-employee panel survey that may offer guidance for a U.S. effort (Statistics Canada, 1995). A pilot test of the Workplace and Employee Survey was conducted in early 1996 of 1,000 establishments and 6,000 of their employees. The production version of the survey will begin in 1998 and continue yearly; the sample will include 5,000 establishments and 30,000 employees. Establishments will be tracked over time with periodic replenishment of the sample; employees will be tracked as long as they remain with the same company and for one period after they leave. The survey content covers a range of topics, including: work force characteristics, compensation, training, business strategy, financial performance, and technology use for employers; and job characteristics, pay and benefits, training, participation in decision making, education, recent work experience, and family situation for employees.

A way to begin providing panel information on U.S. employers for behavioral analysis and to explore feasible methods of data collection would be to build a continuing employer survey into HRS/AHEAD. In the first interview wave, HRS asked information with which to locate sample members' employers and obtain pension and health care plan descriptions from them. The survey also asked employed sample members about benefit plan features and other aspects of their job and work place (e.g., perceptions of employer attitudes toward older workers); see Box 4-9.

At a minimum, it appears desirable and feasible for subsequent waves of HRS/AHEAD to collect employer benefit data. It is important that the collection cover all employed sample members, including those with the same job, because of the likelihood that some employers will change their benefit provisions. If reporting in the Form 5500 series is improved, it would be possible to obtain plan descriptions from this source for a large fraction of HRS/AHEAD respondents without having to contact their employers.

In addition to using the employer benefit plan descriptions for such purposes as estimating future benefit entitlements, the information can be compared to self-reports in HRS/AHEAD. One important question such data would address is whether employees' knowledge of benefit plan features and the implications for how best to prepare for retirement is improving over time. Research has shown that workers often do not know or give incorrect answers to questions about important pension plan provisions, such as whether and at what age early retirement is possible: see, for example, Mitchell (1988), who compared worker responses in the 1983 Survey of Consumer Finances with information provided by employers about the workers' pension plans. For this purpose, it would be useful to ask both the sample members and their employers about employer programs for educating workers about pension and other benefits. The Department of Labor is making such employer education programs a priority initiative. The Social Security Administration is also attempting to provide covered workers with more information about benefit entitlements under current law.[19]

Going further, HRS/AHEAD could conduct a full-fledged survey of sample members' employers, with information on such characteristics as return on investment, benefit plan costs, wage structure, and age distribution of employees. Some of this information could be obtained from publicly available sources, such as the Compustat database, thereby reducing respondent burden.

There are several advantages of incorporating an employer survey into HRS/ AHEAD. The employer sample is readily generated from HRS sample members' responses and would have a built-in longitudinal component. It would provide a vastly richer set of employer characteristics than ever before available with which to analyze individual savings and retirement behavior. However, for analysis of employer behavior as such (e.g., factors in benefit plan decisions), a piggybacked survey is not an efficient sample design. Important categories of employers, such

---

[19]See Employee Benefit Research Institute (1995, 1996b, 1996c) for research, based on case studies and special surveys of workers and participant-directed defined contribution pension plan sponsors, on employer financial education programs and their effects on workers' pension plan contributions.

## BOX 4-9
## DATA ON EMPLOYER CHARACTERISTICS IN HRS
### (for employers of HRS respondents)

### Employer-Provided Information

Health insurance plan provisions
Pension plan provisions (Summary Plan Descriptions)

### Employee Reports of Fringe Benefits

Weeks of paid vacation allowed
Days of paid sick leave allowed
Whether long-term disability insurance provided
Features of pension plan coverage for self (see Box 4-5)
Features of health insurance coverage for self (see Box 4-6)

### Employee Reports of Hours Flexibility for Self

Could respondent reduce hours and what would happen to pay, health
　　insurance benefits, and pension eligibility
Could respondent increase hours on job

### Employee Reports of Employer Accommodation
### for Work Disability

Specific kinds of adjustments made, such as providing transportation,
　　shortening hours, special equipment, etc.

### Employee Reports of Employer Characteristics

Number of employees at this establishment (location)
Number of employees at employer overall
Whether covered by union contract
Industry of employer

### Employee Perceptions of Age-Related Personnel Practices

(Whether agree with following)
In decisions about promotion, employer gives preference to younger
　　people
Co-workers make older people feel they should retire before 65
Employer would let older workers move to a less demanding job with less
　　pay if they wanted

### Employee Characterization of Job Requirements

Whether job requires physical effort, good eyesight, good memory, lots of
　　stress, etc.

as companies with predominantly younger workers, may have high sampling variability and hence large standard errors of estimates.

The alternative, as discussed above, is to design a continuing employer-employee (or employer) panel survey as a wholly separate data collection effort. Thorough analysis will be required to determine the costs and benefits of alternative approaches to obtaining needed longitudinal employer data for behavioral research. At the least, HRS/AHEAD could offer a vehicle to experiment with methods of employer data collection to improve measurement and data quality.

## Recommendations

The development of analytically useful databases on employers for retirement-income-related policy analysis and projection purposes should be an important government goal. At present, important information on the characteristics and determinants of employer benefit plan offerings and employer demand for older workers is lacking, incomplete, or not provided in a usable manner. Given the central role of employers in providing retirement income and health care benefits, the lack of an adequate database is a major handicap to evaluation of alternative policy proposals in these areas.

**5. The U.S. Department of Labor should establish an interagency task force on employer data to specify an integrated plan for collecting retirement-income-related information. The plan should specify short-term and long-term goals that consider user needs, resource constraints, and the problems of obtaining information from employers due to such factors as low response rates, locating the appropriate respondents, and confidentiality concerns. The task force should involve researchers, private benefit consultants, and representatives of public and private employers in its work.**

**6. The employer data collection plan should include short-term and long-term goals for obtaining improved information on the distribution across employers of all benefit plan offerings (including pensions, health insurance, disability insurance, retiree health insurance, life insurance). Comprehensive baseline information is a priority need, along with a plan for regular updating. Needed data elements include benefit plan characteristics and costs, employer characteristics (e.g., number of employees, financial characteristics, wage structure), and work force characteristics (e.g., age structure) for public and private employers and the self-employed.**

**7. The employer data collection task force should give priority to redesigning and enhancing existing data collection systems on employer benefit offerings and related topics. Such systems include the Employee Benefits Survey, which currently provides information for broad categories of em-**

ployees but not for employers, and the Form 5500 data series, which serves regulatory purposes and currently has limited research use.

Consideration should be given to improvements to the Form 5500 series, including:

- making the data more timely and accessible (e.g., on-line);
- linking records over time to provide panel data;
- merging the Form 5500 benefit plan information with the kind of employer financial characteristics found in the Compustat database;
- working to standardize the reporting for health care and disability plans, so that they can be added to the Form 5500 database; and
- finding ways to add information about benefit plan features to the database, perhaps by abstracting analytically useful information from the narrative plan descriptions that are filed with the Form 5500.

8. The employer data collection plan should include short-term and long-term goals for obtaining information on labor demand for older workers and the factors that may affect that demand. Needed data elements include employment patterns of older workers, compensation and benefit costs by age, and worker productivity by age. Very little information on these topics is currently available, and some raise difficult measurement issues. A reasonable short-term goal is to sponsor case studies of employers that can help identify important variables and feasible means of collecting them on a larger scale.

9. The employer data collection task force should consider the feasibility and cost-effectiveness of a panel survey, which is periodically refreshed, that collects detailed information on employers and their workers. Such a survey should cover the full universe, including private for-profit, nonprofit, and government employers, and the self-employed. Longitudinal data from an employer-based survey are needed to analyze the factors that affect employer decisions about recruitment and retention of older workers and benefit plan offerings and how these decisions, in turn, affect workers.

10. HRS and AHEAD should develop and implement a plan for obtaining information on a continuing basis on the pension and health insurance offerings of the employers of the HRS/AHEAD sample members.

## EXPANDED USE OF ADMINISTRATIVE DATA

A recurrent theme in retirement-income-related research is the need for data from administrative records, either as stand-alone databases for analysis or linked with survey data. Such records can often provide important variables for individuals and employers at very low marginal cost. The major difficulty concerns how to provide access to such data for research and modeling purposes when their use raises concerns about maintaining the confidentiality of respondent information.[20]

## Records on Individuals

Greater access to Social Security Administration earnings and benefits records could advance many important areas of retirement-income-related analysis and modeling. As a stand-alone database, SSA records have the potential to improve U.S. data on mortality at older ages and to study the relationship of socioeconomic status (as measured by earnings levels) to mortality.[21] Such studies could be carried out by SSA staff or by researchers who are sworn in as SSA employees to prevent disclosure of confidential data (as has been done for some Census Bureau studies). Given the importance of mortality projections for projecting retirement income security, we urge that priority be given to mortality research with SSA records.

More problematic from the perspective of confidentiality protection are proposals to link SSA records with survey responses. Some studies have been done, but they have been limited. Exact-match files of SSA records with the March 1973 and 1978 CPS, developed by the Census Bureau, were made publicly available (the 1973 file included an exact match with IRS records), as were exact-match files of SSA records with the Retirement History Survey. However, no exact-match files of SSA records with CPS data for years later than 1979 have been developed for public use. The Census Bureau has developed exact-match files of Social Security records with the 1984, 1990, and 1991 panels of the Survey of Income and Program Participation (SIPP), but these files are made available only to SSA analysts with strict restrictions on use. The Census Bureau recently released a public-use, exact-match file of the March 1991 CPS with selected data from IRS administrative tax records. In this file, techniques of data-switching and the addition of noise were used to mask the data so that no sensitive information that could identify specific individuals was released. More extensive matches of IRS data with CPS and SIPP files have been used to evaluate the quality of income reporting in the March CPS and SIPP and for research on improved weighting schemes to reduce the variance of SIPP estimates, but these files are only available internally to Census Bureau staff.

The Department of Labor sponsored a 1977-1978 Survey of Private Pension Benefit Amounts that linked private employer pension plan records on beneficia-

---

[20]See Duncan, Jabine, and deWolf (1993) for a review of confidentiality and access issues for federal statistical data and promising avenues for addressing the difficulties.

[21]If SSA tracked marital status of all beneficiaries, then SSA records could also support needed analysis of the relationship of marital status to mortality.

ries with SSA earnings and benefits records (Office of Pension and Welfare Benefit Programs, 1985). This survey used the Form 5500 database to sample private pension plans and obtain information from plan administrators on benefits paid to individual plan participants. The matched records of pension and Social Security benefits and earnings were used to analyze the contribution of employer pensions to retirement income security (e.g., to calculate earnings replacement rates). The response rate from plan administrators was low (about 50%), and large defined contribution plans were underrepresented. However, the matched data were viewed as more accurate than household survey estimates of pension retirement benefits, which are typically underreported. No public-use files were made available from the survey, and it would presumably be difficult to do so if it were to be repeated.

Legislative restrictions are one reason that publicly available exact-match files of SSA and survey data have not been developed in recent years. Another reason is that statistical agencies have become more concerned with questions of privacy and confidentiality of data and the potentially adverse effects on survey response rates if people believe that their replies are not held in strict confidence.

Nevertheless, there is a strong need for exact-match files. Calculations of expected Social Security benefits require either complete histories of covered earnings or summary variables, such as average indexed monthly covered earnings over a worker's span of employment, that in turn derive from earnings histories. Such histories are difficult to obtain retrospectively in surveys and would require decades of data collection to obtain prospectively. Earnings histories, including earnings above the payroll tax ceiling (available in SSA records beginning in 1979), are also helpful in calculating expected benefits from the types of employer pension plans that calculate benefits on the basis of several years of highest earnings with the employer or that specify employer contributions as a percentage of earnings. Finally, benefit histories are useful to evaluate and augment survey responses of Social Security income.

Plans are now being implemented to make available on a restricted basis exact-match files of HRS/AHEAD and SSA records that will provide very valuable information for analysis purposes. (Links will also be made with HCFA Medicare data and possibly with state Medicaid data.) A three-pronged strategy will be followed to protect confidentiality. First, linked data files with complete earnings and benefits histories will be made available on a limited access basis only to researchers who sign nondisclosure agreements that include penalties for violation. Second, public-use files will include only summary variables derived from the earnings histories. Third, estimated Social Security entitlements that have been computed under a variety of assumptions will be made available to HRS users under restricted conditions (Mitchell, Steinmeier, and Olson, 1996).

We support the preparation of exact-match files that link SSA and other administrative records with HRS/AHEAD and urge that arrangements be made to perform these linkages on a regular basis. We also encourage the Census Bureau and SSA to consider the development of SIPP-SSA exact-match files that can be made publicly available by following the strategy of HRS and AHEAD, namely, to provide summary variables derived from the earnings histories that facilitate the calculation of expected Social Security benefits. (Iams and Sandell [1996], SSA researchers who are using matched SIPP-SSA files for Social Security benefit modeling, make a similar recommendation.) There are plans to include SSA information on Social Security benefit type, and whether the respondent has died, in publicly available SIPP files. We support these efforts and also urge consideration of developing SIPP files for public release that include derived variables from SSA earnings records.

## Records on Employers

Administrative records for employers, such as financial statements that are abstracted in Compustat and the Form 5500 data series, provide useful information for analytic purposes. These particular data sets, unlike SSA records, are derived from public documents, but problems can arise when they are merged with other data for which confidentiality protection is promised (e.g., BLS or Census Bureau surveys).

Employers are sensitive about the release of data that could be useful to competitors, and it can be very difficult to mask such variables as employer size sufficiently to prevent disclosure and at the same time maintain the analytical value of the data. Indeed, microdata from employer surveys, let alone matched survey and administrative records data, are often not made publicly available at all.

Sometimes agencies are willing to retabulate confidential data at the request of researchers. For example, BLS has linked Form 5500 data with the EBS and run analyses for outside researchers. However, the researchers were not themselves given access to the microrecords, and they found this mode of data access very limiting (MacDonald, 1995).

One possible strategy to provide greater access to matched employer data is to adopt the strategy proposed for exact-match files of SSA earnings histories with HRS/AHEAD. Under this strategy, researchers could gain access to the complete data sets under very strict conditions of use. At the same time, public-use files could be developed in which key administrative records variables are summarized in a manner that is most relevant for research needs and other steps are taken (e.g., limited geographic identification) to prevent disclosure. If this approach is adopted for matched employer data, it would be important for agencies to consult with researchers to determine the appropriate summarized variables.

The Census Bureau is pursuing another very promising approach for research access to its employer data files, including the LRD, which have not been available for use except at the Bureau's headquarters. This approach may provide a model for other agencies. Several years ago, the Census Bureau, in collaboration with the National Bureau of Economic Research, a private organization, established a secure Research Data Center at its Boston regional office. Researchers may come to the center, be sworn in as special Census Bureau agents, and use the data sets on site. Census Bureau employees must review any output that researchers take with them to ensure that it does not identify specific respondents. Although more limiting than use of microdata at one's own institution, this arrangement is far preferable for researchers in the Boston area than having to come to the headquarters in the Washington, D.C., area. The success of the Boston data center has led the Census Bureau to set up a second center at Carnegie Mellon University in Pittsburgh, and the agency is exploring researchers' interest in having similar centers in other major cities around the country.

## Recommendations

**11. Matched files of panel survey responses and key administrative records should be regularly produced for retirement-income-related policy analysis and projection purposes. Examples include exact matches of survey records with Social Security earnings histories and benefit records, Medicare and Medicaid records, and the National Death Index. The added information in matched files is obtainable at low marginal cost and is essential for analysis of retirement and savings decisions and the effect of medical care use and expenditures on retirement security.**

**12. Agencies should collaborate on the development and oversight of matched data sets for individuals and employers, with input from researchers on content. They should also vigorously explore creative solutions for providing research access to exact-match files that safeguard the confidentiality of individual responses. Possible solutions include: (1) developing public-use files that contain summary variables derived from the administrative records portion of the matched file; (2) requiring researchers to sign nondisclosure agreements with significant penalties for violations; and (3) providing researchers with access to matched files on site at secure data centers.**

## DATA VALIDATION

Validation of databases that are used in behavioral and projection models is as important as validation of the models themselves. Sampling errors in data inputs are one source of uncertainty of model estimates; more important, nonsampling errors can introduce both uncertainty and bias into model estimates. Data validation is essential to identify the types and magnitudes of such errors. It is also essential for survey methodological research, which should be part of every data collection program to determine procedures for improving data quality at the outset by improving questionnaire design and data collection procedures.

There are many sources of nonsampling errors in both surveys and administrative records. One source is unit nonresponse, that is, failure by a reporting unit to provide any information at all. Panel surveys are subject to cumulative unit nonresponse over time, or attrition, as people become tired of cooperating with the survey or move and cannot be traced. Other sources of error are nonresponse to specific items, overreporting (e.g., a false positive report of pension coverage), underreporting (e.g., reporting an amount less than actually received for an income source), and misclassification (e.g., reporting a defined benefit pension plan as a defined contribution plan or vice versa). Yet another source of error in surveys is undercoverage of the population because the sampling frame does not include all people or employers in the universe or other reasons. For example, household surveys of the general population almost always have low coverage rates of such groups as young minority men.[22]

Surveys and administrative records systems use several methods to try to compensate for nonsampling errors, such as adjustment of survey weights for population undercoverage and attrition, imputation for item nonresponse, and editing for misclassification or inconsistency in reporting. However, these procedures are not likely to maintain all of the underlying relationships and may themselves be a source of bias.

### Validation Methods

Validation involves estimating overall error rates and the contribution of individual sources of error to them, including the contribution of weighting, imputation, and editing procedures. The problem is to determine appropriate benchmarks for comparison. There are several approaches to validation; see Box 4-10 for examples of their use.

*Reinterviews* Asking a sample of respondents the same question in a reinterview cannot establish which answer is correct, but it can indicate whether the responses are robust in the sense that there is a high level of consistency between the answers given originally and in reinterviews.

*Use of Alternative Question Wording* Experimentation with different question wording, or other aspects of questionnaire design (such as the order in which questions are asked) may determine that the responses are sensitive to such

---

[22]Coverage rates are developed by comparing survey population estimates by age, race, and sex to census population estimates updated by births, deaths, and estimated net immigration; Medicare records are used for the elderly.

## BOX 4-10
## SELECTED DATA VALIDATION STUDIES

***Aggregate Reporting Errors in Asset Values by Type***   Smith
(1993:12-13, Table 6) compared aggregate asset values in the first wave
of HRS and the 1989 SCF; the SCF data pertain to households with residents aged 51 to 61, with values inflated to 1992.  Total net worth is
underreported in HRS compared with the SCF, but the extent of underreporting is less than in other surveys.  There are discrepancies in reporting
of asset values by type:

| Asset Type | HRS as Percentage of SCF |
|---|---|
| Total net worth | 88 |
| Vehicles | 172 |
| House equity | 77 |
| Liquid assets | 93 |
| IRA and Keogh accounts | 131 |
| Stocks, mutual funds | 131 |
| Business equity | 62 |

***Aggregate Reporting Errors in Pension Income Amounts***   Coder
and Scoon-Rogers (1994:21-24, Table 2) compared income reporting in
the March 1991 CPS and 1990 SIPP with independent estimates constructed from the National Income and Product Accounts (NIPA).  Their
results, when subtracting an estimate of lump-sum receipts for private
(but not public) employer pensions from the NIPA and making other appropriate adjustments, show a range of differences:

| Pension Type | SIPP and CPS Amounts as Percentage of NIPA |
|---|---|
| Private pensions | 107, 111 |
| Federal employee pensions | 73, 80 |
| Military pensions | 92, 87 |
| State and local government pensions | 75, 77 |

If lump-sum receipts are not subtracted from private pension amounts in
the NIPA, then the SIPP and March CPS estimates are only 50-55 percent of the independent estimate.  It appears that some, but not all, recipients of lump-sum pension distributions are reporting them as regular income in SIPP and the March CPS, contrary to the surveys' intent.

***Imputation Effects on Underreporting of Earnings*** Coder (1991, 1992) compared earnings reports for married couples in the March 1986 CPS and 1990 SIPP with exactly matched IRS records. He found both underreporting and overreporting problems. He further determined that the Census Bureau's imputation procedures for missing reports increased the extent of net underreporting in the surveys.

***Question Wording Effects on Employment Status*** Extensive questionnaire testing, including the use of cognitive research methods, was used to redesign the CPS questionnaire to reflect changes in employment patterns and facilitate response. One set of question changes elicited more reports from women working and fewer reports that classified them as not in the labor force. Use of the new questionnaire and data collection procedures affected some key labor force statistics (see Polivka and Miller, 1995).

***Population Coverage Errors*** Bureau of the Census (1996:Table D-2) reports coverage rates in the March 1994 CPS by age, race, and sex. The worst covered population groups are young and middle-aged black men: coverage rates are 71 percent, 76 percent, 67 percent, and 68 percent, respectively, for black men aged 20-24, 25-29, 30-34, and 35-44. Coverage rates for these groups are similarly low in SIPP (see Jabine, King, and Petroni, 1990:Tables 10.12, 10.13, which report coverage rates in the March 1986 CPS and SIPP). The elderly generally have better coverage rates: 94 percent, 96 percent, 93 percent, and 98 percent, respectively, for black men, black women, nonblack men, and nonblack women aged 65-74 in the March 1994 CPS. Older population groups sometimes have estimated coverage rates of higher than 100 percent due to age reporting errors. (See text for definition and measurement of population coverage rates in surveys.)

variations. In the past 10 years, federal statistical agencies have made increasing use of techniques from cognitive psychology to study in greater depth the ways in which respondents react to and interpret specific question wording. The results of such methods, which include one-on-one sessions in which a researcher probes the respondent after each question to ask what he or she had in mind when answering, have often shown startling differences in perceptions between respondents and survey personnel (see Jabine et al., 1984).

*Aggregate Comparisons of Two or More Surveys* Comparing aggregate estimates from one survey with aggregate estimates from another survey that is believed to be superior can provide an overall measure of data quality. For example, as discussed above, estimates of household wealth from such surveys as HRS or SIPP have been compared with estimates from the SCF. Another example is comparing estimates of retiree pension and health care benefits from the March CPS income supplement with estimates from the detailed supplements that have been conducted occasionally on these income sources (most recently in September 1994; see Pension and Welfare Benefits Administration, 1995b). However, aggregate comparisons do not generally shed light on the sources of error in survey estimates. Also, they need to be carefully made to ensure that definitions of the reporting universe and data items are comparable between the surveys being compared.

*Aggregate Comparisons of Surveys with Administrative Records Data*  Survey and administrative records comparisons are often viewed as a preferred method of measuring overall data quality, on the assumption that the administrative records estimates represent "truth." For example, validation studies of the quality of income data in such surveys as the March CPS and SIPP have used estimates from IRS tax records, food stamps and other program records, and the National Income and Product Accounts (NIPA) as benchmarks.

However, such comparisons often require extensive adjustments of the administrative sources, which cannot always be completely made, for consistency of coverage and definitions with the survey data. Thus, comparing NIPA and survey income estimates requires adjusting the NIPA estimates to exclude income of institutionalized people, Armed Forces members overseas, and others who are not covered in household surveys (including nonprofit institutions in some cases). In another example, comparing the percentage of private wage and salary workers who participate in employer pension plans between the Form 5500 data series and the periodic supplements to the CPS on pensions requires several adjustments (see Beller and Lawrence, 1990). The two series do not include exactly the same types of pensions; also, the Form 5500 series includes nonvested participants who left their jobs less than 1 year previously, and it double counts workers with more than one job in which they are covered.

Finally, administrative sources are not always error free. For example, there is evidence that earnings are underreported to assistance program caseworkers, which suggests that household surveys are not necessarily inaccurate when they find higher proportions of public assistance recipients with earnings than shown in case records. Also, Medicare records are not an entirely accurate representation of the older population, given the problem of phantom enrollees (records for people who have already died).

*Microlevel Comparisons of Survey and Administrative Records*  Exact-match files make it possible to carry out detailed validation studies that decompose overall error levels into specific sources of error, including overreporting, underreporting, misclassification, erroneous imputation for nonresponse. Again, care needs to be taken to assure comparability of universes and data items: for example, not everyone is required to file a tax return.

Because of confidentiality restrictions, the opportunity for microlevel error analyses has generally been limited to federal statistical agency staff. One analysis by outside researchers is Herzog and Rubin (1983), who studied the quality of March CPS Social Security benefit imputations with the publicly available 1973 CPS-SSA-IRS exact-match file. David et al. (1986) carried out a similar study of earnings imputations with a 1981 CPS-IRS exact-match file that they used while working at the Census Bureau as special sworn agents.

## Validation Needs

To improve the capability for accurate modeling and analysis of retirement-income-related policies and behaviors, validation studies of key data sources should be carried out on a regular basis. Such studies can provide important feedback to data collection agencies to improve data quality at the source. They are also needed to enable researchers and policy analysts to determine appropriate strategies to compensate for data problems in their models. For these purposes, it can be useful to develop data quality profiles that are regularly updated as new information becomes available. Quality profiles bring together the results of validation studies for a particular survey or administrative records system into a comprehensive document that describes sources of error and their magnitudes, where known, and that identifies areas for which more validation work is needed (see, e.g., Jabine, King, and Petroni, 1990, which is a quality profile for SIPP.)

Several kinds of data validation studies could be useful for retirement-income-related databases.

***Comparing CPS, SIPP, and HRS Reports of Pension Participation*** SSA recently completed a comparison of the May 1993 CPS pension supplement with 1993 data from the 1992 SIPP panel, finding that participation (coverage) estimates in the two surveys are almost identical (Iams, 1995). A similar analysis should be performed for all three surveys for the HRS age cohort.

***Comparing Household Survey Reports of Pension Participation with Estimates from Employer Administrative Records*** Aggregate comparisons, such as the study by Beller and Lawrence (1990) of the CPS pension supplements and the Form 5500 data series, should be carried out on a regular basis. More work is needed to improve the validity of such comparisons to account, for example, for worker participation in more than one plan and in plans of more than one employer.

Microlevel comparisons of household survey reports of pension plan provisions with employer records are possible and should be carried out for sample members of HRS, although the quality of the analysis may be affected by the relatively low rate of employer response. About 25 percent of sample members' employers did not respond to the request for Summary Plan Descriptions, and another 10 percent provided inadequate information with which to code relevant pension plan features. This level of employer response is typical of the experience of other surveys that have requested the descriptions, such as the 1989 SCF and 1989 NLS-Mature Women (see Juster and Suzman, 1995:44-45).

*Comparing Household Survey Data on Income and Assets Across Surveys and with Administrative Records* Comparisons should be regularly performed of household survey reports with other surveys (e.g., comparing wealth estimates from HRS/AHEAD or SIPP with the SCF) and with NIPA and other administrative records sources (e.g., income tax records). Such comparisons, particularly with administrative records, require considerable care.

With regard to pension income, a major issue is the treatment of the rapidly growing phenomenon of lump-sum pension distributions, which are treated differently in different surveys and records. Lump-sum distributions are included in the NIPA accounts and in income tax returns; according to the income concept of the March CPS, lump sums are not to be reported; SIPP has a separate category to report lump sums of all types; and HRS/AHEAD has questions on several types of lump sums, including pension distributions. Comparisons of March CPS, SIPP, IRS, and NIPA data suggest that some CPS and SIPP respondents may be reporting lump-sum pension amounts as regular income, but the extent to which this happens is not clear (Coder and Scoon-Rogers, 1994:21-24; see also Schieber, 1995). Careful analysis of pension income reporting in the March CPS and SIPP in comparison with HRS/AHEAD for the HRS/AHEAD age range could be helpful, as could cognitive research with respondents to determine their knowledge of types of pension income and, in particular, whether they distinguish lump sums from pension distributions that are spread out over time. To make household surveys more useful for retirement-income-related analysis, it would clearly be desirable to obtain as complete reporting as possible of both regular and lump-sum pension amounts.

To the extent that these and other validation studies identify serious data quality problems, behavioral and projection models will need to be adjusted or their results qualified in an appropriate manner. For example, some microsimulation projection models have a provision to adjust March CPS income data for comparability with NIPA estimates. Such adjustment procedures must be carefully worked out, not only to be sure that the NIPA estimates are in fact comparable with CPS income concepts, but also to preserve key relationships among income amounts and other variables.

## Recommendation

13. Budgets for retirement-income-related surveys should include sufficient resources for regular evaluation of data quality. Evaluation methods include reinterviewing subsamples of respondents to measure consistency of reporting; experimentation with alternative question wording to identify possible reporting problems; and comparing survey estimates with administrative records to determine the completeness and accuracy of survey reporting, taking care to adjust for differences in definitions and other aspects of the two sources.

# 5

# Development of Projection Models

As the concern about retirement income security and the costs to provide it increases over the next few years, decision makers will look to projection models to estimate the likely costs and other effects of alternative policy proposals. Such models will require good data and a solid base of research knowledge with which to project demographic and economic trends and behavioral responses to policy changes and other factors. Outputs from analytical models of the behavior of individuals and employers that receive general consensus should be inputs to projection models. Otherwise, when policy proposals are expected to elicit a behavioral response, projection models will fall short in estimating the likely effects. In the preceding two chapters, we identified critical deficiencies in both data and research. As we discuss below, available projection models are also deficient in many respects. The question is how to allocate limited resources for developing better capabilities for retirement-income-related policy analysis.

As we stress throughout this report, the U.S. Department of Labor (DOL) and other relevant agencies should give priority to effecting needed improvements in data and analytical research before making significant investments in broad-based projection models. Such investments will be misplaced until there is better understanding of key behaviors—such as employer decisions about hiring and compensation policies and individual decisions about savings and consumption—and better data with which to project trends in those behaviors and other factors. Until efforts to improve data and research bear fruit, we recommend that agencies make limited investments in special-purpose models that use the best available data to answer policy makers' specific questions.

At the same time, agencies should consider the kinds of broad-based projection modeling capabilities that it will be important to develop in the future. In this chapter, we address: types of projection models that could be useful; the dimensions of models that should be considered in planning for improved projection capabilities; the capabilities and limitations of existing models; long-term issues in developing models of employers and employer behavior; long-term issues in developing improved individual-level microsimulation models; issues in developing validation capabilities in new and current models; and strategies for projection modeling in the near term with existing models or one-time special-purpose models (including improvements to the model maintained by the Social Security Office of the Actuary).

## CURRENT MODELS AND THEIR USES

### Types of Models

Projection models vary widely in scope, complexity, and modeling strategy. Some of the major types are time-series models, cell-based models, microsimulation models, macroeconomic models, and computable general equilibrium models. Some models incorporate multiple approaches: for example, in the Macroeconomic-Demographic Model (MDM), a macroeconomic growth model interacts with cell-based models of population growth, family formation, the labor market, and other model components. Other models reflect primarily one approach but make use of the outputs of other kinds of techniques; see Appendix C for descriptions of some models.

*Times-Series Models* Time-series models project aggregate historical data into the future on the basis of a function, which can be simple or complex, of the behavior of the data in previous periods. For example, future labor force participation rates for older men can be projected to continue to decline on the basis of trend data from 1950 to 1995. However, the longer the projection period, the more hazardous it is to assume that past trends will continue unchanged into the future. Indeed, for the example just noted, there is currently debate about whether the trend toward early retirement among men has peaked.

*Cell-Based Models* Cell-based models divide the population into groups, such as 5-year age categories by sex, and develop separate projections for each group—for example, separate projections of life expectancies, retirement age probabilities, and so forth. The separate projections may be based on time-series analysis, modified by assumptions about the likely behavioral effects of policy changes (e.g., the effects on retirement age of reductions in initial Social Security benefits). Because a cell-based model reflects differences among groups, the aggregate outcome it projects may differ greatly from the outcome of a simple time-series projection for the population as a whole.

The Office of the Actuary in the Social Security Administration (SSA) uses cell-based techniques to develop 75-year projections of the balance in the trust funds. Such techniques are also used in actuarial models of employer pension fund balances and in models used by the Census Bureau, SSA, and others to develop population projections.

***Microsimulation Models*** Microsimulation models use individual records for large samples of the population, estimating outcomes for each individual on the basis of that person's characteristics and aggregating the results. Such models usually employ stochastic or probabilistic methods to generate distributions for such outcomes as retirement decisions.

DYNASIM2 and PRISM are two dynamic microsimulation models that have been used to evaluate alternative Social Security and employer pension policies. They use dynamic aging techniques to project their samples forward in time. In dynamic aging, characteristics of persons in the sample are altered year by year through the application of transition probabilities to simulate who in the sample will live, die, marry, divorce, stay on the same job, take another job, retire, and so on. Policy simulations are then performed on the samples for 1 or more years. The transition probabilities may come from a variety of sources, including time-series analysis (e.g., for life expectancy) and behavioral analysis (using simple or complex analytical models). Thus, for example, a behavioral equation in DYNASIM2 relates labor force participation to age, race, sex, education, disability, marital status, presence of children, and spouse's earnings and includes a complex error term by which labor force participation changes for an individual are linked across time and with changes in hours and wages.

Another microsimulation projection technique is called static aging, in which the characteristics of the sample are altered by adjusting the sample weights to reflect the expected distributions in the projection year before conducting policy simulations. This method is typically employed for short-range projections (e.g., of tax liabilities or welfare program participants in the next 5 years) and not for the longer range projections that are often required for retirement-income-related policy modeling.

Microsimulation models can estimate the effects of more detailed policy changes for a larger number of groups than is possible with cell-based models. In addition, Burtless (1996) argues that microsimulation provides an organizing framework. It requires model developers and users to think through all of the behavioral links and interactions. It also helps them identify gaps in research knowledge and data and set priorities for filling in key gaps. However, microsimulation models have costs as well as benefits, which must be evaluated vis-à-vis other modeling approaches in the context of users' information needs. In particular, they tend to be complex and difficult to use.

Both microsimulation and cell-based models can be developed for organizations (e.g., employers) as well as for individuals. However, with the exception of the Pension Insurance Management System (PIMS) model recently developed for the Pension Benefit Guaranty Corporation (PBGC) (see Appendix C), we know of no policy projection models of retirement-income-related behavior of employers.

***Macroeconomic Forecasting Models*** Macroeconomic forecasting models are used to make projections for the U.S. economy. They use systems of simultaneous equations, estimated with historical time series, to forecast the effects of aggregate factors, such as rising inflation or changes in the federal budget deficit, on aggregate outcomes, such as gross national product or unemployment.

***Computable General Equilibrium (CGE) Models*** CGE models estimate the longer run effects of proposed policy changes on prices and quantities in markets, taking into account behavioral responses and feedback effects between supply and demand. For example, an increase in marginal tax rates may decrease work effort, thereby leading to reduced labor supply, thereby leading to higher wage rates and increased labor supply until a new equilibrium is reached. As generally implemented, CGE models are macro rather than micro in nature, in that they are not usually disaggregated on many dimensions. However, unlike macroeconomic forecasting models, CGE models are based on explicit theories of the behavior of households and employers rather than on relationships among aggregates.

### Dimensions of Models

There are three key dimensions on which to evaluate projection models:

* the degree to which the model provides accurate estimates of policy outcomes, in that the estimates approximate what would occur if a proposed policy change were implemented;
* the amount of information provided in the model output on the uncertainty of the model estimates and their sensitivity to key assumptions; and
* the degree to which the model incorporates best current professional judgment about the underlying behavior—for example, the best judgment about the appropriate functional form and parameter values with which to estimate changes in personal savings in response to changes in employer pensions or Social Security.

Obviously, it is highly desirable that models be accurate, provide estimates of uncertainty and sensitivity to key assumptions, and incorporate best professional judgment (or be able to use alternative specifications to reflect important disagreements). But determining the accuracy of model outputs is a difficult task at best. Also, models have to date rarely included the capabilities with which to estimate uncertainty, conduct sensitivity analyses, or incorporate alternative model specifications; consequently, little model validation work has been done. With recent advances in computing technology and statistical methods, it is now possible to effect significant improvements in model capabilities in these areas (see "Validation" below).

Other dimensions of projection models include:

- scope, in terms of the types of policies that a model can simulate and the kinds of outcome measures for which it can provide information;
- detail, in terms of how well a model can represent all of the provisions of current law and estimate the effects of changes to one or more provisions;
- extent of disaggregation of model outputs, that is, the extent to which the model can estimate the distributions of outcomes for groups of interest, variously defined, in addition to average tendencies;
- time period, whether the model can develop projections for 5 years or 75 years;
- extent of feedback loops, which permit estimating not only the first-order effects of a policy change, but also the second-order effects, taking into account behavioral responses to the new policy;
- ability to link to other models, either by supplying outputs for other models to use as inputs or by accepting other models' outputs as inputs;
- amount of elapsed time that is required to obtain outputs from the model on one or more policy options, including options that are close variants of current policies and options that differ markedly in one or more respects;
- extent of openness and transparency, that is, how usable and understandable the model is to people other than the developers;
- ease of use and modification as needed; and
- extent of portability, from one computing hardware and software environment to another.

The first five dimensions listed above—scope, detail, disaggregation, time period of projections, and feedback loops—have to do with the breadth and depth of model capabilities. Other things being equal, it is desirable to have a model that can simulate a broad range of policy options and, for each option or combination of options, estimate a broad range of outcomes. Other things being equal, it is also desirable to have a model that can evaluate proposals for fine tuning one or more aspects of complicated sets of program provisions, that can develop projections over long time horizons, and that can provide distributions of outputs for particular groups of interest in addition to population means. As an example, in considering a policy change that increases—or decreases—employer pension benefits, decision makers are likely to be interested in the effects not only for all workers, but also for workers in different industries, age groups, and earnings categories and by size-of-employer categories. Finally, a projection model is more useful to the extent that it can estimate the second-round effects of policy changes, which, because of behavioral responses, are likely to differ from the initially estimated effects. For example, changes designed to increase employer pension coverage, if they also increase employer costs, could lead employers to opt out of pension plans and hence reduce coverage over time.

Desirable though these dimensions are, there are costs to increasing the breadth and depth of model capabilities. For example, models that simulate a wide range of policy outcomes and options are likely to be time and resource intensive to develop and apply. Also, modeling of feedback effects is quite difficult, both operationally and because of the uncertainty of behavioral responses to policy changes. Hence, it may be cost-effective to have different models for answering questions about particular types of policy changes, as well as different models for estimating means versus distributions, effects over shorter versus longer periods, and second-order as distinct from first-order effects. Indeed, the various types of modeling strategies listed earlier, such as cell-based and microsimulation approaches, reflect choices about how much and what kinds of detail to include in models. With a range of models, it becomes critical to consider ways to facilitate links between them (the sixth dimension listed).

The last four dimensions listed—response time, openness and transparency, ease of use, and portability—have to do with operational features that determine how readily a model can be applied during the course of a policy debate, modified as needed to incorporate additional capabilities, and validated and improved. These dimensions, which cut across model types, also have to do with how large a user community develops for a model, which, in turn, is a major factor in how widely a model is used and how rigorously it is evaluated.

Features of models that facilitate a higher level of performance on these dimensions include adequate documentation, public availability of the model to analysts, a user-friendly interface that allows people who are not programmers to operate the model, and other design elements that permit ready modification of the model to simulate newly proposed policy options in a consistent manner and to facilitate multiple runs and specifications for model validation purposes. Many of these features (e.g., real-time response mode or a graphical, point-and-click user-friendly interface) appear more obtainable when a model is designed for microcomputer or workstation computing environments than when it is designed for mainframe or supercomputing environments.

It clearly seems important for models to provide timely response and to be open, easy to use, and portable, whatever their type or breadth and depth of capabilities. However, the costs of achieving high levels of performance on these dimensions must also be considered. As an example, it is typically time and labor intensive to produce good documentation, although, with forethought, it is possible to build features into models to facilitate the documentation process. Also, the nature of an agency's information requirements may dictate trade-offs between, say, the ease of use of a model and its capabilities. For example, a particular set of applications may require computing power that is not available from microcomputers or workstations (e.g., CGE models may require super-computers to attain the level of desired detail of inputs and outputs). In this case, the only modeling option is to invest in a model that has limited access. An alternative is to implement a simpler version of the model on a microcomputer and a more elaborate version—or a version that will process larger numbers of sample cases—on a supercomputer.

## Assessment

There are many projection models available today that relate in some way to retirement income security. Some of these models were developed for very narrowly targeted applications, such as actuarial cell-based models that are de-signed to project the balance of assets and liabilities for a specific company's pension plan. Although these kinds of models serve important purposes, we have not reviewed them because of their lack of generality. Also, our review does not extend to health care financing projection models, although such models are very important to a full assessment of retirement income security, nor to tax revenue models, such as that used by the U.S. Treasury Department.[1] Rather, we have looked primarily at models that can address somewhat broader retirement-in-come-related policy questions, for example, the effects of tax policy changes on accumulations in Individual Retirement Accounts (IRAs) and pension accounts over people's working lives.

Our overall conclusions about existing models are mixed. Some models appear to have useful features for some kinds of applications but, on balance, we conclude that existing models are not adequate to fully inform the retirement income policy debate.

For some important topics, there are currently no available relevant models. Specifically, there are no models of employer behavior with regard to benefit offerings or demand for older workers that could provide input for individual-based models of labor supply and retirement asset accumulation. Rather, existing employer-based models address such issues as pension funding effects on share prices and employer pension policy within a corporate financial setting. The new PIMS microsimulation employer-based model has been developed for the PBGC, but it has a limited focus. PIMS estimates corporate bankruptcies among em-ployers with defined benefit pension plans on the basis of simulating key eco-nomic variables and employer characteristics. It also simulates plan participants and funding status. Finally, it simulates the implications of projected bankrupt-

---

[1]See Office of Technology Assessment (1994) for an evaluation of models that were used in the recent health care reform policy debate.

cies of companies with underfunded plans for the PBGC fund that insures such plans.

For individuals, there are microsimulation models that are broad in scope and provide the capability for detailed, disaggregated analysis. They could be very useful for retirement-income-related policy analysis, but they generally suffer from several deficiencies: they have not been adequately validated and are not designed to facilitate validation; they are based on old or limited data sets; they do not reflect best current professional judgment about underlying behavior; they have little facility for implementing alternative behavioral specifications when there are important disagreements; their provision for feedback loops between policy changes and behavioral responses is weak; they generally have little provision for ready exchange of inputs and outputs with other models; they are not well documented; and they are not open and transparent or readily portable, although they now are generally implemented with personal computing technology.

CGE models that have been developed to answer such questions as the intergenerational benefits and costs of alternative Social Security financing systems are impressive in their treatment of the interactions of the household, government, and private sectors of the economy and in their use of up-to-date information and research knowledge. However, these models deal primarily with "big picture" issues in a highly stylized manner and primarily for the Social Security system, not the much more heterogeneous world of employer pensions. Also, to date, these models have not addressed the limitations of the life-cycle model of savings and consumption (see Chapter 3), and they are usually structured as equilibrium models without unemployment, particularly long-term unemployment, among older workers. These models do not provide distributional detail, nor can they address the effects of very specific policy changes or combinations of changes. Finally, there are as yet no links between these models and cell-based or microsimulation projection models that would provide additional specificity.

A positive trend is that newer models generally follow design principles that encourage use and validation. For example, PIMS, the employer-based model, operates on personal computers and has a design that facilitates model validation. However, newer models, such as PIMS, SSASIM, the Solvency and Individual Retirement model (SIR), and the model under development by Wolf et al. (1995), tend to be limited in scope. SSASIM is a cell-based model similar in structure to the SSA actuarial cost model that uses Monte Carlo methods to characterize uncertainty about forecasts of Social Security trust fund balances. SIR is a cell-based model similar to the SSA actuarial cost model that provides limited distributional information for different types of workers. Wolf is developing a microsimulation model primarily for simulating kinship networks and disability status of the elderly.

Because individual-level microsimulation models potentially offer very important capabilities for retirement-income-related policy analysis, we review aspects of two of the existing dynamic models—DYNASIM2 and PRISM—in Appendix D. The discussion focuses on some weaknesses of these models, not to single them out for criticism, but to support our case for important areas of future development for this type of model.[2]

## LOOKING TO THE FUTURE

We recommend priority attention to data collection and research and analytical modeling over the next few years rather than to significant investments in broad-based projection models. However, we believe it is important to establish goals for projection model development and, in some instances, to move forward on design work, so that implementation can progress expeditiously once invest-ments in data and research bear fruit. Specifically, the federal government should establish goals for the development of employer models (using cell-based or microsimulation techniques) and for a new general-purpose individual-level microsimulation model. Other retirement income modeling tools are needed as well, but it is clearly important to have the projection capabilities that employer models and a new individual-level microsimulation model can provide.

### Employer Models

Employer hiring and compensation policies are critical to retirement income security, most obviously affecting the extent of pension coverage and benefits, but also affecting Social Security benefit levels and the opportunities to contrib-ute to such earnings-linked savings vehicles as IRAs. Employers also often provide other important benefits, such as retiree health care and disability insur-ance, as well as opportunities for part-time, post-retirement work. A full assess-ment of the likely effects of many retirement-income-related policy proposals will not be possible without considering what is happening to and with employ-ers. Shifts in employment across sectors that have historically differed in wage and benefit levels can affect retirement income security, as can employer re-sponses to changes in policies and other factors that alter incentives (e.g., pension simplification may increase the probability that small businesses will set up pension plans).

Employer-based projection models are clearly needed for much retirement income policy analysis. In some instances, decision makers will want informa-

---

[2]For other assessments of microsimulation models, see Citro and Hanushek (1991); the papers cited in Cohen (1991a); Employee Benefit Research Institute (1980a, 1980b, 1981); Reno (1993:29-31); Ross (1991); and U.S. General Accounting Office (1986). Burtless (1989) and Grossman and Watts (1982) focus on behavioral elements of microsimulation models. Anderson (1996) and Hollenbeck (1995) review microsimulation and other projection models that are relevant for retire-ment income policy modeling.

tion about how many employers will take a certain action within a specified time period (e.g., set up a pension plan) and how many workers will be affected. Such information could most likely come directly from an employer model that includes such characteristics as industry and size. In other instances, decision makers will want to know the longer term implications for retirement income flows (e.g., from pension accumulations) for different groups of workers; for this information it will most likely be necessary to produce outputs from employer models that can feed into individual-level models for workers and their families.

At present, there are no models that can project the distribution of employer pension and related benefit offerings or the distribution of employer demand for workers. Moreover, there is little basis on which to develop such models in the near term: the needed data and research knowledge are simply lacking (see Chapters 3 and 4). Resources spent on model development cannot be cost-effective until more complete data are available (e.g., about the distribution of employer benefits) and until there is much better understanding of the factors that influence hiring and compensation decisions for different kinds of employers. Gaining such understanding will require considerable elaboration and testing of alternative theories about employer behavior. The development of employer-based projection models is an important goal for the Department of Labor and other agencies, but one that can only be realized over the long term.

It is important to keep this long-term model development goal in mind as decisions are made about investments in employer-related data and research. In this regard, it could be useful to consider alternative projection model designs and strategies and their requirements. One question is whether to start with a cell-based design that classifies employers on a limited number of important dimensions or to opt for a microsimulation model. A cell-based model would be easier to implement and have fewer data requirements than a microsimulation model, but it would have more limited capability for analysis and for simulation of behavioral response.

It could also be useful to bring together researchers and people with experience in developing projection models to consider possible model designs on the basis of anticipating what research results may show. For example, what would be the design and data requirements for a projection model if employer costs are taken to be the key factor in hiring and compensation policies? What would be the requirements if employee preferences are also deemed to be an important factor?

As new data about employers become available and are analyzed, DOL could sponsor workshops to discuss research findings and their implications for the development of employer-based projection models. Clearly, to make progress toward the goal of model development, it will be important for DOL to give priority to the work of the interagency task force on employer data (see Recommendations 5-9, Chapter 4) and to putting an employer data collection plan on as fast a track as possible.

## Recommendation

**14. The U.S. Department of Labor should consider the development of employer models as an important long-term goal.** Retirement-income-related policy analysis requires models of employer behavior that can project the likely future distribution of benefit plan offerings and the demand for older workers. However, there is little basis on which to design, let alone implement, such models until investments have been made in needed data and behavioral research.

### Microsimulation Models of Individuals and Families

Policy makers often want to know the effects of proposed policy changes on population groups, categorized by age, sex, race or ethnicity, income level, and the like. Cell-based models can provide distributional detail, but the cells must be defined in advance and are difficult to change in response to user needs. In principle, large-scale microsimulation is a much more flexible tool with which to provide detailed information about distributional effects, limited only by sample size constraints on the reliability of small cell estimates. Broad-based microsimulation can also address important interactions among policies, such as how a change in Social Security benefits will likely affect benefits from employer pension plans that are linked to Social Security. Dynamic microsimulation can in principle forecast the long-term effects of policy changes, including behavioral responses: for example, how a change in Social Security benefits will likely change retirement and savings behavior and, ultimately, affect retirement income levels for different cohorts of workers.

We believe that a general-purpose, dynamic microsimulation model is needed to project the distributional effects of policy alternatives on the retirement income security of individuals and families over the medium term and for modeling interactions among policies. Other, more limited modeling tools are often appropriate and cost-effective for specific policy questions. However, as Burtless (1996) argues, it is important to have the capability to address all three legs of the retirement income stool—Social Security, employer pensions, and personal savings—in an integrated modeling framework that can provide needed distributional detail.

Such a modeling framework is also useful because it can help structure related analytical work. The effort to develop and apply a large-scale microsimulation model will invariably identify behavioral interactions and processes that need to be better understood. It will also help determine which parameters are crucial for analysis and which are less important, and it can suggest how concepts and variables should be consistently defined and measured to be useful for modeling purposes.

Unlike the situation for employer models, there are existing individual-level microsimulation models—notably DYNASIM2 and PRISM—that have proven useful for analysis of previous pension and Social Security reform proposals (see Appendices C and D). However, these models use obsolete databases—March Current Population Survey (CPS) files from the 1970s that were exactly matched with Social Security earnings records—and obsolete behavioral parameters, such as retirement probabilities estimated with data from the old Retirement History Survey (RHS). More important, because they were originally implemented with costly and cumbersome mainframe computer technology, these models are not well structured to simulate the effects of policy changes on key behaviors, such as labor force participation. They are also not well developed in other respects (e.g., they do not handle personal savings in any detail).[3]

Rich new data sets, notably the Health and Retirement Survey and the Asset and Health Dynamics Among the Oldest Old survey (HRS/AHEAD), are beginning to provide data with which to reestimate behavioral parameters and address such critical issues as the differences in savings rates across and within cohorts. These new data and associated research can provide the basis for a new individual-level microsimulation model that can address a wide range of retirement-income-related policy issues. Relevant agencies should consider the development of such a model as an important long-term goal.

We believe that it will prove more cost-effective in the long run to develop a new simulation model than to try to update existing models. It is not simply a question of updating existing models with new data and parameter values, but instead of significantly modifying and augmenting their capabilities in a number of ways. Starting fresh is likely to be a more fruitful strategy. However, elements of existing models could contribute to a new model. Specifically, the demographic components (births, deaths, marriages, etc.) of existing models are generally well developed and could form the basis of the demographic components of a new model with updated parameters. Also, the program accounting components of existing models—for example, the calculation of Social Security benefits given an earnings history and the determination of eligibility for Supplemental Security Income (SSI)—are generally well specified and could likely be imported into a new model.

We caution that it would be premature to begin now to construct a new individual-level microsimulation model. The priority need is for investments in data and research, and it would be difficult to invest in a large, complex model at the same time. Moreover, the results of new data collection and research may

---

[3]Another individual-level microsimulation model is CORSIM, which began as an adaptation of DYNASIM2 and has since been redesigned. Operating on both personal computers and super-computers, it provides detailed simulations of demographic histories. However, it has limited capability for simulation of Social Security or employer pension policies, and its asset accumulation modules lack behavioral components (see Appendix C).

suggest a different design from the design that would be adopted for a model on the basis of current knowledge.

Another reason for delaying construction of a new microsimulation model, while data and behavioral modeling issues are addressed, is that it will then likely be possible to build a new class of projection models that are significantly improved over simple extensions of existing models. This possibility exists because of advances in microcomputing technology (including personal computers and even more powerful workstations) that are providing much greater power at cheaper cost than in the past and that are bringing computing applications closer to the end user. These advances, in turn, have spurred the development of new methodologies that promise to improve important model functions that have often been neglected in the past, in particular: validation of model outputs (which includes sensitivity analysis and estimation of uncertainty); documentation of model components, parameters, and data; provision for multiple outputs, including outputs that alert the user to aspects of the model that are more or less robust; and other features that make a model more open and transparent, easy to use, and accessible to a wide range of users. Examples of relevant new methodologies include powerful computer-based statistical techniques for estimating the uncertainty in model outputs; graphical user interfaces that make it possible for analysts to experiment more readily with policy options and alternative model specifications (e.g., varying estimates of parameter values); and hypertext language that can support the development of user-friendly, computer-searchable documentation, which makes a model more accessible to users.

These and other innovative approaches to important model functions are still evolving. Instead of trying to work out a model structure and design on the basis of today's technology and methods, which would lock in the use of technologies that may soon be superseded, it seems worthwhile to await further developments. When new data and research results become available with which to build new models, then choices can be made about how best to take advantage of the latest technological developments for improved model functionality and design.[4]

Of course, there will always be new knowledge and methods that make any current state of the art of projection modeling obsolete in one or more respects. We are not thereby arguing that new microsimulation model development should be deferred indefinitely. To the contrary, improved models are needed and should be developed. However, we do argue that, at the present time, the deficiencies in needed data and research are so great that resources must be concentrated first and foremost on filling data and knowledge gaps before investing in model development.

---

[4]Citro and Hanushek (1991:Chap. 6) discuss principles of microsimulation model design and development; Cotton and Sadowsky (1991), Cohen (1991c), and Hollenbeck (1991) discuss, respectively, relevant advances in computing technology, use of new techniques for estimation of uncertainty, and requirements for model documentation.

## Model Requirements

We stress that construction of a new microsimulation model would be premature; however, consideration of the requirements for such a model could help structure relevant data collection and research. We assume that a new individual-level microsimulation model would be dynamic: that is, it would use dynamic aging techniques to project a broad range of behaviors and processes (see "Types of Models", above). Important characteristics for a new dynamic model include the capability to develop detailed projections in key areas, to simulate a wide range of relevant policies and behavioral interactions, to estimate the effects of health care coverage and costs on the distribution of retirement income, and to interact with employer-based models and with models that simulate longer run effects.

***Detailed Projection Capabilities*** A new individual-level microsimulation model requires detailed demographic, labor supply and retirement, pension coverage and benefits, and savings projection capabilities as integral components.

Existing dynamic microsimulation models have well-developed demographic modules that could likely be adapted for a new model. For example, the mortality module in DYNASIM2 is richly specified: the mortality equation includes marital status and education as determinant variables as well as age, race, and sex. It would be relatively straightforward to evaluate and modify, if necessary, the specific parameter values in existing demographic modules to reflect current best professional judgment.

In contrast, the labor supply and retirement modules in existing models require major revamping for use in a new model. For example, the equations in DYNASIM2 that determine labor force participation, hours, and wages were derived from 1970s data in the Panel Study of Income Dynamics (PSID) and lack policy parameters. The equations for the retirement decision were estimated from the RHS completed in 1979; they include expected Social Security and pension benefits but not other personal savings, and they assume that disability status is exogenous. The hours of work equations in PRISM were estimated from matched CPS files that are now many years out of date; they primarily take the form of simple year-to-year transitions among hours categories. This type of equation is easy to implement, but, over time, its use will negate the very purpose of microsimulation, which is to preserve distributional detail. Such a formulation captures limited information about previous work patterns, so that it will not properly project the work choices of individuals at the extremes of the distribution, such as people who rarely or always worked. Neither DYNASIM2 nor PRISM has a capability for labor supply and retirement decisions to interact with labor demand.

The choice of an appropriate functional form and parameter values for equations to include in new labor supply and retirement modules should look to the results of labor supply research with HRS/AHEAD. Such research will undoubtedly include further development of analytic dynamic programming models (see Chapter 3), which might serve as the labor supply and retirement decision component of a new microsimulation projection model. Because dynamic programming models require reestimating labor supply decisions at each time period in light of all available information (e.g., recalculated expected Social Security benefits), they are currently likely to be computationally intractable for projection modeling purposes. However, if they became more tractable and could be extended in some important ways (e.g., to take account of pension benefits), they could well support a major advance in labor supply and retirement projection capabilities.

The pension coverage and benefits components of existing models are also far from satisfactory for a new model. PRISM simulates more features of pension plans and captures more distributional variation than DYNASIM2, by drawing on a sample of Summary Plan Descriptions filed with Form 5500s. However, this sample has not been updated since 1983, and neither PRISM nor DYNASIM2 reflects the important changes that have occurred in the distribution of types of pension plans since then.

Ideally, given the frequency of changes in pension and other benefit offerings, the pension component of an individual-level microsimulation model would obtain inputs from an employer-based model of benefit distributions. Since it may take longer to develop sophisticated new employer-based projection models than new individual-level models, the pension component of a new individual-level model would necessarily be somewhat undeveloped, without full capability for dynamic projections. However, some improvements could be effected (both in a new model and in existing models). For example, data could be pieced together from HRS/AHEAD and other surveys to obtain an up-to-date baseline distribution of pension plan types for different age cohorts and other characteristics of workers. Also, a crude capability could be implemented to update the distribution of employer types by size and industry, on the basis of aggregate trends, to use to project job characteristics and pension plan features historically associated with different employers. In addition, a crude capability could be developed to project shifts in pension plan types within and among employer classes and to use the estimated distributions to assign pension coverage to workers.

Finally, the personal savings components of existing microsimulation models are very undeveloped. DYNASIM2 and PRISM project IRA contributions but not other kinds of personal savings.[5] Research with HRS/AHEAD and other sources will be required to provide clearer answers about the appropriate analyti-

---

[5]The long-term care submodel of PRISM assigns asset portfolios to people when they reach age 65, and then in each year of the projection it makes a simple adjustment of housing asset values by an assumed inflation rate and of nonhousing asset values by an assumed constant rate of dissaving.

cal model of savings and consumption that can form the basis of a sophisticated projection module for personal savings.

*Policy Simulations and Behavioral Interactions*  A new individual-level microsimulation model should be able to simulate a wide range of policies that relate to the major sources of retirement income: Social Security, employer pensions, IRAs and other forms of personal savings, SSI and other relevant transfer programs, and post-retirement earnings. Moreover, a new model should be able to simulate behavioral responses that can alter the initial or first-round effects of policy changes. Although it is probably not feasible to simulate the equilibrium effects of a policy change, it should be possible to simulate second-round effects that are consequent on important behavioral responses to a proposed policy.

Existing dynamic models, in order to reduce computational burdens, have adopted a strategy in which demographic and employment life histories are dynamically generated and only then used as the basis for retirement-income-related policy simulations. (Alternatively, demographic and labor force transition equations do not include such policy variables as expected Social Security or pension benefits.) This strategy greatly constrains the capability to simulate behavioral responses to policy changes or other factors not included at the stage of generating the life histories (see Burtless, 1989, on this point). We believe that a new model needs to be more dynamic in this respect: that is, it should include the capability for policies to interact with demographic and employment behavior (e.g., simulating the effect on labor force participation of younger workers of significant changes in Social Security or employer pension provisions). Similarly, a new model should have a capability for policies to interact with savings and consumption behavior.

*Health Care Coverage and Costs*  Health care expenditures not covered by insurance (including premiums) are a potential major drain on retirement income, but simulating the effects of health care policy initiatives on medical care needs and expenditures is a daunting task. It would simply be infeasible to try to incorporate a health care policy simulation model into a new individual-level retirement income model. However, a new retirement model could usefully include a component—perhaps off-line from the main model—that estimates the portion of retirement income that remains after expected health care expenditures for different groups of the elderly population. This component would distribute out-of-pocket medical care expenditures among the elderly to agree with out-of-model projections of overall health care costs and the extent of insurance coverage under different health care policy proposals.

*Interactions with Other Models*  A new individual-level microsimulation model should be able to exchange inputs and outputs with other types of models.

Specifically, a new model should accept distributions of jobs and benefit offerings from employer-based models of labor demand and compensation policies to use in simulating the labor supply and pension benefits of workers. In this way, the time path of labor force participation, pension accumulation, and other personal saving can reflect changed behavior by employers.

An individual-level model cannot make use of inputs of jobs and benefit offerings from employer-based models until such models are available, but the design of the individual-level model should facilitate easy future implementation of links with employer models. Whether the design should allow for repeated iterations between worker and employer behavior is a difficult question. Feedback loops between labor supply and demand, and the consequent effects for pension benefits and other savings, are desirable analytically. However, there may be problems of implementation and difficulty in interpreting results.

A new individual-level model should also have a capability to interact with longer run effects models, such as macroeconomic models and CGE models. Burtless (1996) outlines a relatively straightforward macroeconomic model that could accept outputs from a dynamic microsimulation model to use to estimate the effects on gross output and national savings of policy changes that affect Social Security taxes and benefits, employer pensions, and other personal savings. He notes that current projections of the Social Security and Medicare trust fund (from cell-based models) ignore the likelihood that trust fund shortfalls may adversely affect national saving and investment due to the crowding-out effect of increasing the federal budget deficit. In turn, such effects on saving could depress real wage growth and thereby tax collections for Social Security and Medicare, as well as pension accumulations and other savings.

Burtless (1996) also notes the importance for long-term retirement income security projections of allowing important variables—such as inflation; unemployment; market rates of return on housing, stocks, and other assets; and birth and death rates—to exhibit cyclical variation. Existing dynamic microsimulation models usually calibrate their year-to-year simulations to match aggregate projections of births and deaths, employment and unemployment, wage growth, interest rates, and inflation. Most often, they use aggregate values from the intermediate trust fund projections of the SSA Office of the Actuary. However, the latter projections assume that critical economic and demographic variables eventually attain stable values, making no allowance for sudden and unexpected swings (e.g., the intermediate projections assume no economic recessions over a 75-year period).

While an assumption of convergence to stable values may be acceptable for aggregate projections, it is much less so for projections in which distributional outcomes within and across cohorts of workers and retirees are of interest. Hence, a new individual-level microsimulation model should have a capability to incorporate cyclical (or random) variations in key aggregates.

Such a capability is particularly important in light of policy interest in placing more responsibility for retirement and health care planning on individuals. Policy changes in this mode include proposals to increase incentives for defined contribution employer pension plans and other personal savings, to allow tax-advantaged medical savings accounts, and to privatize all or part of Social Security collections. Such policies increase the potential for unexpected gains and losses in retirement income security for particular age cohorts and other groups due to such factors as variation in price inflation, ups and downs in the economy, and stock market booms and busts.

## Database To Be Used

The choice of a primary database on which simulations are performed is critical to the development of a new individual-level microsimulation model with a full range of capabilities. Existing dynamic models use such databases as a 1973 exact-match of the March CPS and SSA earnings histories (DYNASIM2); a 1978 exact-match of the March CPS and SSA earnings histories, which in turn is exactly matched to the March 1979 CPS and the May 1979 CPS pension supplement (PRISM); and decennial census public-use microdata sample files (CORSIM). A model under development by Wolf and his colleagues (Wolf et al., 1995), which focuses on kinship networks and disability status rather than retirement income security per se, uses the 1987-1988 National Survey of Families and Households as its primary database (see Appendix C). Existing models also draw on a variety of other data for such inputs as transition probabilities (to age or project the database records forward in time) and control totals (to calibrate the projections on key aggregates).

The choice of an exact-match March CPS-SSA file as the database for DYNASIM2 and PRISM was to obtain employment and income information for a large population sample linked with earnings histories to use in calculating Social Security and employer pension benefits. However, the lack of a more recent public-use exact-match file is clearly a problem for these models, which must simulate about 20 years of historical data before they can begin projecting into the future. Aggregate information, such as employment and wage rates, can be used to keep the simulations in line with actual historical experience for a handful of key variables, but there is no way to ensure that the models accurately reflect the interrelationships among all of the important variables for that 20-year period.

Even if a new public-use exact-match March CPS-SSA file is developed, however, we question the desirability of continuing to use such a file as the primary database for a new retirement-income-related dynamic microsimulation model. The advantages of the March CPS as a modeling database are that it is a very large sample of the entire population (60,000 households, recently cut back to 50,000), which permits long-term projections, and that it has extensive information on family characteristics, employment, and income. At the same time, it has several disadvantages in terms of data content and quality. It has no information on consumption or on asset holdings (except for a home and what can be inferred from reports of interest and other asset income), limited information on disability status and health insurance coverage, very little information on sample members' employers, and no information on such variables as retirement plans and expectations that research may determine are important to include in labor supply and savings equations. Information on pension coverage is collected in a different supplement that is fielded every 5 years and for which the sample only partially overlaps with the March sample. In addition, there are problems with the quality of the income information, including high nonresponse rates and significant underreporting of income amounts for sources other than earnings.

As we argue with regard to such model functions as validation and documentation, it makes sense to wait to consider the choice of a primary database until new data and research results can support the development of a new generation of models. Some of the possible alternatives that are now on the horizon and may then be worth investigating include the PSID, the Survey of Income and Program Participation (SIPP), and extracts of HRS/AHEAD and other panel surveys.

*Panel Study of Income Dynamics*  The PSID has a rich set of variables and covers the entire age range of the population. However, it has a limited sample size (9,000 households), and it would need to be matched with Social Security earnings records.

*Survey of Income and Program Participation*  Beginning in 1996, SIPP will have an expanded sample size of about 37,000 households; a new panel will be introduced every 4 years. SIPP obtains extensive information on a 4-month, annual, or biannual basis for income and assets, health and disability status, use of health care and health insurance coverage, pension plan coverage and retirement expectations, and family and work histories. Also, evidence indicates that SIPP obtains more complete reporting for most income sources than the March CPS (see, e.g., Coder and Scoon-Rogers, 1994). In the past, nonresponse rates to questions on asset values have been high in SIPP, but, beginning in 1996, SIPP will use the HRS/AHEAD bracketing technique for assets and interest income, which should increase response. SIPP has limited information on sample members' employers; a supplement is being tested that will ask employers to provide information about the employee's pension and health insurance plans and other fringe benefits, but funds have not been provided for the supplement.

Further improvements would need to be made to the SIPP questionnaire to make it suitable for use as a database for a new individual-level dynamic microsimulation model. For example, assuming that the HRS/AHEAD questions on subjective probabilities (e.g., of one's own life expectancy) prove to have analytical power, similar questions would need to be added to SIPP. The modular design of SIPP, with a core income and employment module and a series of rotating topical modules, lends itself to such additions. In contrast, it is very difficult to add questions to the March CPS income supplement because of the overriding need to keep the supplement from impairing response to the main labor force survey (which is the source of the official monthly unemployment statistics).

In practice, however, SIPP has not proven to be as flexible to modify as its design suggests. A major constraint on questionnaire changes and experimentation has been the concern of the Census Bureau to standardize data collection and processing procedures for a large survey. This situation could change in the future as agencies seek to use SIPP for more kinds of policy analysis: for example, DOL is considering a transfer of funds from the CPS to SIPP for an improved supplement on pension coverage, and the SIPP questionnaire is being altered to make it more suitable for poverty measurement.

Finally, SIPP would need to be matched with Social Security earnings records. SSA is currently using exact matches of the 1984 and 1990 SIPP panels with SSA data for limited kinds of retirement income modeling (see "Near-Term Modeling Strategies," below); however, these files are not available to researchers outside SSA. Plans are under way to append year of death and type of Social Security benefit from SSA records to SIPP files for public release, but there are no plans as yet to make available SIPP files with linked SSA earnings data.

***Extract of HRS/AHEAD and Other Panel Surveys*** Data from HRS/ AHEAD and other panel surveys (for age groups that HRS/AHEAD does not cover), linked with SSA earnings variables, could be used for microsimulation modeling. The major advantage of HRS/AHEAD as a primary database is that it will be used for much of the analytical modeling that will presumably underlie the behavioral components of a new projection model. Researchers will mine the rich data in HRS/AHEAD, including previously unavailable information (e.g., expectations, detailed descriptions of pension plans), to develop improved analytical models of retirement-income-related behavior. Ideally, a projection model should have available the same rich data for performing simulations as were used analytically. The projection model should not have to fall back on behavioral parameters that, of necessity (due to the limitations of the primary database), have been reestimated with fewer input variables than were incorporated in state-of-the-art research.

The principal drawback to the use of HRS/AHEAD for simulation purposes is that it does not contain information for people younger than age 51 (except for some spouses of sample members). Because people may retire as young as ages 55-60, this limitation restricts the time horizon of projections to 5-10 years (although time horizons can be longer for projections that pertain to older people, say, those aged 65 and older or 70 and older). A possible solution to this problem is to merge other data sets with HRS/AHEAD. The new and filler HRS/AHEAD cohorts will be introduced in 1998-1999, and first-wave data should be available for them by 1999-2000. By merging data from these cohorts with data from the original HRS/AHEAD cohorts, the National Longitudinal Survey of Youth (NLSY), and NLS-Young Women, it would be possible to obtain a sizable database for women aged 33-40 and 44 and older and for men aged 33-40 and 51 and older in 1998 (see Figure 4-1 in Chapter 4). Assuming that the missing years could be filled in by some procedure (which would be relatively easy for women and more difficult for men, given a larger missing age range), the resulting database would permit projections of retirement behavior for 20 years or more into the future. (A 20-year projection could estimate retirement status and income security for people aged 53 and older in 2018; a 30-year projection could provide the same estimates for people aged 63 and older in 2028.) If HRS/ AHEAD is to be merged with other panel surveys for projection modeling purposes, it will be critically important to review the survey questionnaires to identify ways to make them as compatible as possible.

**Design Considerations**

Each of the requirements and features discussed above stretches the capabilities of existing dynamic microsimulation models. Considerable thought will be needed to determine potentially useful approaches for implementation: for example, how best to capture the inherent heterogeneity of employer and worker behavior in linkages between individual and employer-based models. While agencies should remain focused on data collection and basic research in the near term and not work on the development of new large-scale projection models, some continuing discussions about design could help pave the way for the development of the next generation of models. Such discussions could help rationalize individual data collection and analytical modeling efforts by indicating priorities for projection modeling and raising issues that relate to the feasibility of implementing data and research results in new projection models.

Discussions about model design issues should involve multiple agencies, including DOL and SSA, and people from both the academic and projection modeling communities. Analysts and modelers have had little communication in the past, and links must be forged. A useful, low-cost activity could be to involve microsimulation modelers in the workshops on early results that are being held to present findings from HRS/AHEAD. They could be asked to comment on research papers from the perspective of the feasibility of using analytical models and research results in a microsimulation context. Microsimulation modelers could also contribute to discussions among agency staff and the principal investigators of the major individual-level panel surveys on changes and improvements in their content and design.

## Recommendation

Large-scale, general-purpose microsimulation in principle is a useful technique for projecting the distributional effects of policy alternatives on the retirement income security of individuals and families and for modeling interactions among policies (e.g., between Social Security or Medicare and employer benefits). However, needed data and estimates of key behavioral parameters are lacking for a useful model, and existing models do not provide an adequate structure on which to build an improved model.

**15. The relevant federal agencies should consider the development of a new integrated, individual-level microsimulation model for retirement-income-related policy analysis as an important long-term goal, but construction of such a model would be premature until advances are made in data, research knowledge, and computational methods. Some continuing design discussions could help structure relevant data collection and research. Some elements of existing projection models might contribute to a new model.**

## VALIDATION

Validation is important for the data sources that are used for retirement-income-related analytical and projection modeling and for the models themselves. This section discusses validation issues for projection models. In view of the long time periods for which projections are often required and the range and complexity of policies and behaviors that are typically simulated, it is critically important to devote a significant portion of available projection modeling resources to validation activities.

### Validation Goals and Methods

As we indicate above, projection models—of whatever type and range of capabilities—should: (1) provide accurate estimates of policy outcomes; (2) provide as outputs information on the uncertainty of model estimates and their sensitivity to key assumptions; and (3) incorporate best current professional judgment about the underlying behaviors. These are very stringent criteria. Indeed, for the first criterion, one might ask how one can know whether a model's estimates are accurate when the policy change has not yet happened and may never happen (see Citro and Hanushek, 1991:72-78; Chap. 9).

Clearly, one cannot know at the time a model is estimating the effects of a proposed policy change that the estimates are, in fact, accurate. However, one can conduct a series of ex post external validation studies to establish a degree of confidence in a model's track record. Sometimes it is possible to compare a model's estimates with what actually occurred. More commonly, it is necessary to conduct "ex post forecasting" studies, in which one puts oneself in the place of an analyst who, say, 10 or 20 years ago, was asked to simulate a policy change to take effect in some future year. One chooses the "future" year to be in the recent past so that measures of what happened are available from administrative records or other sources. Correspondingly, one chooses the policy change to be the actual policy in effect during the comparison year. (An alternative approach is to use a current model to develop "backcasted" estimates of policies for earlier years.)

Because differences between a model's estimates and what actually occurred may be due to economic or social changes that the model could not have been expected to forecast (e.g., an unanticipated recession or an unexpected increase or decrease in fertility rates), it will be helpful to conduct ex post forecasting (or backcasting) studies that use actual values for the factors that could not have been anticipated and focus on the accuracy of the model with regard to other elements. Also, in many instances, the important criterion will be whether the model accurately projected the *differences* in the outcomes under two or more policy alternatives and not the more stringent criterion of whether it accurately projected the *levels* of outcomes for a specific alternative.

In addition to studies that help establish confidence in a model's track record, it is important to develop estimates of the range of uncertainty of a model's estimates. On average, a model may produce unbiased estimates, but the results of any particular model run may have a wide band of uncertainty around them. The sources of error in model simulations can be summarized in four broad categories: (1) sampling variability in the input database, which is only one of a family of possible data sets that could have been obtained; (2) sampling variability in other inputs, such as imputations, regression coefficients, and control totals; (3) errors in the database and other inputs; and (4) errors due to model misspecification.

Advances in statistical methodology that take advantage of modern computing power have made it possible to estimate the uncertainty in model estimates due to such sources as sampling variations in the input data. One such technique is the bootstrap (see Cohen, 1991c), which, simply put, measures variability by using the observed sample distribution in place of the unobserved population distribution. The strength of this approach is that variance estimation becomes a function of computing power rather than an exercise in solving multidimensional integrations for complex estimators and distributions.

For complex models, like dynamic microsimulation models, sample reuse techniques can be used to measure the uncertainty in a model's estimates due to the two kinds of sampling variability. However, the uncertainty due to the two kinds of errors may be difficult to put into a probabilistic context. Sensitivity analysis, which is carried out by developing and running one or more alternative versions of one or more model components, can help assess the uncertainty in model estimates due to the choice of a particular model structure or specification.

For example, one could use sensitivity analysis to investigate the effects of a particular equation for simulating the labor supply response to a change in the retirement age for Social Security or employer pensions. In its simplest terms, sensitivity analysis is a diagnostic tool for ascertaining which parts of an overall model could have the largest impact on results and therefore are the most important to scrutinize for potential errors that could be reduced or eliminated (see Citro and Hanushek, 1991:89-96; Chap. 9). Sensitivity analysis is particularly important for retirement income modeling in view of the long time horizon for most projections, which will compound any errors in model specification or assumptions.

For various reasons, external validation studies, estimation of uncertainty, and sensitivity analysis have rarely been carried out for projection models.[6] Historically, one reason was that such studies were very costly and time-consuming. However, if models are implemented in computing environments that provide ready, cost-effective access to users for multiple runs and model respecifications, then validation becomes very feasible.

Another reason there are few estimates of uncertainty is that decision makers usually want only point estimates, without measures of uncertainty. It is important, therefore, to develop innovative ways to convey estimates of uncertainty that decision makers will take into account in debates about policy alternatives (see Citro and Hanushek, 1991:86-88). This task may be easier for retirement-income-related policy projections because decision makers have somewhat more experience with estimates of uncertainty for such projections than for estimates on other topics. Thus, because of the long time horizon, the SSA Office of the Actuary routinely presents high-cost, intermediate, and low-cost scenarios for the balance in the Social Security trust funds under current law. However, this approach to bounding uncertainty is problematic (see "SSA Model Validation," below). Moreover, there is no comparable record of regularly projecting the long-term funding status of employer pensions, even though this source of retirement income may be more uncertain than Social Security (see Burtless, 1993; also, Schieber and Shoven, 1993, develop such a projection for defined benefit and defined contribution plans).

Finally, an essential feature of an acceptable projection model is that it incorporate best professional judgment about relevant factors, particularly for aspects of the model to which estimates are sensitive. "Best" professional judgment is not always the newest theory or latest academic model, which may be too new to have been properly evaluated. Also, because there is a range of professional opinion in many areas, it will be important to conduct sensitivity analyses of alternative specifications before selecting a particular approach to use for a

---

[6]See Cohen (1991a) for a review of validation studies that have been done of social welfare policy analysis microsimulation models, including DYNASIM2 and PRISM.

central or base case. Yet it is clear that when important changes have occurred—for example, in worker productivity or savings rates or mortality rates—a model that uses data or estimates of behavioral parameters that do not reflect those changes will not be helpful in informing the policy debate. Also, given that relatively little work has been done to date to conduct external validation studies or sensitivity analyses of models, the extent to which a model incorporates best professional judgment is often the only indicator of the likely level of model performance.

## SSA Model Validation

The Social Security actuarial cost model, which uses cell-based methods to carry forward the results of time-series analysis, is an exception to our statement that model validation and assessment of uncertainty are rarely performed. The Office of the Actuary's 75-year projections of trust fund balances under current law, which are revised every year, are often evaluated by comparing them to what actually occurred in the short run and by looking at the patterns of yearly revision (see, e.g., Schieber and Shoven, 1993). Also, the Office of the Actuary routinely prepares trust fund balance projections for low-cost, intermediate, and high-cost scenarios, thereby providing a type of sensitivity analysis (similar to that provided for Census Bureau population projections). SSA also provides sensitivity analyses of the separate effects of key assumptions. In these analyses, the high-cost, intermediate, and low-cost values are used for one assumption, such as fertility, while the intermediate values are used for all other assumptions.

However, as Burtless (1993) points out, the assumptions underlying the low-cost and high-cost scenarios are not chosen so as to bound the likely range of potential experience in any manner that approximates a statistical confidence interval. Hence, they are less useful to policy makers, analysts, and the public because they do not indicate the probability of a best-case or worst-case outcome relative to the intermediate projection. Also, the assumptions may be internally inconsistent. For example, the growth rate of real wages (for which a higher value is a favorable outcome for the Social Security system) may be negatively correlated with real interest rates (for which a higher value is also a favorable outcome for the system).

Finally, key assumptions of the central or intermediate scenario may not always reflect current best professional judgment. For example, the mortality forecasts developed by SSA are at one extreme of the range of available forecasts: they represent a more pronounced slowing of the rates of mortality decline observed in this century than is forecast by others (see Lee and Skinner, 1996). The implication of the SSA forecasts is that people will not live as long as forecast by others and, hence, that the growth in the elderly population, particularly of the oldest old (those aged 85 and older), will be less pronounced. Consequently, the use of the SSA forecasts, even from the high-cost scenario, could result in overly optimistic assessments of the ability of employer pensions or personal savings to provide adequate retirement income support over retirees' life spans. The use of the SSA forecasts is also problematic for assessments of the Social Security system, even though the relevant population estimate is not the number of elderly per se but the old-age dependency ratio (people aged 65 and older as a ratio of people aged 20-64). While a lower mortality rate than that forecast by SSA will increase income to the system (more younger people will be alive to contribute payroll taxes), it will also increase payouts from the system, and the relative increase in outgo will exceed the relative increase in taxable payrolls (see Board of Trustees [OASDI], 1994:132-133).

Lee and Carter (1992) provide a credible alternative to the SSA mortality forecasts. Their method essentially projects into the future the rate of mortality decline observed over the twentieth century, which has been fairly steady despite periods of faster and slower progress. SSA's method extrapolates cause-specific death rates over the preceding 20 years, which necessarily results in a marked slowing in the rate of mortality decline, as the more rapidly declining causes of death come to claim a smaller and smaller share of total mortality. Of course, it is impossible to know which of the two methods will ultimately prove more accurate.

A major advantage of the Lee and Carter approach, noted by Lee and Skinner (1996), is that it provides probability intervals describing the uncertainty in their extrapolative method. However, the Lee and Carter estimates of uncertainty do not allow for model specification error or the possibility of "structural breaks" in time series, such as the sharp decline in age-specific mortality rates that occurred between the nineteenth and twentieth centuries. Hence, Lee and Carter probably underestimate the extent of uncertainty in their forecasts of mortality rates.

Recently, Lee and Tuljapurkar (1994) extended the methods of Lee and Carter to develop stochastic population forecasts with consistent and meaningful probability intervals for all items forecast (e.g., age categories of the population, taking account of all demographic processes). Lee and Tuljapurkar formulated models of age-specific fertility (from Lee, 1993) and age-specific mortality (from Lee and Carter, 1992), in which they estimated a single time-varying parameter for each process by using standard time-series analysis techniques. (Net immigration could also be handled in the same manner, but it was treated as deterministic at the level assumed in the Census Bureau projections.) They then used these fitted models of stochastically varying rates as inputs to the population renewal process and carefully tracked the propagation and sources of error. They used analytic methods to find both the expected value of the forecast and the probability intervals.

Similar results could be obtained with Monte Carlo methods, that is, by repeated stochastic simulations using the stochastic models of vital rates. The SSASIM model, recently developed with support from SSA, uses Monte Carlo techniques to characterize uncertainty in the Social Security trust fund balance forecasts (Holmer, 1995a, 1995b; see also Sze, 1995, and Appendix C). SSASIM implements stochastic processes for all of the key demographic and economic variables that are used in the SSA actuarial cost model in a general framework that can accommodate different expectations (specified by the user) about the dynamics of each variable over time and in association with other variables. For example, a policy analyst can assume that such variables as rates of mortality decline follow a consistent trajectory over the span of the projection period (as does the SSA actuarial cost model) or that the time trend will exhibit cyclical fluctuations. The analyst's assumptions are used to specify the means, standard deviations, and correlation coefficients of a multivariate normal distribution; multiple runs with different random draws from the distribution for a particular set of assumptions generate the expected values of variables and the probability bounds.

The use of scenarios by SSA and the Census Bureau to convey uncertainty about forecasts stands in contrast to the use of probabilistic methods. To build scenarios, an analyst develops one forecast on the basis of the "expected" trajectories for each demographic or economic process. The analyst then also develops alternative trajectories for each process above and below the expected trajectories and combines them in various ways to produce high and low forecasts with which to bound the intermediate or expected forecast. For example, because trust fund balances are influenced by the old-age dependency ratio, SSA combines low fertility with low mortality for its high-cost scenario. The Census Bureau, on the other hand, combines high fertility with low mortality into a high scenario for total population growth. As a consequence, the Census Bureau's high and low estimates of the elderly population cover a wider band than the SSA estimates, while the Census Bureau's high and low estimates of the old-age dependency ratio cover a narrower band.

The SSA high- and low-cost scenarios for the population aged 65 and older and the old-age dependency ratio cover a somewhat narrower band than the 95 percent probability intervals generated by Lee and Tuljapurkar (1994). One could use the Lee and Tuljapurkar upper and lower bounds to produce new population scenarios. However, as Lee and Skinner (1996) point out, the problem with any method of constructing scenarios is that there is no means by which to attach probability intervals to the resulting forecasts. The scenario approach assumes—unrealistically—that the high, medium, or low trajectory for each demographic process is followed consistently over the entire time span. In contrast, the stochastic forecasts of Lee and Tuljapurkar treat fertility and mortality as random variables at every iteration, producing true probability bounds for the projections at each period (e.g., each 5-year interval).

Although stochastic methods may underestimate the uncertainty in demographic and economic forecasts, depending on how the parameters of the stochastic process are estimated, they represent a major step forward over the scenario approach for conveying estimates of uncertainty to policy makers. The use of stochastic methods to estimate the uncertainty of projections of demographic and economic variables seems imperative for the kinds of long-range forecasts that are often used in retirement-income-related policy debates. In this regard, it would be very useful to further develop the capabilities of the SSASIM model for estimating the uncertainty of the projections in the SSA model, including work on alternative methods with which to estimate the parameters of the stochastic process.

## Recommendation

**16. Models that project policy outcomes over long periods should routinely assess the accuracy and uncertainty of the projections and report prediction errors in previous forecasts. To be able to evaluate a model's projections in a cost-effective manner, the model design must explicitly include a capability for sensitivity analysis (e.g., how much the outputs vary with alternative assumptions and versions of model components) and a capability to estimate uncertainty from such sources as sampling variability in the database and other model inputs.**

## NEAR-TERM MODELING STRATEGIES

The kinds of investments we recommend in data and research will take time to return benefits for retirement-income-related policy analysis. In addition, the development of needed employer models and a new large-scale individual-level microsimulation model, which must await advances in data and research knowledge, cannot be completed in the near term. In the meantime, the Department of Labor and other agencies must be able to answer decision makers' questions about the likely effects of alternative policies. They cannot respond that they are unable to provide requested information because data and knowledge are lacking with which to develop improved projection models.

In order to be responsive to decision makers' legitimate information demands without incurring significant model development costs that could well be misdirected, agencies should try to frame policy questions as specifically as possible and use limited special-purpose models together with the best available data and research knowledge to answer those questions. Depending on the issue, a special-purpose model may already exist, or, more likely, it will be necessary to adapt one from another model or to construct one on the spot.

Admittedly, limited ad hoc models may not provide very reliable answers to policy questions, and, in particular, they are not likely to be able to handle important policy interactions. Also, special-purpose models may be able to model behavioral responses to policy changes only very crudely, although they should incorporate such responses when reasonable parameters are available and feasible to implement. However, the alternative of trying at this time to develop more complex models, when needed data and research knowledge are lacking, will not likely give a better result and will very likely waste scarce resources.

We acknowledge that a phased approach to retirement income modeling, as we recommend, may not provide useful answers before there is actually a retirement income crisis that requires extensive evaluation of alternative policy proposals in a comprehensive framework. However, there will be continuing need for retirement-income-related modeling capabilities (as is true for health care policy), and without investments in data and behavioral research, government agencies will never be in a position to develop markedly improved projection models. (The health care agencies have recognized this point by redesigning and expanding their surveys.) Again, we are concerned about the use of scarce resources in the near term. We believe they are best used for data and research instead of extensive development (or redevelopment) of large-scale models. To the extent that limited investments can lead to better special-purpose models for specific questions, we support those investments.

## The CBO Approach

The modus operandi that we have in mind is that of the Congressional Budget Office (CBO), whose analysts regularly prepare ad hoc, special-purpose models, often using spreadsheet tools, to develop estimates of the likely costs and other effects of proposed policy changes. CBO staff combine data and parameter estimates in their ad hoc models from a wide range of sources, sometimes including as inputs the outputs of larger, more formal projection models with the results adjusted as seems appropriate. Sometimes they make additional "out-of-model" adjustments, for example, to provide crude estimates of the likely effects of behavioral response to policy changes. (See Citro and Hanushek, 1991:41-51, for a case study of the modeling tools used by CBO and the U.S. Department of Health and Human Services in the late 1980s for estimating the effects of welfare reform.)

In general, CBO staff develop their models only to the point to which they can answer the question at hand. For example, projections for a few years might be developed with distributional detail, while longer term projections are developed on a very aggregate basis. Or a model might be developed to handle only the particular policy change that is under consideration. However, in instances in which the same kind of question arises frequently, CBO will develop more formal models that are intended for repeated use and that can handle a wider range of variations in a particular policy area. As just one example, CBO developed a hospital-based model that is designed to estimate the cost and distributional effects of changing various provisions of the Medicare prospective payment scheme used to reimburse hospital costs.

The problem with an ad hoc approach to model building is that there is virtually no incentive to provide for such desirable model features as openness or portability or to document a model for use by others. More important, there is no incentive to perform more than the crudest type of model validation. However, the strategy of special-purpose model development, when carried out by knowledgeable analysts, can provide answers to specific policy questions with minimum staff resources and time. The answers will very likely be limited and of highly variable quality, but they can assist the policy debate, and the process of developing them can identify issues to consider in the design of new, improved large-scale models for use in future policy projections.

The problem for retirement-income-related projection modeling for the executive branch in the near term (and in the long term, too) is that there is no equivalent of CBO in a cabinet department. CBO will itself prepare estimates for retirement-income related policy proposals, but the executive branch needs its own modeling capability, particularly when proposals are being drafted and have not yet been sent to the Congress. There is no staff group in the executive branch that is in a position to take a broad view of policy analysis in this area, much less to make effective use of available data, research, and modeling tools to develop the best possible estimates in the most direct manner in response to decision makers' questions. There are clusters of analysts in such agencies as DOL and SSA, but it would be helpful to have a larger critical mass working together on a regular basis.

For example, SSA analysts are currently working on models of the distribution of Social Security benefits by using matched SSA earnings records and SIPP data. The SSA analysts initially developed models with which to project earnings histories for 1984-1993 for members of the 1984 SIPP panel on the basis of prior earnings histories, and they obtained reasonable results. They then used these models to project future earnings histories for members of the 1990 SIPP panel (Iams and Sandell, 1996; Sandell and Iams, 1996). The SSA analysts propose to extend their models to project pension income, as well as Social Security benefits, on the basis of earnings histories and other characteristics of SIPP sample members. If successful, and if a savings income projection capability is also added, this approach could offer some useful policy modeling capability without requiring a full-fledged dynamic microsimulation model (assuming that policy changes can be factored into the projections in some manner).

SSA analysts are also working on cross-sectional microsimulation models of SSI and the disability insurance (DI) component of the Social Security system with matched SIPP and disability program data from SSA records. As part of this effort, they are developing ways to simulate the multistage disability application and determination process (see Lahiri, Vaughan, and Wixon, 1995). Initially they expect to be able to make estimates of the number of people in the civilian noninstitutional population who are likely to meet SSA disability criteria. Estimates of those categorically eligible on the basis of disability will then be combined with estimates of financial eligibility for SSI and DI insured status. A subsequent model of the application decision is also planned and will be used to introduce selectivity adjustments to the estimates of the pool of those eligible for disability benefits.

This SSA modeling work should be well known and available to other analysts, such as those in the Pension and Welfare Benefits Administration in DOL. Similarly, work that PWBA analysts may do with employer pension issues should be well known and available to analysts in other relevant agencies. It is probably not feasible to establish a cross-agency retirement income modeling group with authority to prepare estimates on behalf of the executive branch, but perhaps it is possible to establish coordinating mechanisms. For example, it would be useful to establish an interagency users group that meets regularly to review retirement-income-related projection model developments at the member agencies. Such meetings could contribute to the design of new, improved models in the future.

## Improvements to Existing Models

In the near term, while large investments in projection model development are in abeyance, it is important to seek opportunities for cost-effective improvements to existing retirement-income-related projection models and to make them known and available across agencies. For example, it may be possible to marginally improve the pension components of such models as DYNASIM2 and PRISM, even though major improvements in pension simulation capability will depend on the development of new models that use greatly improved data.

An important model for which it appears feasible to effect useful improvements in the near term is the SSA actuarial cost model. The SSA model is the linchpin of retirement-income-related projection modeling. It produces relatively few outputs (principally, the trust fund balances over a 75-year time horizon), but its projections are critical in setting the tone for policy debates. Also, many other models calibrate their outputs to components of the SSA projections, such as the forecasted population size by age and sex and wage growth and other economic factors.

We urge attention to extending the SSA model in several ways.[7] First, it is critically important to develop probabilistic estimates of uncertainty for each of the variables projected in the model and then to develop estimates of uncertainty of the model's outputs as a whole, taking account of covariances among the various time series (mortality, labor force participation, wage growth, etc.). Such estimates should replace the current scenario approach, which has no probabilistic structure. Work is under way at SSA along these lines (see the previous discussion in "SSA Model Validation"), and we urge that it be continued.

Second, it would be highly useful to add a capability to the model for limited

---

[7]The 1994-95 Advisory Council on Social Security Technical Panel on Assumptions and Methods (1995:60-66) has made similar recommendations.

distributional analysis of the effects of current and proposed Social Security provisions. For example, it would be useful to be able to project costs and benefits of policy alternatives for low, middle, and high earners among the population. Such projections would be helpful in evaluating outputs of more disaggregated models, and vice versa. A distributional component of the SSA model should include a capability to simulate the effects of cyclical or random variations in key aggregate variables, such as interest rates and growth in wages.

Third, because of the importance of mortality projections for estimates of the retirement-age population, we urge SSA to evaluate the sensitivity of the model's outputs to mortality projections that are disaggregated by such characteristics as marital status and income levels. If the analysis suggests a strong degree of sensitivity, it would be important to undertake research on the best form of such projections for use in the model. SSA administrative data could provide the basis for a comprehensive study of the relationship of mortality to earnings for people of retirement age. (Studying the relationship of mortality to marital status with these data would require SSA to track the marital status of all beneficiaries, which could also be useful for projections of beneficiaries.) SSA also has several SIPP panel files to which it is appending year-by-year mortality records. These files could permit a rich, multivariate analysis of mortality correlates for a limited sample.[8]

Finally, it would be highly useful to develop means by which to document and provide research access to the model. Outputs of the SSA actuarial cost model are so widely used for inputs to other models that it would be very helpful if outside analysts could more readily learn about and have access to the model. Such access would also facilitate outside reviews of the model's properties to identify other improvements.

## Recommendations

**17. To respond to immediate policy needs, agencies should use limited, special-purpose models with the best available data and research findings to answer specific policy questions. Although such models may not provide very accurate estimates, the alternative of developing complex new individual-level microsimulation or employer models in advance of needed improvements in data and research knowledge has little prospect of producing better results and will likely represent, in the immediate future, a misuse of scarce resources.**

---

[8]Panis and Lillard (1996) recently developed mortality models with data on age, race, sex, marital status, and household income of surviving sample members and decedents in the PSID. They used these models to simulate the effects of proposed Social Security changes, such as increasing the contribution rate and decreasing benefits, on the net present value of Social Security benefits for prototypical types of beneficiaries.

**18.** The Social Security Administration should consider enhancements to the SSA actuarial cost model in the near term. This model provides useful outputs for other models and helps frame the overall retirement income security policy debate. Priority improvements include the following:

• replacing the scenario approach with probabilistic estimates of uncertainty for the model's projections that take into account covariances among the various time series (mortality, labor force participation, wage growth, etc.);

• adding a capability for limited distributional analysis of the effects of current and proposed Social Security provisions (e.g., of costs and benefits for low, middle, and high earners);

• evaluating the sensitivity of the model's outputs to mortality projections that are disaggregated by such characteristics as marital status and income levels and planning to develop such projections, if warranted; and

• developing means to document and provide research access to the model.

# 6

# Furthering Coordination for Data Collection, Research, and Modeling

There are many pieces to the retirement-income-security policy puzzle, and many research, data collection, policy, and program agencies are involved in one or more aspects of the topic. There are strengths to having a variety of perspectives; however, we believe that mechanisms for coordinating agency efforts and setting priorities within a broader perspective are needed.

There is also a need for greater involvement of the private sector and academic research community in retirement-income-related data collection, analysis, and modeling. Such involvement expands the community of people who can contribute to improved databases and behavioral analyses that are most relevant for policy and to the development and evaluation of projection models that appropriately use data and research results.

## ORGANIZATIONAL ISSUES

As noted in Chapter 1, responsibility for the major policies that affect retirement income security, such as employer pension regulation, Social Security, tax policy, and health care programs, is spread among several agencies in different departments. The responsibility for relevant data collection and research is spread among several policy, statistical, and research agencies as well. There are benefits of having many players in this complex area. Different agencies can develop expertise in particular aspects of data collection, analysis, and policy formulation and can bring perspectives to the table that might otherwise be overlooked. Also, it would not make sense to combine such functions as private pension regulation with support of basic behavioral research or broad-based data collection in the same agency—the concerns and skills required to be effective in these different capacities are very different.

At the same time, there are clearly drawbacks to having the responsibilities for retirement-income-related policies, data, and research dispersed across so many agencies, each with its own perspective. For data on individuals, for example, existing panel surveys, which are sponsored by different agencies with different agendas, do not complement each other as well as they might. Even more problematic are data on employers. As just one example, the U.S. Department of Health and Human Services (HHS) is undertaking a large new survey of employer health insurance plans and costs, without reference to the need for data on pensions and other benefits. Such a course makes sense from the department's orientation toward health policy issues, but it does not necessarily make sense from the government's broader interest with issues of retirement income security policy.

More generally, having a large number of agencies involved in retirement-income-related data collection and analysis increases the likelihood that there will be both unnecessary overlap and duplication of effort and significant gaps in needed information. We conclude that more attention should be given to interagency coordination to improve the quality and utility of data and research knowledge, to identify priority areas in which more work is needed, and, conversely, to identify areas in which overlap could be reduced. Highly constrained budgets for data and research make it all the more urgent to achieve effective coordination of agencies' agendas and plans.

The challenge is to devise appropriate coordination mechanisms that facilitate making hard choices among agencies' priorities, but do not stifle initiative and innovation or introduce bureaucratic layers of review and approval. Attempts to develop a "unified" budget for retirement-income-related data collection or research, for example, would undoubtedly require a very heavy hand from the U.S. Office of Management and Budget (OMB) and be largely futile, in any case, in part because the budget authority for the various agencies that would be affected is split among a number of congressional committees. In contrast, interagency committees and forums, which are often very effective as a means of sharing information, are typically much less effective as a means by which to set priorities or to induce agencies to alter their agendas in any significant manner. Indeed, a former official in the Department of Education once said that "coordination in the government is an unnatural act." The characteristics of existing interagency groups that are or could be relevant to the retirement area only underscore this point.

One such group is the Federal Committee on Statistical Methodology. It has been very hard-working throughout its 20-year existence and has a string of outstanding publications to its credit, several of which treat topics that are important for improving retirement-income-related data (see, e.g., Federal Committee on Statistical Methodology, 1988, 1990). The committee had a strong chair, the late Maria Gonzalez of the Statistical Policy Division of OMB, and has been able to enlist substantial contributions from staff of many member agencies. But this committee has not sought to determine data gaps and overlaps or set priorities; its major tasks have been to review data quality issues and describe best statistical practice.

Another such group is the Interagency Forum on Aging-Related Statistics, established in 1986 and led by the Census Bureau, the National Center for Health Statistics (NCHS), and the National Institute on Aging (NIA). It has served as a forum for information exchange in twice-yearly meetings and has tried at times to go beyond that function. Its working groups have had some success in such areas as identifying core sets of data items that aging-related surveys should include. However, the forum has found it difficult to sustain efforts that could affect agencies' survey plans.

Recently, a combination of circumstances led agencies within HHS to develop an integrated design for health-related data collection. The circumstances included the glaring weaknesses in relevant data and research knowledge that became apparent in the 1993-1994 health care reform debate, constrained budgets, and the pressures for departmental restructuring and agency cooperation from the "reinventing government" initiative (Hunter and Arnett, 1996). The result has been a plan that integrates several surveys, which were previously independently conducted by different agencies, in a way that will, it is hoped, serve a variety of health status and health care policy analysis needs in a cost-effective manner. HHS has also established a senior-level Data Council, with overall responsibility for addressing data issues across the department. The challenge for work on retirement is that coordination mechanisms for surveys and administrative record systems must involve agencies both within and across departments.

## COORDINATION MECHANISMS

### Data Collection

We believe there are opportunities to work toward integration of retirement-income-related data collection for employers and individuals. What will be required is a decision to avoid the example of health care reform, in which embarrassing deficiencies led to integration after the fact, and, instead, try to make priority investments in anticipation of policy needs.

### Employer Data Task Force

We recommend that the U.S. Department of Labor (DOL) establish a task force on retirement-income-related employer data that is led by the Bureau of Labor Statistics (BLS) and the Pension and Welfare Benefits Administration (PWBA) and involves other relevant agencies (see Chapter 4). We urge the task force to obtain input from benefit consultants, representatives of different types of employers, and academic researchers.

A priority for the task force should be to review the major government employer data collection systems and to analyze the implications of alternative ways of building on their strengths in terms of both costs and benefits. For example, what are the prospects and what would be the costs of making the DOL/ PWBA Form 5500 data series more useful for research purposes and linking it to the BLS Employee Benefits Survey (EBS) (and perhaps the Employment Cost Trends Survey as well)? Alternatively, is it possible to expand the HHS National Employer Health Insurance Survey to cover benefits more widely and at what cost? If such an expansion is possible, would it be possible or desirable to reduce the scope of the EBS or Form 5500 data series and with what potential cost savings?

The task force should look for other ways to leverage existing data series and to identify unnecessary overlap so funds would be available for needed new data collection. For example, what are the possibilities of incorporating selected private data sets into an integrated employer database? Should the periodic pension coverage supplement in the Current Population Survey (CPS) be eliminated in favor of continuing and improving the annual pension information collected in the Survey of Income and Program Participation (SIPP)? In fact, PWBA is now actively exploring this last possibility with the Census Bureau. There is evidence that the SIPP pension data are of equal quality (Iams, 1995), and SIPP has the advantage of obtaining considerably more information than the CPS that would be useful to analyze together with pension data.

Finally, the task force should consider the costs and benefits of alternative models for obtaining panel data on employers and their workers. One model is to build on the Health and Retirement Survey (HRS). Another model is to launch a brand-new survey.

While the task force will not be able to compel agencies to alter their agendas, its cost-benefit analyses, if well done, would provide considerable insight into the advantages and disadvantages of alternative plans. Its analyses could facilitate collaborative decisions by agencies to streamline existing data systems where feasible and thereby make resources available for important unmet data needs.

**Panel Survey Review Group**

We recommend that NIA facilitate collaborative efforts among sponsors and principal investigators to regularly review the questionnaire content and data collection practices of the major retirement-income-related panel surveys of individuals: HRS and AHEAD (Health and Retirement Survey and Asset and Health Dynamics Among the Oldest Old survey), the various cohorts in the National

Longitudinal Surveys (NLS), and the Panel Study of Income Dynamics (PSID). The Survey of Consumer Finances (SCF) and SIPP should also be included in these reviews (see Chapter 4). NIA is well suited for this role, given its focus on aging research, which includes the economic well-being of the elderly, and its sponsorship of HRS/AHEAD.

There appear to be significant opportunities to improve the overall utility and quality of the data from panel surveys of individuals for retirement-income-related behavioral analysis. As just one example, adding wealth and pension modules to the National Longitudinal Survey of Youth (NLSY) would make it possible to determine why there are such great disparities in savings and wealth by the time people reach their 50s (the age cohort of HRS). Because the NLSY cohort is now well past the age when most schooling is obtained, it is possible to make room for retirement-income-related modules by scaling back previously important modules on education and training.

We do not make detailed recommendations about what could or should be done to each survey (see our general recommendations in Chapter 4); rather we stress the importance of periodically bringing together the sponsor agencies and principal investigators to conduct broad oversight reviews. These reviews should seek to identify the best data collection practices that should be universally adopted, to consider core question content that would facilitate cross-survey and pooled data analyses, and to consider modules to add and delete that could make the surveys more useful for analysis of retirement income security while not compromising their other goals.

## Forum Working Group on Data Quality

It would be helpful for the employer data task force and the panel survey review group to share their analyses and conclusions periodically with the Interagency Forum on Aging-Related Statistics. In addition, we suggest that the forum, perhaps working with the Federal Committee on Statistical Methodology, establish a working group to conduct important cross-survey studies of the quality of retirement-income-related data. We expect that each survey or administrative records data system regularly conducts its own quality reviews; however, we believe it would be useful for an interagency working group to undertake and publish cross-cutting studies on key issues (see the list in Chapter 4 for examples). The working group could also review completed validation studies, whether performed by the group or by individual data system sponsors, to identify priority areas for data quality improvement.

## Projection Modeling

We suggest that analysts who are working on special-purpose projection models for retirement-income-related policy analysis in different agencies get together on a regular basis to share information and learn from one another (see Chapter 5). Meetings of the group could be the source of ideas for the design and, ultimately, implementation of new employer-based models and a new individual-level microsimulation model, after new data and research results become available. Members of the group should have input to the employer data collection task force and the panel survey review group regarding the content of specific surveys, such as HRS/AHEAD, to ensure that policy-relevant variables are included in formats that are tractable for new projection models.

Such a users' group should include academic and private sector analysts with relevant interest and experience in projection modeling, as well as agency staff. In general, it is important for agencies to involve outside researchers and private sector representatives in retirement-income-related data collection and modeling. Actively reaching out to the private sector and academia can have benefits ranging from a better climate for collection of relevant employer data to a larger community of researchers who are actively engaged in the development and use of policy-relevant behavioral and projection models.

## Recommendation

**19. Relevant agencies should establish coordination mechanisms to help improve the quality and utility of retirement-income-related data, reduce unnecessary duplication of effort, and identify priorities. Coordination mechanisms should recognize the need for flexibility and experimentation and not impose added bureaucratic requirements. Responsibilities for retirement-income-related policy analysis, research, and data collection are widely dispersed across government agencies, yet much work in this area requires an integrated, cross-agency perspective, as well as the involvement of academic researchers and private sector representatives.**

## INVOLVING THE PRIVATE SECTOR AND ACADEMIA

Working out ways to increase the involvement of academic and private sector analysts in retirement-income-related data collection and projection modeling, in addition to relevant behavioral research, is important for obtaining a full return on agencies' limited investment dollars. There are precedents for such involvement in the area of data collection but not, to date, in the area of development of projection models.

### Data Collection

HRS and AHEAD offer a model of successful involvement of the research community in generating databases that appear to have extraordinary analytical promise for explaining key retirement-income-related behaviors and contributing to the development of a new generation of projection modeling tools. The start-up phase of HRS and AHEAD obtained input on design and content issues from literally hundreds of researchers in several disciplines. Interdisciplinary steering committees of researchers have continued to guide the development of the two surveys and have maintained a strong focus on data needs for behavioral analysis and experimentation with new questions and procedures to improve policy relevance and data quality. Federal agencies have had input to HRS/AHEAD through an interagency review group coordinated by NIA.

We urge that this approach be extended to employer surveys. In this area, it is particularly important to involve private sector representatives as well as academic researchers in issues of survey design, content, and data collection procedures. Success in obtaining needed employer data is unlikely if employers themselves are not consulted about feasibility issues and if they are not made aware of the value of improved data, not only for government planning and policy analysis, but also for use by the private sector. As key participants in the U.S. system of pension, health care, and disability benefits, employers have a stake in having access to the best data and analytical models with which to make decisions about benefit offerings and about personnel and compensation practices more broadly.

### Projection Modeling

In the area of projection modeling, there are as yet no success stories of effective collaboration of agencies and their contractors with the academic community more broadly. Historically, the research community has been largely disassociated from the development and application of projection models for policy analysis (as distinct from analytical models to study behavior). Reasons for this disassociation include the complexities of many models (e.g., microsimulation models have been viewed as "black boxes") and limited access to them. Also, academic research incentives emphasize new findings and theoretical applications rather than estimations of the costs and distributional implications of proposed policy changes (see discussion in Citro and Hanushek, 1991:281-289).

We stress that the federal government should give priority to retirement-income-related data collection and research, not to investment in large-scale projection models. At the same time, we support some continuing discussion of the requirements for a new generation of employer-based and individual-level microsimulation projection models (see Chapter 5). We suggest that modelers provide input to the task force on employer data and the panel survey review group and that a projection modeling users' group involve interested academics and private sector analysts. In this way, a dialogue could begin on such issues as the feasibility of integrating behavioral models of particular types and with particular input variables into projection models.

When investments in data collection and associated research begin to bear fruit so that it makes sense to actively plan for the development of a new generation of projection models, it will be important to continue a dialogue between the model builders and academic researchers. Complete integration of the work of researchers and projection modelers is not likely a feasible goal: it seems unrealistic to expect that researchers working in different areas could all develop look-alike, "plug-compatible," analytical models for use as modules in a projection model. Research will inevitably proceed in different directions with differing implications for the adaptation of research results to projection model needs. However, it should be possible to involve researchers from key analytical fields—labor supply, savings and consumption, employer behavior—more closely in the development of useful projection models than has been the case in the past. When it becomes appropriate to establish steering groups for new models, such groups should include researchers as well as agency and contractor staff, similar to the approach of HRS/AHEAD. The use of discussion groups and World Wide Web sites on the Internet can provide a low-cost way to maintain an active dialogue among steering group members. Periodically, they could use the Internet to obtain critical reviews from other researchers about the design elements for new projection models (e.g., the functional form and input variables for particular behavioral components).

From participation in such a dialogue may well come increased interest on the part of the research community in projection modeling, including the key issue of model validation, and an enhanced capability of researchers to make effective contributions in this area. Ultimately, the combined efforts of people working in the public, private, and academic sectors will be needed to develop improved projection models—built on improvements in data and research knowledge—that can support more informed debate about the effects of alternative policies on the retirement income security of current and future generations of Americans.

## Recommendation

**20. Collaboration between government agencies and the research community and private sector should be developed to spur improvements in retirement-income-related data and research knowledge that can support the development of improved projection models. The model for such collaboration is the involvement of large numbers of researchers from several disciplines in the design and content of HRS and AHEAD, which has had high payoff for the relevance and quality of the data. For employer data collection systems, this model should also involve private sector representatives as well as academic researchers in design and content issues.**

# APPENDICES

# APPENDIX
# A
# Contents, *Assessing Knowledge of Retirement Behavior*

The papers in *Assessing Knowledge of Retirement Behavior* (Hanushek and Maritato, 1996) were originally presented in September 1994 at the panel's Conference on Modeling the Impact of Public and Private Policies on Retirement Behavior and Income: What Do We Know and What Do We Need to Know? They were subsequently modified to incorporate the comments of discussants at the conference, panel members, and reviewers. The papers and the workshop discussion contributed significantly to the panel's work and our report.

# APPENDIX
# B

# Retirement-Income-Related Data Sets

This appendix describes federally-sponsored data sources of the following types: panel surveys of cohorts of individuals; other panel surveys of families and households; repeated cross-sectional surveys of households; and administrative and survey data sources on employers and employees.

## PANEL SURVEYS FOR COHORTS OF INDIVIDUALS

***Asset and Health Dynamics Among the Oldest Old (AHEAD)*** Ongoing (Hurd et al., 1994): Panel survey of people aged 70 and older at the time of the original interview and their spouses. Collects detailed information on demographic background, dissaving and Medicaid eligibility, family structure and in-kind and financial transfers, housing, income and assets, physical and cognitive health, use of community and nursing home services and out-of-pocket service costs; future questionnaires will be more similar between AHEAD and HRS (e.g., both will include employment status), and the section on medical care costs and sources of health insurance coverage will be expanded. Data will be linked with Medicare files, SSA earnings and benefits files, state Medicaid files (if possible), and the National Death Index.

First interview conducted in 1993-1994, second interview in 1996; 8,223 respondents, drawn from both the HRS screener sample with an oversample of blacks, Hispanics, and Florida residents and from the Medicare Master Enrollment File for people aged 80 and older. Funding has been approved for 2 more interviews and to introduce a cohort in between HRS and AHEAD of people and their spouses, beginning in 1999 when they are aged 69-75. Conducted by the University of Michigan for NIA.

*Health and Retirement Survey (HRS)* Ongoing (Juster and Suzman, 1995; see also Rust, 1993; Smith, 1988): Panel survey of people aged 51-61 at the time of the original interview and their spouses. Collects comprehensive information on demographic background, disability, employment status and job history, family structure and transfers, health and cognitive conditions and status, health insurance and pension plans, housing, income and net worth, retirement plans and perspectives, and attitudes, preferences, expectations, and subjective probabilities; includes experimental modules. Data will be linked with Medicare files, SSA earnings files, and the National Death Index; health and pension benefit plan descriptions were obtained from employers in the first interview.

First interview conducted in 1992, second interview in 1994, third interview in 1996; 12,654 respondents with an oversample of blacks, Hispanics, and Florida residents. Funding has been approved for one more interview; funding has also been approved to collect data on a new cohort of people and their spouses, beginning in 1998 when they are aged 51-56. (The same size for the HRS and AHEAD new cohorts will be about 7,000 people.) Conducted by the University of Michigan for NIA.

*Longitudinal Study of Aging (LSOA)* Ongoing (National Center for Health Statistics, 1992): Based on two studies, the Supplement on Aging (SOA) to the 1984 National Health Interview Survey (NHIS) and the Second Supplement on Aging (SOA II) to the 1994 NHIS. Everyone 55 years of age and older in a 1984 NHIS household was eligible for the SOA; participants aged 70 and older were subsequently interviewed by telephone in 1986, 1988, and 1990 to obtain information about changes in their functional status and living arrangements. SOA II involved interviewing 10,000 people in the NHIS who were aged 70 and older, beginning in October 1994 through March 1996. Elderly people in black households were oversampled. Participants will be followed up every 2 years, beginning in 1997, for one or more waves. Data linked with Medicare records and the National Death Index. Conducted by the Census Bureau for NCHS and NIA.

*Medicare Current Beneficiary Survey (CBS)* Ongoing (Adler, 1994): Rotating panel survey of Medicare enrollees. First panel began in fall 1991; the original sample of about 15,000 beneficiaries was continued with replenishment each fall for several years. The rotating design began in 1994; a new panel is introduced each fall. Sample members are retained in a panel for 4 years and interviewed 3 times per year; about 16,000 cases are included in each interview. Collects information on health status, access to care, satisfaction with care, and health insurance in the first fall interview; collects information on health care utilization and cost in subsequent interviews and on income and assets each spring. Survey data are linked to Medicare claims records (except for people enrolled in health maintenance organizations, for which no claims records exist).

*National Longitudinal Survey of Mature Women (NLS-MW)* Ongoing (Center for Human Resource Research, 1995a, 1995b; Fahy, 1995): Panel survey of women aged 30-44 at the time of the original interview; some data collected also for spouse. Collects detailed information (not always at every interview) on current labor force and employment status; characteristics of current or last job, including some characteristics of employer; work experience prior to initial interview in 1967; work experience since most recent interview; demographic background, including parents' characteristics; migration; education and training; health and physical condition; marital and family characteristics, including caregiving responsibilities; net family assets and family income by type; attitudes and perspectives (e.g., how feels about job); retirement expectations and self and spouse retirement eligibility; hypothetical job offer; volunteer work; local area labor market conditions. Descriptions were obtained from employers of sample members' pension plans in 1989; information was obtained on post-retirement health insurance coverage for self and spouse in 1992.

First interview conducted in 1967; sample of 5,000 women, including oversample of blacks, followed at 1- to 3-year intervals; most recent interview in 1995 when the women were aged 58-72. Conducted by the Census Bureau for the Ohio State University Center for Human Resource Research under a contract with BLS.

*National Longitudinal Survey of Older Men (NLS-OM)* Completed (Center for Human Resource Research, 1995a, 1995b; Fahy, 1995): Panel survey of men aged 45-60 at the time of the original interview, who also reported information for their wives. Collected detailed information (not always at every interview) on current labor force and employment status; characteristics of current or last job; work experience prior to initial interview in 1966; work experience since most recent interview; demographic background, including parents' characteristics; migration; education and training; health and physical condition of self and spouse; marital and family characteristics; net family assets and family income by type; attitudes and perspectives (e.g., how felt about job); retirement expectations and retirement eligibility; hypothetical job offer; volunteer work; local area labor market conditions. 1990 reinterview collected information on social support networks and long-term care use and financing.

First interview conducted in 1966; sample of 5,000 men, including oversample of blacks, followed at 1- to 2-year intervals until 1983 when they were aged 62-77; surviving members of the sample (or next-of-kin for decedents) reinterviewed in 1990 when they were aged 69-84. Conducted by the Census Bureau for the Ohio State University Center for Human Resource Research under a contract with DOL; NIA provided funding for the 1990 reinterview.

*National Longitudinal Survey of Young Men (NLS-YM)*  Completed (Center for Human Resource Research, 1995a, 1995b; Fahy, 1995):  Panel survey of men aged 14-24 at the time of the original interview; some data collected also for spouse.  Collected detailed information on current labor force and employment status; characteristics of current or last job; work experience prior to initial interview in 1966; work experience since previous interview; demographic background, including parents' characteristics; migration; education and training; health and physical condition; marital and family characteristics; net family assets and family income by type; military service; attitudes and perspectives (e.g., how felt about job); hypothetical job offer; local area labor market conditions.

First interview conducted in 1966; sample of 5,000 men, including oversample of blacks, followed at 1- to 2-year intervals from 1966 to 1981 when they were aged 29-39.  Conducted by the Census Bureau for the Ohio State University Center for Human Resource Research under a contract with DOL.

*National Longitudinal Survey of Young Women (NLS-YW)*  Ongoing (Center for Human Resource Research, 1995a, 1995b; Fahy, 1995):  Panel survey of women aged 14-24 at the time of the original interview; some data collected also for spouse.  Collects detailed information (not always at every interview) on current labor force and employment status; characteristics of current or last job, including some characteristics of employer; work experience prior to initial interview in 1968; work experience since most recent interview; demographic background, including parents' characteristics; migration; education and training; health and physical condition; marital and family characteristics, including child care arrangements; net family assets and family income by type; attitudes and perspectives (e.g., how feels about job); hypothetical job offer; volunteer work; local area labor market conditions.

First interview conducted in 1968; sample of 5,000 women, including oversample of blacks, followed at 1- to 3-year intervals; most recent interview in 1995 when they were aged 41-51.  Conducted by the Census Bureau for the Ohio State University Center for Human Resource Research under a contract with BLS.

*National Longitudinal Survey of Youth (Young Men and Women) (NLSY)*  Ongoing (Center for Human Resource Research, 1995a, 1995b; Fahy, 1995):  Panel survey of people aged 14-21 at the time of the original interview; some data collected also for spouse.  Collects detailed information on current labor force and employment status and characteristics of current or most recent job; work experience since January 1, 1978, or previous interview; characteristics of jobs with more than 10 or 20 hours per week and more than 9 weeks in duration since January 1, 1978, or previous interview; demographic background, including parents' characteristics; migration; education, vocational training, and government jobs or training programs; health and physical condition; marital and family characteristics; family income, assets, and program participation; military service; work attitudes; educational and occupational aspirations and expectations; other social and psychological variables; discrimination problems in employment; significant others; school discipline; delinquency, drugs, and alcohol use; reported police contacts; time use; child care arrangements; looking for work; local labor market conditions.

First interview conducted in 1979; sample of 13,000 followed annually until 1994 and biennially beginning in 1996; most recent interview in 1994 when they were aged 29-36. An oversample of people in the military was discontinued after 1984; an oversample of economically disadvantaged whites was discontinued after 1990; the current sample size is about 10,000. Conducted by the National Opinion Research Center (NORC) for the Ohio State University Center for Human Resource Research under a contract with BLS.

***National Long-Term Care Survey (NLTCS)*** Ongoing (Manton, Corder, and Stallard, 1993): Panel survey of Medicare eligible people age 65 and older and chronically disabled at the time of the original interview with refreshment, together with a repeated cross-section survey of disability incidence among Medicare eligible people age 65 and older. For disabled and institutionalized people, collects detailed information on demographic background, health care services used, housing and neighborhood characteristics, income and assets, medical conditions and recent medical problems, out-of-pocket medical care payments and other sources of payment, physical and cognitive functional limitations, and services (formal and informal) received by impaired individuals and source of payment. Linked to Medicare service records.

First interview conducted in 1982; 35,000 people were screened to determine disability status (defined by one ADL or IADL impairment of 90 days or more duration), and the 6,400 people who were identified as chronically disabled, community residents received detailed in-home interviews. These disabled people and also people identified in 1982 as living in institutions were reinterviewed in 1984. Also, in 1984, 12,100 community residents who were not disabled in 1982 were rescreened to determine disability status in 1984, and a new sample of 4,900 people who turned age 65 between 1982 and 1984 was drawn from Medicare files and screened. Disabled and institutionalized people identified in these screenings received detailed interviews. In 1989, sample members identified as chronically disabled or institutionalized in 1982 or 1984 were reinterviewed in 1989. Also, 5,000 community residents who were not disabled in 1984 were rescreened, and a new sample of 4,900 people who turned age 65 between 1984 and 1989 was drawn from Medicare files and screened. Disabled and institutionalized people identified in these screenings received detailed interviews. The 1994 survey followed the same pattern as the 1989 survey; in addition, oversamples were drawn of people aged 95 and older and nonwhites.

Conducted by the Census Bureau for NIA, Duke University, and HHS/ASPE; HCFA and AHCPR provided funding for earlier rounds.

*New Beneficiary Survey (NBS) and New Beneficiary Followup (NBF)* Completed (U.S. Social Security Administration, 1993, 1994): Two-wave panel survey of people who began receiving Social Security benefits in a 12-month period in 1980-1981 and of people aged 65 or older at that time who were covered by Medicare but not receiving Social Security benefits.

First interview (NBS) conducted in 1982; sample of 9,100 retired workers, 5,200 disabled workers, 2,400 wife or widow beneficiaries, and 1,400 Medicare recipients not receiving Social Security. Collected information on demographic characteristics, marital and childbearing history, employment history, current income and assets, and health.

Second interview (NBF) of survivors and spouses of decedents conducted in 1991. Collected information on economic circumstances, health, family contacts, post-retirement employment, and changes in life circumstances that might explain changes in economic status (e.g., death of a spouse, episode of hospitalization, change in residence). Disabled worker beneficiaries were asked about efforts to return to work, experiences with rehabilitation services, and knowledge of SSA work incentive provisions.

Data were linked with selected information from SSA, SSI, and Medicare records. Conducted by Temple University for the Social Security Administration. NIA, HCFA, ASPE, AHCPR, and the Office of the Assistant Secretary for Health also contributed funding support.

*Retirement History Survey (RHS)* Completed (U.S. Social Security Administration, no date; see also Rust, 1993): Panel survey of people aged 58-63 at the time of the original interview, including men and women with no husband in the household (considerable information was also collected for wives and widows of male sample members). Obtained information on respondent's work experience, retirement and retirement plans, family composition and support patterns, expenditures, social and leisure activities (in most interviews), health status, health care utilization, health care expenditures, migration, assets and debts (except in 1973, which had a shortened interview), income sources and amounts, spouse's work experience, labor force participation and financial experience of recent widows.

Data were linked with SSA earnings and benefits records. First interview in 1969; sample of 11,150 people selected from the Current Population Survey and followed every 2 years until 1979 when they were aged 68-73. Conducted by the Census Bureau for the Social Security Administration.

## OTHER PANEL SURVEYS OF FAMILIES AND HOUSEHOLDS

*National Survey of Families and Households (NSFH)* Completed (Sweet and Bumpass, 1996): Interviewed a sample of 13,000 families in 1987-1988, including an oversample of minorities and households containing single-parent families, stepfamilies, recently married couples, and cohabiting couples. In each household, a randomly selected adult was interviewed; also, a shorter, self-administered questionnaire was completed by the spouse or cohabiting partner of the primary respondent. Collected information on detailed household composition, family background, adult family transitions, couple interactions, parent-child interactions, education and work, economic and psychological well-being, and family attitudes.

The original sample was reinterviewed in 1992-1994. Personal interviews were conducted of primary respondents and their spouse or cohabiting partner. Telephone interviews were conducted with children and a randomly selected parent of the main respondent; proxy interviews were obtained with the spouse or other relative of a deceased or seriously ill original respondent. Collected information on life history since the original interview, health and well-being, family process, kinship, social support and interhousehold exchanges, and current labor force involvement, income sources, assets, and debts.

Conducted by Temple University for the University of Wisconsin under a grant from NIA and NICHD.

*Panel Study of Income Dynamics (PSID)* Ongoing (Duncan and Hill, 1991; Hill, 1992): Follows a sample of families on an annual basis (beginning in 1997, the survey will be biennial). Collects the most detailed information about family heads and, since the late 1970s, about wives and cohabitors. The core content includes demographic characteristics; current employment and employment history in past year; annual income by type for the head (most detail), and other family members; in-kind public assistance; estimate of federal taxes paid; housing value, mortgage and property taxes, or rent; average weekly expenditures on food; financial assistance to people living elsewhere; housework time; geographic mobility; socioeconomic background; health; religion; military service; county labor market conditions. Supplements asked occasionally have covered a wide range of topics, such as disability and illness, extended family and kinship ties, fringe benefits, inheritances, retirement plans and experiences, retrospective histories, and wealth. In 1990, there were some links to Medicare records.

The current sample size is 9,200 families, including original sample families who were first interviewed in 1968, new families formed from them (e.g., by adult children), and a sample of Hispanic families added in 1990. A sample of immigrant families will be added in 1997. Conducted by the University of Michigan with funding from NSF and other agencies.

*Survey of Income and Program Participation (SIPP)* Ongoing (Citro and Kalton, 1993; Jabine, King, and Petroni, 1990): Repeated panel survey of samples of families interviewed at 4-month intervals. The core content includes demographic characteristics; monthly information on labor force participation, job characteristics, and earnings for each person age 15 or older; monthly information on public and private health insurance coverage; and monthly (or 4-month) information on detailed sources and amounts of income from about 65 sources of cash income and seven in-kind programs for each person age 15 or older. Topical modules asked once or twice in each panel cover annual income and taxes; educational financing and enrollment; eligibility for selected programs (including expenditures on shelter, out-of-pocket medical care costs, and dependent care); employee benefits (1984 panel only); housing costs and finance; individual retirement accounts; personal history; retirement expectations and pension plan coverage; financial and property assets and liabilities. A topical module with variable content in each panel responds to needs of policy analysis agencies. Topics covered to date include characteristics of job from which retired; child care; child support; functional activities; health status and use of health care; home health care; long-term care; and others. The 1984, 1990, and 1991 panels were exactly matched with Social Security earnings and benefit records for the use of SSA analysts; other panels have been exactly matched with IRS earnings data for evaluation of data quality within the Census Bureau.

From 1983-1993, the survey followed samples of adults for 32 months; a new panel was introduced each February with an initial sample size of from 12,500 to 23,600 families. Under a redesign introduced in 1996, the survey is following a sample of adults and children in about 37,000 families for 48 months; a new panel will be introduced every 4 years. The 1992 and 1993 panels will continue to be followed at annual intervals from 1997-2002 in the Survey of Program Dynamics (SPD), which was mandated by the Personal Responsibility and Work Opportunity Act of 1996. The SPD will focus on gathering information with which to monitor and evaluate the effects of changes in social welfare programs on families with children. Conducted by the Census Bureau.

## REPEATED CROSS-SECTIONAL SURVEYS OF HOUSEHOLDS

***Consumer Expenditure Survey (CEX)*** Ongoing (Jacobs and Shipp, 1990): Interview Survey component interviews 5,000 consumer units each quarter. Household addresses remain in sample for 5 quarters.[1] Collects demographic characteristics; work experience of consumer unit members aged 14; detailed quarterly information for expenditure categories that comprise an estimated 60-70 percent of total expenditures; global or usual quarterly expenditures for categories that comprise an additional estimated 20-25 percent of total expenditures; previous 12 months' expenditures for some items; inventory of real assets at initial interview and changes in ownership and mortgages each quarter; financial assets and

---

[1]Surveys like the CEX and CPS have a panel component in that sample units are interviewed more than once. However, the sample units are addresses, not household members. Whoever is residing at the address is interviewed; people who move are not followed.

changes in them over past 12 months at 5th interview; income in prior 12 months at 2nd and 5th interviews; taxes at 2nd and 5th interviews.

Diary Survey component obtains 2-week expenditure diaries from 6,000 consumer units spread out over the year. Interview and Diary information are combined to form estimates of total expenditures. Conducted by the Census Bureau for BLS.

**Current Population Survey (CPS)** Ongoing (Bureau of the Census, 1996; Pension and Welfare Benefits Administration, 1994, 1995b): Interviews 60,000 households each month about previous month's labor force participation, job characteristics, and demographic characteristics (the sample was recently cut to 50,000). Household addresses remain in the sample for 4 months in one year and the same 4 months a second year. The March income supplement also includes military in civilian housing and an additional sample of 2,500 housing units that had contained at least one adult of Hispanic origin as of the preceding November interview.

The March income supplement collects information on labor force participation and job history in the prior calendar year for each person aged 15 or older; annual income for the prior calendar year for each person aged 15 or older by source (about 30 types of regular cash income); participation in noncash benefit programs; health insurance coverage. The March 1973 and March 1978 CPS files were exactly matched with Social Security earnings records and made publicly available. Later March CPS files have on occasion been matched with IRS earnings records for evaluation of data quality within the Census Bureau.

The April (or May) employee benefits supplement (administered in 1972 and every 5 years beginning in 1979) collects information for workers about employer-provided pension and health care plan coverage; reasons for pension noncoverage for workers in companies with plans; years of service with employer; size of employer; annual earnings and family income; whether covered by union contract; type of pension plan; self-reported vested status; percent of pay contributed to 401(k)-type plan; percentage of employer match; whether ever received, amount, and uses of lump-sum payments; whether and amount contributed last year to IRA; whether self and/or family covered by employer health plan, spouse's employer plan, or other plan; for experienced unemployed workers aged 25-64, whether covered by former employer's health plan; for covered workers aged 46 and over, expectations about availability of health care coverage after retirement. (This supplement may be discontinued in favor of using the pension and health care plan coverage information in SIPP.)

The September 1994 supplement collected information on pension benefits received by retirees and health care insurance coverage of retirees. It asked detailed questions of people aged 40 and over about receipt and amounts of pension annuity and lump-sum benefits based on former employment and about continuation of employment-based health insurance coverage during retirement.

The supplement updated information collected in December 1989 on pension benefit amounts and in August 1988 on retiree health insurance coverage.

Conducted by the Census Bureau for BLS; other agencies provide funding for supplements.

***National Medicare Expenditure Survey (NMES); renamed Medical Expenditure Panel Survey (MEPS)*** Ongoing (Hunter and Arnett, 1996): 1987 survey interviewed a sample of 14,000 households, including oversamples of blacks, Hispanics, people aged 65 and older, low-income people, and people with functional limitations. Households were interviewed 5 times between February 1987 and July 1988 about their utilization, expenditures, and sources of payment for all major forms of medical care and demographic and socioeconomic characteristics. Surveys were also conducted of physicians and health care facilities providing care to members of the household sample during the period and of employers and insurance companies responsible for their insurance coverage. The 1987 NMES also included an institutional survey of 13,000 residents of nursing and personal care homes.

Similar surveys were conducted in 1980 and 1977. Beginning in 1996, the survey will be conducted on a continuing basis as a repeated panel survey. Samples of families will be interviewed over 2-year periods, with a new panel introduced every year. The sample will be drawn from households in the National Health Interview Survey. Conducted by Westat, Inc., for AHCPR, HCFA, and NCHS.

***Survey of Consumer Finances (SCF)*** Ongoing (Avery and Elliehausen, 1986; Avery, Elliehausen, and Kennickell, 1987; Kennickell and Shack-Marquez, 1992; Kennickell and Starr-McCluer, 1994; Kennickell and McManus, 1994; see also Curtin, Juster, and Morgan, 1989): First conducted under the current design in 1983 and every 3 years thereafter (predecessor surveys were conducted as early as 1963). Originally included a panel component: the 1986 SCF was a reinterview of the 1983 sample, and the 1989 SCF included a subset of the 1983 sample in addition to a new cross-sectional sample. However, the 1983 survey data were not used because of quality problems, and, for cost reasons, the 1992 and 1995 surveys have not repeated the panel feature of the 1989 survey. Collects comprehensive information on household wealth from a household sample together with a sample of high-income households drawn from Internal Revenue Service files who agree to participate; total sample size is about 3,000-4,000 households. In most years, has obtained descriptions of sample members' pension plans from their employers. The 1983, 1986, and 1989 surveys were conducted by the University of Michigan for the Federal Reserve Board; the 1992 and 1995 surveys were conducted by the National Opinion Research Center for the Federal Reserve Board.

## DATA SOURCES ON EMPLOYERS AND EMPLOYEES

***Employee Benefits Survey (EBS)***   Ongoing (Bureau of Labor Statistics, 1992a, 1994; see also MacDonald, 1995):   Obtains descriptions of various types of benefits offered to full-time and part-time workers in specified occupations by employers from a sample of about 6,000 nonfarm private sector establishments and state and local governments (mid- and large-size private employers with 100 or more employees are surveyed in one year and small private employers and state and local governments the next year).   Tabulates numbers of workers covered by or participating in various benefits by occupation.   (For private sector employees, the categories are professional, technical, and related; clerical and sales; production and service.   For public employees, the categories are regular employees; teachers; police and firefighters.)   No tabulations are provided by number of employees, and tabulations by employer characteristics are very limited (geographic region and 1-digit SIC code).

The EBS began in 1979 with surveys of benefits provided to full-time workers in medium and large establishments (100 or 250 or more employees, depending on the industry), with limited coverage in the service sector.   The 1987 survey examined benefits provided to full-time employees in state and local governments with 50 or more employees; the 1988 and 1989 surveys covered full-time employees in medium and large establishments with 100 or more employees in all industries; the present system began in 1990.   Work is under way to integrate the EBS more fully with the Employment Cost Trends Survey and the Occupational Compensation Survey Program, which obtains compensation data for specific areas.   Conducted by BLS.

***Employment Cost Trends Survey (ECT)***   Ongoing (Bureau of Labor Statistics, 1992b):   Serves as the basis for the Employment Cost Index (ECI), which provides quarterly estimates of changes in wage and benefit costs and annual estimates of the level of wage and benefit costs, developed from samples of establishments and occupations.   The ECT uses the same sample as the EBS.   Conducted by BLS.

***Form 5500 Data System***:   Ongoing (Pension and Welfare Benefits Administration, 1995a):   Private employers are required to file information annually with the IRS about pension and welfare benefit plans.   (Fringe benefit plans are a class of welfare benefit plans that include group legal services, cafeteria plans, and educational assistance.   Other types of welfare benefit plans are medical and dental insurance, life insurance, apprenticeship and training, scholarship funds, severance pay, disability, etc.)   Employers with pension or welfare plans with 100 or more participants must file Form 5500 and relevant schedules; employers with pension or welfare plans with fewer than 100 participants file a shorter Form 5500-C/R; the self-employed with a pension plan that has only one participant or one participant and that participant's spouse file Form 5500EZ. Plans for which forms are *not* to be filed include unfunded and/or uninsured welfare plans with fewer than 100 participants (i.e., plans that are paid for from general assets); unfunded pension or welfare plans whose benefits go only to a select group of management or highly compensated employees; and model simplified pension plans, which include most simplified employee pension (SEP) plans. Also, one-time or special "window" plans are not documented.

Information collected includes type of plan; number of participants (plans with 100 or more participants also report the number of active participants, retired and separated participants entitled to future benefits, beneficiaries of deceased participants, participants who left the employer with less than 100 percent vesting); whether plan ever amended or terminated; total number of employees and those excludable from plan for various reasons; asset amounts by type; liability amounts by type; net assets; income by type; expenses by type; contributions by employers and employees during the year; actuarial assumptions used as basis for plan funding.

DOL/PWBA makes available data files that contain the universe of filers of Forms 5500, 5500-C, and 5500-R, including pension and welfare benefit plan filers. These files have been edited to some extent by the IRS for consistency of financial information and arithmetic errors.

DOL/PWBA also makes available a research database of all pension plans filing Form 5500 and a weighted, 5 percent sample of all pension plans filing Form 5500-C. These data have been further edited to identify such problems as truncation of financial entries by multi-billion dollar plans and incorrect entries for such items as type of plan. Corrections are made on the basis of analysts' judgment and are not verified with the filer. The database contains some recoded variables, including designation of pension plans as primary or supplemental in the case of employers with multiple plans. Researchers have sometimes prepared exact-match files of the Form 5500 pension plan research database with financial information abstracted by Compustat from annual reports filed with the SEC.

A similar research database does not exist for welfare benefit plan filers. DOL/PWBA indicates that inconsistencies in welfare plan reporting severely limit the usefulness of Form 5500 data on these plans for research purposes.

***Longitudinal Research Database (LRD)*** Ongoing (Center for Economic Studies, 1995; Troske, 1995): Contains annual data beginning in 1972 for nearly all large U.S. manufacturing plants from the Annual Survey of Manufactures and data every 5 years for all manufacturing plants from the Census of Manufactures, linked over time to create a panel data set. Includes such information as total value of output, cost of materials, investment, and employment.

LRD data have been exactly matched with data on workers from the 1990 census long form, including demographic characteristics, occupation, and income by type, to form the Worker-Establishment Characteristics Database

(WECD). The WECD contains records for about 200,000 manufacturing workers matched to 16,000 establishments. The match rate varied by worker and plant characteristics; weights have been created to adjust for these differences. Plans are to expand the WECD to all workers, which can be done if the proposed American Community Survey (the equivalent of asking the long-form questions throughout the decade) goes forward. Data for other economic sectors would come from an exact match with the Longitudinal Business Database (LBD) that is under development at the Census Bureau.

Maintained by the Center for Economic Studies at the Census Bureau; accessible only by special arrangement.

*National Employer Health Insurance Survey (NEHIS)* Ongoing (Hing et al., 1995; Hing and Euller, 1996; Hunter and Arnett, 1996; Sommers, Chapman, and Moriarity, 1996): First conducted in April-December 1994 in order to provide needed data for the health care reform policy debate (planning work begun in June 1993; final estimates to be released in early 1997). Will be conducted on an annual basis, beginning in 1997, and coordinated in terms of questionnaire content with the Health Insurance Plans Survey (HIPS) component of MEPS. The ongoing NEHIS sample size will be about 25,000 establishments.

Collects information from employers on whether they provide health insurance now and in last 5 years; employer characteristics, including type of business, number of branches or locations, number of full-time and part-time employees, wage rate distribution of employees, total payroll, spending on health care; eligibility requirements for employee health care coverage (including for retirees); other benefits offered; characteristics of health insurance plans offered (or a subsample in the case of employers with many plans), including type of plan, number of people enrolled (employees, retirees, dependents), whether self-insured, total premiums, benefits paid for claims incurred, administrative costs, employee contributions to premiums, deductibles, coinsurance rates, maximums, waiting period for pre-existing conditions, types of services covered.

The 1994 survey included 39,000 establishments (36,000 private sector, 3,000 public sector). Sample drawn from Dun and Bradstreet file of private establishments, 1992 Census of Governments, and national sample of self-employed individuals from the 1993 NHIS.

1994 NEHIS conducted by Westat for NCHS; ongoing NEHIS conducted by the Census Bureau for AHCPR, HCFA, and NCHS.

# C
# Examples of Retirement-Income-Related Projection Models

This appendix describes examples of three types of retirement income models: microsimulation models, cell-based models, and intergenerational models. It lists the major references for information about the model.

## MICROSIMULATION MODELS

*CORSIM* (Caldwell, 1993; Caldwell et al., 1993; see also LOGISIL, 1994): Dynamic microsimulation model of people and households; projects life histories for people of all ages, year by year; first version developed in 1986-1988 as adaptation of DYNASIM2 (see below); rebuilt in 1989-1993; written in C language; operates on desktop personal computers; being rewritten to also run on parallel-processing supercomputers. Processes modeled include fertility, immigration, mortality; first marriage, remarriage, divorce, custody of children, leaving home, education level; weeks worked and earnings; employment-related transfer income, welfare-related transfer income, pension-related transfer income; Social Security payroll taxes, federal and state income taxes, property taxes, estate taxes; family earned income, family transfer income, family asset income; consumption, savings; home ownership, market value, mortgage debt; ownership of other assets, market value, debt; asset changes from savings, asset changes from appreciation, asset transfers at death, asset transfers at divorce, income from assets; smoking, alcohol, diabetes. Being expanded and enhanced by the Canadian government as DYNACAN; additions include simulation of the Canadian public and private pension systems; enhancements include making it possible to compare a baseline program and a policy alternative in one instead of two runs and more flexibility in specifying output for policy analysis and validation purposes.

*DYNASIM2 (Dynamic Simulation of Income Model)* (Johnson and Zedlewski, 1982; Johnson et al., 1983; Zedlewski, 1990): Dynamic microsimulation model of people and households; projects life histories for people of all ages, year by year; first version completed in 1975; redesigned version completed in the early 1980s with elements of original DYNASIM, the PENSIM model developed by James Schulz to simulate private pension alternatives, and other features for analyzing retirement-income-related policy issues; written in FORTRAN; operates on mainframes and minicomputers; recently rewritten to operate on desktop personal computers. Processes modeled include death, birth, marriage, divorce, disability, leaving home, education level, migration; labor force participation, annual hours of participation, hourly wage, whether unemployed, proportion of labor force hours unemployed; job change, industry, pension coverage, plan participation; pension eligibility, type of plan, benefit formula, plan constants, benefit computation; Social Security retirement benefit eligibility, retirement benefit computation, disability benefit, spouse benefit, children's benefit; participation in Individual Retirement Account (IRA), accumulations, distribution; whether retiring from job, whether accepting new job; Supplemental Security Income (SSI) eligibility, benefits, participation; federal income taxes, Social Security payroll taxes.

*PIMS (Pension Insurance Management System)* (Holmer, 1993): Dynamic and stochastic microsimulation model of private employers with defined benefit pension plans insured by the Pension Benefit Guaranty Corporation (PBGC); written using the object-oriented capabilities of the C++ language; input data on firms (from Compustat) and sponsored plans (from 5500 forms) organized as a relational database; developed to operate on a personal computer platform. Monte Carlo methods are used to characterize uncertainty about the future course of the economy, industries, and individual firms, as well as uncertainty about future asset returns. The PIMS economy module generates future values for each employer of asset-debt ratios, employment, and market-value equity, and then uses the economy and firm variables to compute a bankruptcy probability using a logit equation estimated with pooled corporate data. The plan module simulates changes in age-service matrices of active plan participants, terminated vested participants, and retired participants. The plan module also simulates each firm's annual contributions to sponsored plans, plan benefits, and several measures of plan liabilities. The PBGC module simulates risk-based pension insurance premium income and expenses involved in pension insurance claims resulting from the past and future bankruptcy of firms that sponsor one or more underfunded plans.

*PRISM (Pension and Retirement Income Simulation Model)* (Kennell and Sheils, 1986, 1990; see also Rivlin and Wiener, 1988): Dynamic microsimulation model of people and households; projects life histories for people alive in base year (1979), year by year; developed in 1980 for the President's Commission on Pension Policy; long-term-care module added in 1986; written in FORTRAN; operates on mainframe computers; recently converted to operate on desktop personal computers. Processes modeled include death, birth, marriage, divorce, education level, disability; annual hours of work, hourly wage; job change, industry, pension coverage, pension plan assignment; decision to retire and accept pension, decision to retire and accept Social Security; IRA adoption, contributions; employer pension benefit computation; Social Security retirement benefit eligibility, retirement benefit computation, disability benefit, spouse benefit, children's benefit; IRA distribution; SSI eligibility, benefits, participation; federal and state income tax, Social Security payroll tax. The long-term care module uses the basic PRISM model, with some modifications, to project family structure, employment, income, assets, and private health insurance coverage for the elderly; the module simulates disability status of the elderly, their use of and expenditures for nursing home and home care services, and their accumulation and spending down of assets to gain Medicaid eligibility.

*Treasury Individual Income Tax Simulation Model (OTA Model)* (Cilke et al., 1994): Static microsimulation model of taxpayers and families; written in FORTRAN; operates on minicomputers; includes a two-stage static routine to update and project the database for a total of 10 years (first stage applies growth rates on each dollar amount to reflect actual and projected per capita real growth and inflation; second stage adjusts the weights of family heads to hit aggregate targets for different variables). Models federal and state income tax and Social Security payroll tax liabilities under current law and alternatives, based on samples of individual income tax returns filed with the IRS.

*Wolf et al. Model for Simulating Life Histories of the Elderly [under development]* (Wolf et al., 1995; McNally and Wolf, 1996): Dynamic microsimulation model of people and households being developed with funding from the National Institute on Aging; will initially develop longitudinal histories for people aged 48 and older in 1988; will focus on kinship networks and functional (disability) status; will project total income for each family but will not, at least initially, identify separate sources of income, such as pensions. Progress has been made in creating the synthetic starting population for the simulation runs and in developing a capability to project kinship availability. Progress is also being made in developing multi-equation models of income dynamics, labor market and retirement behavior, and marriage and divorce, with data from the Panel Study of Income Dynamics and a multivariate random-effects specification, and in simulating disability dynamics on the basis of the Grade of Membership (GoM) model developed by Kenneth Manton, Eric Stallard, and others at Duke University.

## CELL-BASED MODELS

*AARP [American Association of Retired Persons] Solvency and Individual Return Model (SIR)* (Cohen and Beedon, 1994a, 1994b): Cell-based model of the Social Security system; develops year-by-year projections for 75-year period. Uses the Social Security Office of the Actuary's intermediate demographic and economic assumptions for simulating the effects of changing the tax or benefit formulas for workers who retire at different times and with high, medium, or low wages over their work life; can also simulate the effects of privatization schemes. Outputs include years for workers to recover contributions, ratio of benefits to contributions, and Old-Age and Survivors Insurance and Disability Insurance (OASDI) trust fund reserves as a percent of outgo.

*Macroeconomic-Demographic Model (MDM)* (Anderson, 1984, 1990a, 1990b): System of large cell-based models linked to a macroeconomic growth model; originally developed in 1979 for the President's Commission on Pension Policy and the National Institute on Aging to address interactions of Social Security and the private pension system; subsequently expanded to simulate the effects of population aging on the health care system. System models pertain to population growth, the labor market, pension benefits, family formation, consumer expenditures, housing demand, health care expenditures, and health care benefits; macroeconomic model includes two goods (investment and consumer goods) and two factor inputs (labor and capital services).

*Schieber and Shoven Model* (Schieber and Shoven, 1993): Cell-based model of the funding status of the private pension system; develops year-by-year projections for 75-year period of assets, benefits, contributions, investment income, net inflow (current and real), and total payroll for defined benefit and defined contribution plans, separately for private employer, state and local, and federal plans. Uses the Social Security Office of the Actuary's projections of the population by age, sex, and work force participation for each year; distributes the work force into private, state and local, and federal employment by tenure and pension participation status; accounts for mortality, job leaving, job entrance, and job change; projects employer and employee contributions using the Social Security Office of the Actuary's assumptions about real wage growth.

*Social Security Actuarial Cost Model* (Board of Trustees [OASDI], 1996): Cell-based set of models of the funding status of the Social Security system; develops year-by-year projections for 75-year period of payroll taxes, investment income, and benefits for retirement, survivors, disability, and other components of the Social Security system. Develops projections of the population by age and sex on the basis of assumptions about fertility, mortality, and net immigration; develops projections of labor force participation for men by 5-year age group and marital status and for women by 5-year age group, marital status, and presence of children; projects earnings and payroll tax contributions on the basis of assumptions about real wage growth; projects benefits on the basis of projected earnings and assumptions about retirement age; projects investment income on the basis of assumptions about interest rates. Projections are usually developed for high-cost, intermediate, and low-cost scenarios.

*SSASIM* (Holmer, 1995a, 1995b): Dynamic and stochastic cell-based model of the Social Security system; written using the object-oriented capabilities of the C++ language; input data on starting values of population and economic variables as well as policy and behavioral assumptions organized as a relational database; developed to operate on a personal computer platform. Monte Carlo methods are used to characterize uncertainty about the future course of thirteen key demographic and economic input variables used in the Social Security actuarial cost model, as well as uncertainty about future asset returns. The model's logical structure is similar to that of the Social Security actuarial cost model except that numerous economic feedback effects are modeled and that program-related risks are explicitly represented using Monte Carlo methods. Operating in a non-stochastic mode, SSASIM can replicate each of the three scenarios presented in the Trustees Report. The original development of SSASIM was sponsored by the 1994-95 Social Security Advisory Council to support the evaluation of alternative asset allocation policies for the trust fund; subsequent model enhancements, which will permit evaluation of individual account reform proposals, are being sponsored by the Employee Benefit Research Institute.

## INTERGENERATIONAL MODELS

*Aaron, Bosworth, and Burtless Model* (Aaron et al., 1989): Computable general equilibrium model in which labor supply and private saving patterns are based on observed profiles and are assumed to be exogenous. Future labor supply patterns are based on the demographic projections of the Social Security Office of the Actuary. Capital accumulation is derived from the identity that relates saving and investment; an assumed production function determines the relative returns to capital and labor. Model incorporates a detailed characterization of the U.S. Social Security system, which it was developed to analyze.

*Auerbach and Kotlikoff Model* (Auerbach and Kotlikoff, 1987; Auerbach, Kotlikoff, and Skinner, 1983; Auerbach et al., 1989): Computable general equilibrium model with three sectors: household (with 75 overlapping 1-year generations), production, and government. For each sector a system of nonlinear equations relates endogenous behavioral variables (e.g., consumption or labor supply) to predetermined economic variables and taste and technological parameters. Individual model components are fairly simple, but the interactions are complex. By solving for the economy's general equilibrium transition path, the model simulates the major feedback effects between policy and demographic changes and changes in the time paths of wages, interest rates, labor supply, and the capital stock.

Model has been used to address such issues as how much Social Security contribution rates must be increased to maintain current benefit levels; effects on national saving rates and real wages of changing population age structure; effects on international capital flows of changes in saving rates and real wages; effects on overall well-being of people in different generations of economic changes associated with demographic transition; effects on economic performance and generational welfare of reductions in Social Security benefits.

Differs from the Aaron, Bosworth, and Burtless model in modeling household saving and labor supply behavior as endogenous, based on an optimizing life-cycle model and the assumption of perfect foresight.

***Imrohoroglu, Huang, and Sargent Model*** (Imrohoroglu, Huang, and Sargent, 1994): Computable general equilibrium model; assumes households want to smooth consumption and insure against lifetime uncertainty but have access to restricted set of assets and risk-sharing arrangements; assumes households are identical when first formed but that luck makes their wealth and consumption diverge as they age; specifies preferences, technologies, information and demographic structures, and government policies in ways that permit rapid computation of decision rules; models the effects of transitions between Social Security policies (e.g., from an unfunded system to a fully funded system).

Differs from the Auerbach and Kotlikoff model in allowing households to face uncertainty about preferences, income, and life-span.

APPENDIX
# D

# Major Aspects of DYNASIM2 and PRISM

DYNASIM2 and PRISM are dynamic microsimulation models that have been used to analyze a range of retirement-income-related policy proposals.[1] The two models are much broader than the cell-based Social Security actuarial cost model (see Appendix C): they simulate not only Social Security taxes and benefits, but also employer pension and Individual Retirement Account (IRA) contributions and benefits, Supplemental Security Income (SSI) eligibility and benefits, and federal income taxes. PRISM has a long-term care financing module that simulates long-term care utilization and financing for the elderly. The two models take some account of asset income (e.g., dividends and savings interest) but do not simulate wealth.[2]

Because they use dynamic microsimulation techniques, both DYNASIM2 and PRISM are able to provide highly disaggregated outputs for each year of a projection period (e.g., for population groups categorized by level of earnings and employment status). They can simulate complex policy provisions and interactions. For example, for Social Security, they have been used to simulate options that the cell-based Social Security actuarial cost model could not handle (e.g., provisions to credit homemaker spouses with a share of the employed spouse's earnings).

Both models can be obtained by others and are documented to some extent.

---

[1]DYNASIM2 has been used for other types of policy analysis as well, such as the effects on welfare program costs of alternative rates of teenage childbearing.

[2]The PRISM long-term care financing module does treat assets to some extent.

The documentation for DYNASIM2 is more complete than that for PRISM. (For DYNASIM2, see Johnson and Zedlewski, 1982; Johnson, Wertheimer, and Zedlewski, 1983; Zedlewski, 1990; for PRISM, see Kennell and Sheils, 1986, 1990; Rivlin and Wiener, 1988.) The accessibility of the models in practice is limited: they were designed well over a decade ago for mainframe (or minicomputer), batch-oriented computing environments, and they lack user-friendly design features. However, both models were recently moved to a personal computing platform (the PRISM long-term care financing submodel has operated for some years on personal computers). They have had relatively little formal validation, although some older validation studies for DYNASIM2 are available (e.g., Haveman and Lacker, 1984; Hendricks and Holden, 1976; Wertheimer et al., 1986).

DYNASIM2 and PRISM illustrate the power and richness of the microsimulation approach to policy projections. They also illustrate the limitations of existing models for addressing many current retirement-income-related policy issues. Their limitations are partly a function of their design, which was optimized for an older generation of computing technology. Even with a newer design, however, the lack of key data and behavioral parameters for such important elements as savings decisions of individuals and benefit offering decisions of employers would limit their utility. As we note throughout this report, significant improvements in microsimulation modeling capabilities require improvements in data and research knowledge.

This appendix briefly reviews how DYNASIM2 and PRISM work (drawing on Ross, 1991) and comments on key limitations involving their ability to simulate behavioral responses to policy changes and to simulate the effects on workers and retirees of employer benefit and labor demand decisions (drawing on Burtless, 1989; Ross, 1991; and a review of the pension simulation components of the two models by panel member Olivia Mitchell).

## HOW THE MODELS WORK

Both DYNASIM2 and PRISM take an initial database and age the records forward for every year by means of a dynamic approach. These starting databases are exact-match files that contain records for the members of households from the Current Population Survey (CPS) March income supplement matched with their personal earnings histories from Social Security Administration (SSA) administrative records. For DYNASIM2, the starting database is the March 1973 CPS-SSA exact-match file. For PRISM, the starting database is the March 1978 CPS-SSA exact-match file, which, in turn, is matched with the March 1979 CPS and the May 1979 CPS pension supplement.[3] The earnings histories in these files are

---

[3]Because there is only partial overlap between the March 1978, March 1979, and May 1979 CPS samples, the PRISM database has considerably fewer records than the DYNASIM2 database.

essential for computing Social Security payroll contributions and benefit entitlements; they are also useful for simulating employer pension contributions and benefits.

Then, for every year after the base year, DYNASIM2 and PRISM age the characteristics of the records in the file; they not only age each person by 1 year, but also, on the basis of probabilities, simulate whether or not each person will go to school, marry, have a child, divorce, die, change employment status, change jobs, participate in a pension plan, retire, and so on. Both models use outside aggregates, such as the Social Security Office of the Actuary's population projections, to control the simulation results for each projected year.

The essence of the models is the creation of longitudinal histories for each person in the original cross-sectional database. These histories are created in DYNASIM2 and PRISM by a set of modules that simulate each event in the following sequence: death, birth, marriage, divorce, labor force participation, unemployment. Starting with the first year, the modules run in turn for each individual. Then year two is simulated, starting with the first individual, from death through unemployment, and ending with the last individual. After the longitudinal histories are created, policy simulations (e.g., of tax liabilities) are run on the records.

Given this sequence of events, demographic events can influence labor force events occurring in the same year (and demographic events occurring earlier in the sequence can affect those simulated later in the sequence), while events happening later in the sequence affect events in the following year. Events or characteristics that are simulated after the longitudinal histories are created are affected by those histories (e.g., SSI or Social Security benefits), but they cannot affect the sequence of demographic and labor force events. Therefore, the decision to include certain events in the simulation of longitudinal histories is an important one. Table D-1 lists the events included in the simulation of longitudinal histories and the events that are simulated using the synthetic histories for the two models. Tables D-2 and D-3 provide additional information on the determinants of major events simulated by DYNASIM2 and PRISM, respectively.

Originally, both DYNASIM2 and PRISM modeled birth, death, marriage, divorce, disability, and labor force events, and DYNASIM2 also modeled education, migration, and leaving home. The objective in developing DYNASIM2 was to be able to simulate a range of demographic and economic events for many different policy purposes. Thus, for example, the model simulates the education of children and young adults, including those born during the simulation and added to the file, because a labor force simulation might find these children as prime-age workers and a simulation with a very long time horizon might find these children as retirees. PRISM, in contrast, was designed to simulate incomes and long-term care utilization of the elderly through the year 2025. Given this time horizon, the model originally did not attempt to simulate life histories for people who were younger than age 20 in the base year (1979) or for those who

TABLE D-1  Basic Features of DYNASIM2 and PRISM

| Feature | DYNASIM2 | PRISM |
|---|---|---|
| Input Data | Exact match of March 1973 CPS and Social Security earnings records | Exact match of March 1978 CPS and Social Security earnings records; also matched with March and May 1979 CPS |
| | | Retirement Plan Provisions database[a] |
| Simulation Base Year | 1972 | 1979 |
| Information in Simulation Database | | |
| Demographic | 1973 | 1978-1979 |
| Income | 1972 | 1977-1978 |
| Employment | 1972-1973 | 1977-1979 |
| Quarters of Social Security Coverage | 1937-1972 | 1937-1977 |
| Social Security Taxable Earnings | 1951-1972 | 1951-1977 |
| Pension Characteristics | | 1979 |
| Events Simulated to Create Longitudinal Histories | | |
| Demographic | Death Birth Marriage Divorce Disability Education level Leaving home Migration | Death Birth Marriage Divorce Disability Education level |
| Labor Force | Participation Annual hours of participation Hourly wage Whether unemployed Proportion of labor force hours unemployed | Annual hours of work Hourly wage |
| Job and Pension Characteristics | | Job change Industry Pension coverage Pension plan assignment |

## TABLE D-1  Continued

| Feature | DYNASIM2 | PRISM |
|---|---|---|
| Retirement and Benefit Acceptance | | Pension acceptance<br>Social Security acceptance |
| Individual Retirement Account (IRA) | | Adoption<br>Contributions |
| Simulations Based on Longitudinal Histories | | |
| Job and Pension Characteristics | Job change<br>Industry<br>Pension coverage<br>Plan participation | |
| Employer Pension | Pension eligibility<br>Type of plan<br>Benefit formula<br>Plan constants<br>Benefit computation | Benefit computation |
| Social Security | Retirement benefit<br> eligibility<br>Retirement benefit<br> computation<br>Disability benefit<br>Spouse benefit<br>Children's benefit | Retirement benefit<br> eligibility<br>Retirement benefit<br> computation<br>Disability benefit<br>Spouse benefit<br>Children's benefit |
| Individual Retirement Account (IRA) | Participation<br>Accumulations<br>Distribution | Distribution |
| Retirement | Whether leave job<br>Whether accept new job | |
| Supplemental Security Income | Eligibility<br>Benefits<br>Participation | Eligibility<br>Benefits<br>Participation |
| Taxes | Federal income tax<br>Social Security payroll tax | Federal income tax<br>Social Security payroll tax<br>State income tax |

aDeveloped by the original contractor for PRISM, ICF Incorporated.

NOTE:  Table does not include the PRISM Long-Term Care Financing Model.

SOURCE:  Ross (1991:Table 1).  The data for DYNASIM2 come from Johnson, Wertheimer, and Zedlewski (1983) and Johnson and Zedlewski (1982); the data for PRISM come from Kennell and Sheils (1986).

TABLE D-2  Determinants of Major Events Simulated by DYNASIM2

| Event or Characteristic | Variables Used to Determine Event |
| --- | --- |
| *Simulation of Longitudinal Histories* | |

Demographic Event
Death

| | |
| --- | --- |
|   Married Women 45-64 | Age, race, sex, marital status, education, number of children |
|   All Others | Age, race, sex, marital status, education |
| Birth | Age, marital status, number of children, race, education |
|   Multiple Birth | Race |
|   Sex of Newborn | Race |

Marriage

| | |
| --- | --- |
|   Age 18-29 | Age, race, sex, previous marital status, income, education, region, weeks worked, hourly wage, asset income, welfare, unemployment compensation |
|   Other Ages or Ever Married | Age, race, sex, previous marital status |
| Mate Matching | Difference in age, difference in education |
| Leaving Home[a] | Age, race, sex |
| Divorce | Distribution over time of expected divorces for this marriage cohort, age at marriage, education, previous marital status, presence of young children, weeks worked, wages |
| Education | Race, sex, age, years at current school level, parents' education |
| Mobility | Number of years married, size of family, age and sex of head, education of head, race, region, size of metropolitan statistical area (MSA) |

Disability

| | |
| --- | --- |
|   Onset | Age, race, sex, marital status |
|   Recovery | Age, race, sex, marital status, education |

Labor Force Events

| | |
| --- | --- |
|   Labor Force Participation | Age, race, sex, education, South, disability, marital status, student, children, spouse earnings |
|   Hours in the Labor Force | Age, transfer income, expected wage, disability, marital status, children |

TABLE D-2  Continued

| Event or Characteristic | Variables Used to Determine Event |
| --- | --- |
| Wage Rate | Race, sex, age, South, disability, marital status, education, student |
| Unemployment | Age, sex, race, education, marital status, South, disability, children |

Simulation of Jobs, Pensions, and Retirement,
Using Longitudinal Histories

| | |
| --- | --- |
| Job Characteristics and Pension Plans | |
| Job Change | Age, sex, tenure on current job, industry |
| Industry of New Job | Sex, education, previous industry |
| Pension Coverage on New Job | Sex, industry, earnings level |
| Pension Plan Participation | Age, tenure on job, full- or part-time status, sex |
| Type of Pension Coverage | Industry |
| Pension Eligibility and Benefits | |
| Retirement Eligibility | Age, industry, years of service, type of pension |
| Vesting | Industry |
| Benefit Formula | Industry and type of pension coverage |
| Benefit Plan Constants | Benefit formula, industry, type of pension coverage |
| Individual Retirement Accounts | |
| Plan Participation | Sex, earnings |
| Retirement[b] | |
| Probability of Leaving Job | Age, sex, disability, marital status, pension eligibility and amounts, Social Security eligibility and amounts, wage, earnings |
| Probability of Taking New Job | Age, disability, marital status, pension eligibility and amounts, Social Security eligibility and amounts, imputed wage |

[a]Leaving home for reasons other than marriage, birth of a child, divorce, or death.

[b]The retirement module's choice of retirement age for an individual overrides whatever pattern of labor force participation may have been modeled earlier in the simulation of the individual's longitudinal history.

SOURCE: Ross (1991:Table 2). The data come from Johnson, Wertheimer, and Zedlewski (1983) and Johnson and Zedlewski (1982).

TABLE D-3  Determinants of Major Events Simulated by PRISM

| Event or Characteristic | Variables Used to Determine Event |
|---|---|
| Simulation of Longitudinal Histories | |
| Demographic Events | |
| Death | Disability status, age, sex, years of disability |
| Disability | |
| Onset | Age, sex |
| Recovery | Age, sex, years of disability |
| Divorce | Age of husband and wife |
| Marriage | Age, sex, previous marital status |
| Mate Matching | Age of male, age of female |
| Birth | Marital status, age, number of children, employment status last year |
| Labor Force Events | |
| Hours Worked per Year | Hours last year, age, sex, marital status, education, composite of hours in previous 3 years, female with young children, female divorced or widowed this year, receiving pension or Social Security income |
| Wage Rate | Age, sex, whether changed job this year, whether unemployed this year |
| Job Change | Hours worked, age, years on job |
| Industry | Age, education, previous industry, full- or part-time status |
| Pension Characteristics | |
| Pension Coverage | Age, industry, full- or part-time status, wage rate |
| Pension Plan Assignment | Industry, multi- or single employer plan in 1979, hourly or salaried status |
| Retirement | |
| Pension Acceptance | Age, sex (conditional on eligibility) |
| Social Security Acceptance | Age, sex (conditional on eligibility) |
| Individual Retirement Accounts | |
| Adoption | Age, family earnings, pension coverage |
| Contributions | Sex, marital status, family earnings |

SOURCE: Ross (1991:Table 3). The data come from Kennell and Sheils (1986).

were born during the simulations. In 1993, PRISM was modified to simulate educational attainment and life histories for all people alive in the base year.

## PENSION COMPONENTS

### DYNASIM2

DYNASIM was designed in the 1970s and updated to DYNASIM2 in the early 1980s as a microdemographic model focused primarily on family formation and dissolution and active worker employment, and only secondarily on retirement. DYNASIM2's labor market segment is contained in the Family and Earnings History Model. It is a recursive system in which demographic characteristics are first simulated for each person for each year. The last of these is a disability probability, which is determined as a function of age, race, sex, marital status, and education. Disability status, in turn, is then used to determine earnings and labor force participation. Earnings, labor force participation, disability, and hours variables are determined for all years of the simulation before pension accruals or benefits (or taxes) are determined and before retirement outcomes are set.

The Jobs and Benefits History segment of DYNASIM2 takes as input the results from the first-stage simulation just described and inputs several additional outcomes, including retirement age, Social Security and SSI benefits (if entitled), IRA account accumulations, and job history variables. People are also given a pension coverage probability, which depends on sex, industry, and earnings level; if covered, a plan participation outcome is determined, which depends on age, tenure, sex, and full- or part-time status. These participation and coverage probabilities are taken from 1979 CPS data. People assigned positive pension participation are then assigned one of four pension plan types based solely on industry of employment: single-employer defined benefit, single-employer defined contribution, multi-employer defined benefit, or multi-employer defined contribution. There appears to be no provision for a worker to have more than one pension plan from a given employer, although multiple plans have become quite widespread in recent years.

The actual determination of pension benefits is done in an Employer Pension Module subroutine attached to the Jobs and Benefits History segment of DYNASIM2. This module is used whenever a termination benefit must be computed for a covered vested worker or when a worker is simulated to retire in order to evaluate retirement benefits. The kernel of the Employer Pension Module is that it determines the parameters of each worker's pension plan, including the early, normal, and special early retirement ages, probability of full vesting after 10 years of service, defined benefit formula type, and specified constant terms within the defined benefit formula. Maximum service and minimum benefit amounts are also set.

Each of these parameters is assigned on a randomized basis. Factors used to assign the parameters are age, years of service, and industry, drawing from a number of different data sets where available. Pension eligibility requirements for normal and early retirement are based on a 1974 defined benefit plan database of the Bureau of Labor Statistics (BLS). Vesting assignments are determined solely on the basis of industry, using a 1976 data set. Benefit formulas for defined benefit plan participants are assigned annual contribution rates of 7 percent and a nominal rate of interest on their account balances of 7 percent. There are some arbitrary assumptions in the Employer Pension Module. For example, the documentation notes that pre-retirement survivor protection probabilities are arbitrarily set at .02, and the probability of joint and survivor benefits at .75 for men and .25 for women.

Pensions are also considered in the Retirement Model. Once the simulated worker is old enough, the probability of leaving a job and taking a new one is computed as a function of age, sex, disability, earnings, pension and Social Security wealth, and changes in pension and Social Security wealth if retirement is delayed a year. This model differs dramatically from the other job change models in DYNASIM2 in that many more economic variables are allowed to enter on the right-hand side as explanatory factors. One problem with this model is that the pension and Social Security wealth terms assume that people die with certainty at age 85, rather than using a more actuarially correct declining survival table.

DYNASIM2 is a useful model for many policy purposes, but it is limited in a number of ways for retirement income policy analysis in the 1990s and beyond. Although DYNASIM2 could be useful in a partial equilibrium simulation of some retirement income policies, such as the effects of Social Security benefit changes on retirement behavior, doing so requires the assumption that nothing else changes—a questionable assumption for many policy scenarios. Thus, for instance, simulation of changes in payroll taxes would have to assume no labor demand response, since no employer behavior is included in the model. Changes in the taxability of retirement income could be simulated, but the structure of the model would not permit these tax changes to influence earnings, labor supply, or retirement.

Although the model can be used to examine how exogenous changes in pension benefit parameters might influence retirement, it cannot do a good job of examining the effects of changes in nondiscrimination laws or the pension tax treatment of employer contributions, since employers' decisions about pension offerings and the consequences for employees are not included. Similarly, it cannot be used to examine the effect of mandated pensions, since no demand-side behavior is built in—there is no provision for job losses that might result or for depressed earnings. DYNASIM2 is primarily a labor supply model, and thus no labor demand consequences can be examined regarding effects of changes in payroll taxes, effects of privatizing a piece of Social Security, etc. Finally, since only a few "hypothetical" pension plans are included in the model and their parameters are not constrained to be internally consistent with each other or for the employees they cover, there is not much room for estimating how changes in specific rules (e.g., nondiscrimination rules) would affect employees through the effects on employers' compensation decisions or their willingness to offer pensions at all.

## PRISM

PRISM is a microdemographic model designed in the early 1980s to simulate retirement income from public and private sources. The model simulates earnings, employment, retirement, and benefits from employer pensions, Social Security, and SSI. It also generates retiree health care coverage outcomes. It does not model asset accumulation or savings in general, though it does have an IRA savings segment. The PRISM model was augmented in the mid-1980s to include a long-term-care financing module. This module assigns asset portfolios to people when they reach age 65 and then in each year of the projection makes a simple adjustment of housing asset values by an assumed inflation rate and of nonhousing asset values by an assumed constant rate of dissaving.

The structure of the model is recursive. The people in the starting database are "aged" by using background information on such characteristics as earnings histories, pension coverage, and employment. The paths of demographic outcomes are determined first, which in turn feed into the labor force segment. Labor supply outcomes (hours of work, job and industry assignment, pension coverage, date of pension benefit acceptance) are determined next, as a function of such exogenously specified factors as pension plan provisions. Wage growth is also determined at this step, independently of benefit accruals and taxes. (Disability, job change, and entry to the labor force do not depend on benefits or pay.) Next, retiree income levels are specified, including Social Security and pension benefits, using as input the labor force outcomes. Finally, long-term-care outcomes are simulated.

The PRISM pension module includes more than 400 different pension plans in comparison to a handful of generic types in DYNASIM2. Pension coverage is determined in the labor force module. Pension plan coverage is allocated on the basis of 1979 and 1983 CPS coverage rates, assigned as a function of industry, age, wage, and full- or part-time status. Plan type is assigned on the basis of very tight assignment criteria: industry, firm size, Social Security coverage, union, multi- or single-employer status, and hourly or salary status. The model also accounts for the person's 1979 CPS pension plan type, vesting, contributions, and participation in a supplemental plan as a way to benchmark starting values. Retirement benefits depend on pension benefit formulas, cost-of-living adjustments, and pre- as well as postretirement survivors' options. The probability of accepting pension benefits depends on sex and age, but not on benefit amounts. The probability of participating in a savings or thrift plan depends on wages and employer contributions, and employee contributions are always assumed to be the maximum allowed by the plan. A probability distribution estimated from CPS data is used to determine whether a lump-sum distribution is rolled over. (Most small distributions are not rolled over in the model.) All defined contribution accounts are assumed to be annuitized at the individual annuity rate rather than the group annuity rate. Workers are assumed to receive benefits when they retire from all vested defined benefit plans from all prior jobs (although retirees must actually apply for deferred vested benefits from jobs they left before retirement, and some proportion may not do so).

Many pension parameters are drawn from a Retirement Plan Provisions database. Information on a total of 475 plans was collected for 325 plan sponsors, so that in many cases both a primary and a secondary plan was obtained. Private single-employer and multi-employer plans and nonprofit plans came from a stratified random sampling of a 1981 filing of Form 5500 reports. Data for the public employer plans came from a random sample of a 1982 listing of public plans with more than 200 participants. Self-employed plans were also added to the sample, and weights were calculated. The 1981 information was updated in 1983; however, the database does not include 401(k) plans, so, in simulations, savings and thrift plans are assumed to grow to the requisite numbers.

Most pension parameters in the model are taken as fixed numbers, rather than being developed endogenously. Thus, industry pension coverage rates are constraints, and pension plan provisions are assumed not to change over time. Normal, early, and disability retirement formulas are given, as are Social Security integration rules and employer and employee contribution amounts. Employees are assumed to contribute 5 percent of their earnings in profit-sharing plans and to contribute the maximum possible amount to defined contribution plans that require employee money.

The PRISM model is a second-generation approach to what DYNASIM was seeking to accomplish with regard to pension policy simulation. It is still limited, however, for today's pension and retirement income policy needs. One strength of the model is its richness of detail on pensions, both private and public. The Retirement Plan Provisions database with its several hundred pension plans, including their lengthy vector of plan parameters, builds into this model a more realistic degree of cross-sectional variability than the DYNASIM2 format. However, the database has not been updated since 1983, and it is essentially static. Presumably, the sample weights could be altered to allow for changes in the distribution of types of employers and type of plans, but there is no provision for interaction between labor supply and labor demand behavior that could alter the distribution of plan offerings. Also, there is no feedback of pension plan provisions and changes in them to workers' labor supply decisions or wage growth.

## LIMITATIONS

Both DYNASIM2 and PRISM are limited by the old age of their starting databases. Neither model has switched to a newer initial database because in the face of confidentiality concerns and resource constraints, government agencies have not been willing to prepare new exact-match files, although this situation may be changing (see discussion in Chapter 4). The consequence is that both models must simulate more and more years of historical data before they can begin projecting into the future. Aggregate information, such as employment rates and total payroll contributions, can keep the simulations in line with actual historical experience for a handful of key variables for years up to the present, but there is no way to ensure that the models accurately reflect the interrelationships among all of the important variables for those years.

In addition, the models have not been revised to incorporate newer research findings about the underlying behaviors. Many of the key transition probabilities—for example, estimates of labor force participation and retirement—are based on old analytical studies (e.g., in DYNASIM2, on the 1969-1979 Retirement History Survey and early years of the Panel Study of Income Dynamics) and use overly simplistic functional forms. As an example, the labor force simulation in PRISM is based on a simple Markov probability model of transitions between categories of hours of work estimated from matched files of the March 1978 and 1979 CPS. This functional form, over time, will not preserve the characteristics of the distribution of hours worked in the population. Such a formulation captures limited information about previous work patterns, so that it will not properly project the work choices of individuals at the extremes of the distribution—people who rarely or always worked.

With regard to employer-provided pensions, the models do not incorporate more recent knowledge about trends in pension plan coverage, such as the growth in defined contribution plans. Similarly, neither model reflects well the trend toward increasing heterogeneity of labor force behavior, in which an individual may "retire" from a succession of jobs. Also, many pension-related assumptions in both models allow little or no variation over time or across workers: for example, assuming fixed contribution rates for defined benefit plans, that employees always contribute the maximum to defined contribution plans, or that workers receive all of the benefits from defined benefit plans from all prior jobs that the model's pension rules say they are entitled to when they retire.

A reason that neither model has been revised to update key transition probabilities or to incorporate more appropriate functional forms that reflect newer understanding of behavior has to do with the cost and time constraints imposed by their mainframe-oriented design. Because the models are not easy to modify, it is not in the modelers' interest to invest in redesign until substantial funding is available and there are clear research findings about appropriate functional forms and parameter estimates. In addition, since the 1983 Social Security amendments, there has been relatively little demand for retirement-income-related modeling until now. Moreover, the decade of the 1980s saw important changes in labor markets and employee benefits that have made it difficult to determine the best professional judgment about key parameters to incorporate in models.

Another limitation of the models is their lack of a ready capability to estimate the feedback effects of policy changes on behavior, also because of their design. That design separates the construction of longitudinal year-by-year demographic and economic "histories" for each person in the database from policy simulations as such. Because creating longitudinal histories was expensive on a mainframe, the practice has been to generate one set of histories (or a few sets under different reasonable assumptions) and then run a large number of program simulations on that longitudinal file. As noted above, events or characteristics that are simulated after the creation of the longitudinal histories are affected by those histories but cannot in turn affect the sequence of demographic and labor force events. For example, in both models, changes in the Social Security system cannot lead to compensating changes in labor supply over an individual's work life unless the longitudinal histories are re-created with a new set of labor supply equations incorporating the expected response. Although it would be possible for other models to simulate the second-round effects of policy changes that are initially simulated by DYNASIM2 or PRISM, neither model has a ready capability to link with second-round effects models.

Finally, the models allow very few employee decisions to be endogenously determined by pension or tax parameters. Thus, the pension parameters are treated as exogenous to the simulation, and retirement plans are more or less "dropped" on workers, with few or no consequences for their decisions to take a job, change jobs, retire, save, or consume. Ideally, models to evaluate retirement income policy would take pensions as endogenously determined by interactions between employees and employers, in the context of regulatory and overall economic constraints. Because neither DYNASIM2 and PRISM makes pensions endogenous, these two models do not afford the opportunity to investigate how entire classes of policy changes might affect pension sponsorship and participation, pension accumulation and investments, and, finally, pension decumulation. The broader missing piece is employers' demand for labor, including the trade-offs between benefits and wages and employment as well as pay decisions.

# References

Aaron, Henry J., Barry Bosworth, and Gary Burtless
  1989    *Can America Afford to Grow Old?* Washington, D.C.: The Brookings Institution.
Adler, Gerald S.
  1994    A profile of the Medicare Current Beneficiary Survey. *Health Care Financing Review* Summer:153-163.
1994-95 Advisory Council on Social Security Technical Panel on Assumptions and Methods
  1995    *Final Report.* Population Aging Research Center Working Paper Series. Philadelphia: University of Pennsylvania.
1994-95 Advisory Council on Social Security Technical Panel on Trends and Issues in Retirement Saving
  1995    *Final Report.* Population Aging Research Center Working Paper Series. Philadelphia: University of Pennsylvania.
Anderson, Joseph M.
  1984    *Macroeconomic-Demographic Model.* National Institute on Aging. Washington, D.C.: U.S. Department of Health and Human Services.
  1990a   *Macroeconomic-Demographic Model of Health Care and Consumer Expenditures.* NIH Publication No. 90-2986. National Institute on Aging. Washington, D.C.: U.S. Department of Health and Human Services.
  1990b   Micro-macro linkages in economic models. Pp. 187-220 in Gordon H. Lewis and Richard C. Michel, eds., *Microsimulation Techniques for Tax and Transfer Analysis.* Washington, D.C.: The Urban Institute Press.
  1996    *Retirement Policy Analysis: Models, Data, and Requirements for the Future.* Report prepared for the American Society of Actuaries. Chevy Chase, Md.: Capital Research Associates.
Antoniewicz, Rochelle
  1994    A Comparison of the Household Sector from the Flow of Funds Accounts and the Survey of Consumer Finances. Working Paper. Division of Research and Statistics, Federal Reserve Board, Washington, D.C.

*213*

Auerbach, Alan J., and Laurence J. Kotlikoff
1987    *Dynamic Fiscal Policy.* Cambridge, England: Cambridge University Press.
Auerbach, Alan J., Laurence J. Kotlikoff, Robert P. Hagemann, and Giuseppe Nicoletti
1989    The economic dynamics of an ageing population: The case of four OECD countries. *OECD Economic Studies* 12(Spring):97-130.
Auerbach, Alan J., Laurence J. Kotlikoff, and Jonathan Skinner
1983    The efficiency gains from dynamic tax reform. *International Economic Review* 24(1):81-100.
Avery, Robert B., and Gregory E. Elliehausen
1986    Financial characteristics of high-income families. *Federal Reserve Bulletin* (March):163-177.
Avery, Robert B., Gregory E. Elliehausen, and Arthur B. Kennickell
1987    Changes in consumer installment debt: Evidence from the 1983 and 1986 Surveys of Consumer Finances. *Federal Reserve Bulletin* (October):761-778.
Bajtelsmit, Vickie L.
1996    Corporate performance and pension plan design. Pp. 123-139 in Phyllis A. Fernandez, John A. Turner, and Richard P. Hinz, eds., *Pensions, Savings, and Capital Markets.* Pension and Welfare Benefits Administration. Washington, D.C.: U.S. Department of Labor.
Bandeian, Stephen H., and Lawrence S. Lewin
1994    What we don't know about health care reform. *Issues in Science and Technology* Spring:52-58.
Barringer, Melissa W., and Olivia S. Mitchell
1993    Health insurance choice and the older worker. Pp. 125-140 in Olivia S. Mitchell, ed., *As the Workforce Ages—Costs, and Benefits & Policy Challenges.* Ithaca, NY: ILR Press.
Beller, Daniel J., and Helen H. Lawrence
1990    Trends in private pension plan coverage. Pp. 59-96 in John A. Turner and Daniel J. Beller, eds., *Trends in Pensions 1992.* Pension and Welfare Benefits Administration. Washington, D.C.: U.S. Department of Labor.
Betson, David M., Constance F. Citro, and Robert T. Michael
1997    The Report of the Panel on Poverty and Family Assistance: Summary and Follow-up. Discussion Paper. University of Notre Dame, Indiana.
Bilheimer, Linda, and Robert Reischauer
1996    Confessions of the estimators: What didn't we know and when will we know it? [including discussion by Len Nichols and Jon Sheils]. Pp. 147-165 in Henry J. Aaron, ed., *The Problem That Won't Go Away.* Washington, D.C.: The Brookings Institution.
Board of Trustees [HI]
1996    *1996 Annual Report of the Board of Trustees of the Federal Hospital Insurance Trust Fund.* Health Care Financing Administration. Washington, D.C.: U.S. Department of Health and Human Services.
Board of Trustees [OASDI]
1994    *1994 Annual Report of the Board of Trustees of the Federal Old-Age and Survivors Insurance and Disability Insurance Trust Funds.* Washington, D.C.: U.S. Social Security Administration.
1996    *1996 Annual Report of the Board of Trustees of the Federal Old-Age and Survivors Insurance and Disability Insurance Trust Funds.* Washington, D.C.: U.S. Social Security Administration.
Buck Consultants, Inc.
1993    *Postretirement Nonpension Benefit Design: A Delicate Balance.* New York: Buck Consultants, Inc.
1995a   *1994: The Health of America's Pension Plans.* New York: Buck Consultants, Inc.

1995b    *Analysis of Postretirement and Postemployment Benefit Disclosures from Corporate Financial Statements.* New York: Buck Consultants, Inc.
Bureau of the Census
1996    *Poverty in the United States: 1995.* Prepared by Eleanor Baugher and Leatha Lamison-White. Current Population Reports, Consumer Income, Series P60-194. Washington, D.C.: U.S. Department of Commerce.
Bureau of Labor Statistics
1992a    The Employee Benefits Survey. Chapter 9 in *BLS Handbook of Methods.* Bulletin 2414 (September). Washington, D.C.: U.S. Department of Labor.
1992b    Employment Cost Index. Chapter 8 in *BLS Handbook of Methods.* Bulletin 2414 (September). Washington, D.C.: U.S. Department of Labor.
1994    *Employee Benefits in Medium and Large Private Establishments, 1993.* Bulletin 2456. Washington, D.C.: U.S. Department of Labor.
Burkhauser, Richard, and Joseph Quinn
1994    Changing policy signals. Pp. 237-262 in Matilda White Riley, Robert L. Kahn, and Anne Fowler, eds., *Age and Structural Lag.* New York: Wiley.
Buron, Lawrence, Robert Haveman, and Owen O'Donnell
1995    *Recent Trends in U.S. Male Work and Wage Patterns: An Overview.* Discussion Paper 1060-95. Institute for Research on Poverty. Madison: University of Wisconsin.
Burtless, Gary
1989    Labor Supply Response to Microsimulation Models. Paper prepared for the Panel to Evaluate Microsimulation Models for Social Welfare Programs, Committee on National Statistics, National Research Council. The Brookings Institution, Washington, D.C.
1993    The Uncertainty of Social Security Forecasts in Policy Analysis and Planning. Paper prepared for the Public Trustees of the Social Security and Medicare Boards of Trustees. The Brookings Institution, Washington, D.C.
1996    A framework for analyzing future retirement income security. Pp. 244-272 in Eric A. Hanushek and Nancy L. Maritato, eds., *Assessing Knowledge of Retirement Behavior.* Panel on Retirement Income Modeling, Committee on National Statistics, National Research Council. Washington, D.C.: National Academy Press.
Caldwell, Steven B.
1993    CORSIM 2.0—Model Documentation Version 5. Draft. Department of Sociology, Cornell University, Ithaca, N.Y.
Caldwell, Steven B., Rajat Gupta, Blair Habig, Sameer Kalbag, Andrew Payne, and Aaron Peromsik
1993    CORSIM 2.0—User & Technical Documentation. Draft. Department of Sociology, Cornell University, Ithaca, N.Y.
Center for Economic Studies
1995    *Center for Economic Studies. Annual Report 1994-95.* Bureau of the Census. Washington, D.C.: U.S. Department of Commerce.
Center for Human Resource Research
1995a    *NLS Handbook 1995.* Columbus: Ohio State University
1995b    *NLS Users' Guide 1995.* Columbus: Ohio State University.
Chapman, David W., Christopher L. Moriarity, and John Sommers
1996    Should Firms Be Used as Sampling Units for Selecting Establishments for the 1997 National Employer Health Insurance Survey? Paper prepared for the Joint Statistical Meetings, Chicago, Ill. Klemm Analysis Group, Washington, D.C.
Christianson, Anders, and Robert D. Tortora
1995    Issues in surveying businesses: An international survey. Pp. 237-256 in Brenda G. Cox et al., eds., *Business Survey Methods.* New York: John Wiley & Sons, Inc.

Cilke, James, Bob Gillette, C. Eric Larson, and Roy A. Wyscarver
  1994    *The Treasury Individual Income Tax Simulation Model*. Office of Tax Analysis. Washington, D.C.: U.S. Department of the Treasury.
Citro, Constance F., and Eric A. Hanushek, eds.
  1991    *Improving Information for Social Policy Decisions: The Uses of Microsimulation Modeling, Vol. 1, Review and Recommendations*. Panel to Evaluate Microsimulation Models for Social Welfare Programs, Committee on National Statistics, National Research Council. Washington, D.C.: National Academy Press.
Citro, Constance F., and Graham Kalton, eds.
  1993    *The Future of the Survey of Income and Program Participation*. Panel to Evaluate the Survey of Income and Program Participation, Committee on National Statistics, National Research Council. Washington, D.C.: National Academy Press.
Citro, Constance F., and Robert T. Michael, eds.
  1995    *Measuring Poverty: A New Approach*. Panel on Poverty and Family Assistance, Committee on National Statistics, National Research Council. Washington, D.C.: National Academy Press.
Clark, Robert L., and Ann A. McDermed
  1990    *The Choice of Pension Plans in a Changing Regulatory Environment*. Washington, D.C.: The AEI Press.
Coder, John
  1991    Exploring Nonsampling Errors in the Wage and Salary Income Data from the March Current Population Survey. Paper prepared for the Allied Social Sciences Association/Society of Government Economists meeting, Washington, D.C. Bureau of the Census, U.S. Department of Commerce, Washington, D.C.
  1992    Using administrative record information to evaluate the quality of the income data collected in the Survey of Income and Program Participation. In *Proceedings of Statistics Canada Symposium 92—Design and Analysis of Longitudinal Surveys*. Ottawa: Statistics Canada.
Coder, John, and Lydia Scoon-Rogers
  1994    Evaluating the Quality of Income Data Collected in the Annual Supplement to the March Current Population Survey and the Survey of Income and Program Participation. Bureau of the Census, U.S. Department of Commerce, Washington, D.C.
Cohen, Lee M., and Laurel E. Beedon
  1994a   Options for balancing the OASDI trust funds for the long term. *Journal of Aging & Social Policy* 6(1/2):77-93.
  1994b   Social Security Principles and the Range of PAYGO Options for Long-Term OASDI Solvency. Paper prepared for the Gerontological Society of America meetings, Atlanta, Ga. American Association of Retired Persons, Washington, D.C.
Cohen, Michael L.
  1991a   Evaluations of microsimulation models: Literature review. Pp. 237-254 in Constance F. Citro and Eric A. Hanushek, eds., *Improving Information for Social Policy Decisions: The Uses of Microsimulation Modeling, Vol. 2, Technical Papers*. Panel to Evaluate Microsimulation Models for Social Welfare Programs, Committee on National Statistics, National Research Council. Washington, D.C.: National Academy Press.
  1991b   Statistical matching and microsimulation models. Pp. 62-85 in Constance F. Citro and Eric A. Hanushek, eds., *Improving Information for Social Policy Decisions: The Uses of Microsimulation Modeling, Vol. 2, Technical Papers*. Panel to Evaluate Microsimulation Models for Social Welfare Programs, Committee on National Statistics, National Research Council. Washington, D.C.: National Academy Press.

1991c    Variation estimation of microsimulation models through sample reuse. Pp. 237-254 in
         Constance F. Citro and Eric A. Hanushek, eds., *Improving Information for Social Policy
         Decisions: The Uses of Microsimulation Modeling, Vol. 2, Technical Papers.* Panel to
         Evaluate Microsimulation Models for Social Welfare Programs, Committee on National
         Statistics, National Research Council. Washington, D.C.: National Academy Press.
Congressional Budget Office
1993     *Baby Boomers in Retirement: An Early Perspective.* Washington, D.C.: U.S. Govern-
         ment Printing Office.
Cotton, Paul and George Sadowsky
1991     Future computing environments for microsimulation modeling. Pp. 141-234 in Constance
         F. Citro and Eric A. Hanushek, eds., *Improving Information for Social Policy Decisions:
         The Uses of Microsimulation Modeling, Vol. 2, Technical Papers.* Panel to Evaluate
         Microsimulation Models for Social Welfare Programs, Committee on National Statistics,
         National Research Council. Washington, D.C.: National Academy Press.
Cox, Brenda G., David A. Binder, B. Nanjamma Chinnappa, Anders Christianson, Michael J.
         Colledge, and Phillip S. Kott
1995     *Business Survey Methods.* New York: John Wiley & Sons, Inc.
Curtin, Richard T., F. Thomas Juster, and James N. Morgan
1989     Survey estimates of wealth: An assessment of quality. Pp. 473-522 [including comments
         by Eugene Smolensky] in Robert E. Lipsey and Helen Stone Tice, eds., *The Measurement
         of Saving, Investment, and Wealth.* Chicago: University of Chicago Press.
David, Martin, Roderick J.A. Little, Michael E. Samuhel, and Robert K. Triest
1986     Alternative methods for CPS imputation. *Journal of the American Statistical Association*
         81(393):28-41.
Duncan, George T., Thomas B. Jabine, and Virginia A. de Wolf, eds.
1993     *Private Lives and Public Policies: Confidentiality and Accessibility of Government Sta-
         tistics.* Panel on Confidentiality and Data Access, Committee on National Statistics,
         National Research Council, and the Social Science Research Council. Washington, D.C.:
         National Academy Press.
Duncan, Greg J., and Martha S. Hill
1991     Panel Study of Income Dynamics: Research uses and recent innovations. *ICPSR Bulletin*
         February:1-4.
Employee Benefit Research Institute
1980a    *The Application of Modeling Techniques to Retirement Income Policy Issues.* An EBRI
         Workshop. Washington, D.C.: Employee Benefit Research Institute.
1980b    *Modeling Analysis for Retirement Income Policy: Background and Overview.* Washing-
         ton, D.C.: Employee Benefit Research Institute.
1981     *Employee Benefit Programs and Policy: Modeling Research.* Washington, D.C.: Em-
         ployee Benefit Research Institute.
1994     *Baby Boomers in Retirement: What Are Their Prospects?* EBRI Issue Brief, No. 151
         (July). Washington, D.C.: Employee Benefit Research Institute.
1995     *Are Workers Kidding Themselves? Results of the 1995 Retirement Confidence Survey.*
         EBRI Issue Brief No. 168 (December). Washington, D.C.: Employee Benefit Research
         Institute.
1996a    *Contribution Rates and Plan Features: An Analysis of Large 401(k) Plan Data.* EBRI
         Issue Brief No. 174 (June). Washington, D.C.: Employee Benefit Research Institute.
1996b    *Participant Education: Actions and Outcomes.* EBRI Issue Brief No. 169 (January).
         Washington, D.C.: Employee Benefit Research Institute.
1996c    *Worker Investment Decisions: An Analysis of Large 401(k) Plan Data.* EBRI Issue Brief
         No. 176 (August). Washington, D.C.: Employee Benefit Research Institute.

England, Robert Stowe
1994     Mixed reviews. *Plan Sponsor* September:16-22.
Fahy, Terry W., ed.
1995     *NLS—Annotated Bibliography, 1968-1995 Edition.* Center for Human Resource Research.
         Columbus: Ohio State University.
Federal Committee on Statistical Methodology
1988     *Measurement of Quality in Establishment Surveys.* Statistical Policy Working Paper No.
         15. Washington, D.C.: U.S. Office of Management and Budget.
1990     *A Comparative Study of Reporting Units in Selected Employer Data Systems.* Statistical
         Policy Working Paper No. 16. Washington, D.C.: U.S. Office of Management and
         Budget.
Freedman, Vicki A., and Beth J. Soldo, eds.
1994     *Trends in Disability at Older Ages—Summary of a Workshop.* Committee on National
         Statistics, National Research Council. Washington, D.C.: National Academy Press.
Garfinkel, Steven A.
1995     Self-insuring employee health benefits. *Medical Care Research and Review* 52(4):475-
         491.
Ghilarducci, Teresa
1996     Innovative firms and pension plans. Pp. 141-161 in Phyllis A. Fernandez, John A. Turner,
         and Richard P. Hinz., eds., *Pensions, Savings, and Capital Markets.* Pension and Welfare
         Benefit Administration. Washington, D.C.: U.S. Department of Labor.
Grossman, Jean B., and Harold W. Watts
1982     *The Structural Needs of Microsimulation Modeling of Labor Supply and Retirement Be-
         havior.* A report to the Economic Studies Program, Program for Research on Retirement
         and Aging. Washington, D.C.: The Brookings Institution.
Gustman, Alan L., and F. Thomas Juster
1996     Income and wealth of older American households:  Modeling issues for public policy
         analysis. Pp. 11-60 in Eric A. Hanushek and Nancy L. Maritato, eds., *Assessing Knowl-
         edge of Retirement Behavior.* Panel on Retirement Income Modeling, Committee on
         National Statistics, National Research Council. Washington, D.C.: National Academy
         Press.
Gustman, Alan L., and Olivia S. Mitchell
1992     Pensions and labor market activity: Behavior and data requirements. Pp. 39-114 in Zvi
         Bodie and Alicia H. Munnell, eds., *Pensions and the Economy—Sources, Uses, and Limi-
         tations of Data.* Pension Research Council, Wharton School, University of Pennsylvania.
         Philadelphia: University of Pennsylvania Press.
Gustman, Alan L., and Thomas L. Steinmeier
1991     Changing the Social Security rules for work after 65. *Industrial and Labor Relations
         Review* 44(4):733-745.
Hanushek, Eric A., and Nancy L. Maritato, eds.
1996     *Assessing Knowledge of Retirement Behavior.* Panel on Retirement Income Modeling,
         Committee on National Statistics, National Research Council. Washington, D.C.: Na-
         tional Academy Press.
Haveman, Robert H., and Jeffrey M. Lacker
1984     *Discrepancies in Projecting Future Public and Private Pension Benefits: A Comparison
         and Critique of Two Micro-Data Simulation Models.* Institute for Research on Poverty
         Special Report 36. Madison: University of Wisconsin Press.
HayGroup
1993     *1993 Hay/Huggins Benefits Report, Vol. I, Prevalence of Benefits Practices and Execu-
         tive Summary.* Washington, D.C.: HayGroup.

Hendricks, Gary, and Russell Holden
  1976    The role of microanalytic simulation models in projecting OASDI costs. In *Proceedings of the Business and Economic Statistics Section*. Washington, D.C.: American Statistical Association.

Herzog, Thomas N., and Donald B. Rubin
  1983    Using multiple imputations to handle nonresponse in sample surveys. Pp. 209-245 in William G. Madow, Ingram Olkin, and Donald B. Rubin, eds., *Incomplete Data in Sample Surveys, Vol. 2, Theory and Bibliographies*. Panel on Incomplete Data, Committee on National Statistics, National Research Council. New York: Academic Press.

Hewitt Associates
  1995    *Salaried Employee Benefits Provided by Major U.S. Employers in 1995*. New York: Hewitt Associates.

Hill, Martha S.
  1992    *The Panel Study of Income Dynamics: A User's Guide*. Part of the series, *Guides to Major Social Science Data Bases*. Newbury Park, Calif.: Sage Publications, Inc.

Hing, Esther, and Roald Euller
  1996    Comparability of 1996 National Employer Health Insurance Survey (NEHIS) estimates with other employer surveys. In *Proceedings of the Social Statistics Section*. Alexandria, Va.: American Statistical Association.

Hing, Esther, Pat McDonnell, Katherine Levit, and Gail Poe
  1995    The 1994 National Employer Health Insurance Survey (NEHIS). Paper prepared for the American Statistical Association Annual Meeting. National Center for Health Statistics, U.S. Department of Health and Human Services, Washington, D.C.

Holden, Karen
  1991    Social Security Policy and the Income Shock of Widowhood. LaFollette Institute of Public Affairs Working Paper No. 3. University of Wisconsin, Madison.

Hollenbeck, Kevin M.
  1991    Documentation for microsimulation models: TRIM2, MATH, and HITSM. Pp. 333-351 in Constance F. Citro and Eric A. Hanushek, eds., *Improving Information for Social Policy Decisions: The Uses of Microsimulation Modeling, Vol. 2, Technical Papers*. Panel to Evaluate Microsimulation Models for Social Welfare Programs, Committee on National Statistics, National Research Council. Washington, D.C.: National Academy Press.
  1995    A Review of Retirement Income Policy Models. Paper prepared for the Panel on Retirement Income Modeling, Committee on National Statistics, National Research Council. W.E. Upjohn Institute for Employment Research, Kalamazoo, Mich.

Holmer, Martin
  1993    Variance Reduction in Corporate Bankruptcy Simulation. Paper prepared for the Pension Benefit Guaranty Corporation. HR&A, Inc., Washington, D.C.
  1995a   *Demographic Results from SSASIM, A Long-Run Stochastic Simulation Model of Social Security*. HR&A Working Paper. Washington, D.C.: HR&A, Inc. Also published as Appendix A in 1994-95 Advisory Council on Social Security Technical Panel on Assumptions and Methods, *Final Report*. Population Aging Research Center Working Paper Series. Philadelphia: University of Pennsylvania.
  1995b   HR&A Response to SSA-RFP-95-2528, Volume II, Technical Proposal. HR&A, Inc., Washington, D.C.

Hunter, Edward L., and Ross Arnett, III
  1996    Survey "reinventing" at Health and Human Services. *Chance* 9(3):54-57.

Hurd, Michael, Willard Rodgers, Beth Soldo, and Robert Wallace
  1994    Asset and Health Dynamics Among the Oldest Old: An Overview of the Survey. Institute for Social Research, University of Michigan, Ann Arbor.

Iams, Howard M.
1995    A tale of two 1993 pension surveys: The SIPP and the CPS. *Social Security Bulletin* 58(4):125-130.
Iams, Howard M., and Steven H. Sandell
1996    Past is Prologue: Simulating Lifetime Social Security Earnings for the Twenty-First Century. Paper prepared for the U.S. Bureau of the Census Annual Research Conference. U.S. Social Security Administration, Washington, D.C.
Imrohoroglu, Selahattin, He Huang, and Thomas J. Sargent
1994    Transition Between Social Security Systems. Unpublished paper. School of Business, University of Southern California; Department of Economics, University of Chicago; Hoover Institution, Stanford, Calif.
Jabine, Thomas B., Karen E. King, and Rita J. Petroni
1990    *Survey of Income and Program Participation: Quality Profile.* Bureau of the Census. Washington, D.C.: U.S. Department of Commerce.
Jabine, Thomas B., Miron L. Straf, Judith M. Tanur, and Roger Tourangeau, eds.
1984    *Cognitive Aspects of Survey Methodology: Building a Bridge Between Disciplines.* Advanced Research Seminar on Cognitive Aspects of Survey Methodology, Committee on National Statistics, National Research Council. Washington, D.C.: National Academy Press.
Jack Faucett Associates
1990    *The 1988 U.S. Establishment and Enterprise Microdata (USEEM) and the 1984-1988 Weighted Linked U.S. Establishment Longitudinal Microdata (USELM)—Final Report.* Report prepared for the U.S. Small Business Administration. Washington, D.C.: U.S. Department of Commerce, National Technical Information Service.
Jacobs, Eva, and Stephanie Shipp
1990    A history of the U.S. Consumer Expenditure Survey: 1935 to 1988. In *Proceedings of the Social Statistics Section.* Alexandria, Va.: American Statistical Association.
Jacobson, Jonathan E., and John L. Czajka
1994    Using Panel Data to Simulate the Impact of Policy Changes on Women's Labor Supply and Welfare Participation. Paper prepared for the Joint Statistical Meetings, Toronto. Mathematica Policy Research, Inc., Washington, D.C.
Johnson, Jon, Richard Wertheimer, and Sheila R. Zedlewski
1983    *The Dynamic Simulation of Income Model (DYNASIM), Vol. I, The Family and Earnings History Model.* Revised. Washington, D.C.: The Urban Institute Press.
Johnson, Jon, and Sheila R. Zedlewski
1982    *The Dynamic Simulation of Income Model (DYNASIM), Vol. II, The Jobs and Benefits History Model.* Washington, D.C.: The Urban Institute Press.
Juster, F. Thomas, and Kathleen A. Kuester
1991    Differences in the measurement of wealth, wealth inequality and wealth composition obtained from alternative U.S. wealth surveys. *The Review of Income and Wealth* 37(1):33-62.
Juster, F. Thomas, and Richard Suzman
1995    An overview of the Health and Retirement Study. *The Journal of Human Resources* 30(Supplement 1995):S7-S56.
Kalleberg, Arne L., ed.
1986    *America at Work: National Surveys of Employees and Employers.* Report to the U.S. Department of Labor. Advisory Group on a 1986 Quality of Employment Survey. New York: Social Science Research Council.
Karoly, Lynn A., and Jeannette A. Rogowski
1994    The effect of health insurance on the decision to retire. *Industrial and Labor Relations Review* 48(1):103-123.

Kennell, David, and John F. Sheils
  1986    The ICF Pension and Retirement Income Simulation Model (PRISM) With the ICF/
          Brookings Long-Term Care Financing Model. Draft Technical Documentation. ICF
          Incorporated, Washington, D.C.
  1990    PRISM: Dynamic simulation of pension and retirement income. Pp. 137-172 in Gordon
          H. Lewis and Richard C. Michel, eds., *Microsimulation Techniques for Tax and Transfer
          Analysis*. Washington, D.C.: The Urban Institute Press.
Kennickell, Arthur B.
  1996    Using Range Techniques with CAPI in the 1995 Survey of Consumer Finances. Paper
          prepared for the Joint Statistical Meetings, Chicago, Ill. Federal Reserve Board, Wash-
          ington, D.C.
Kennickell, Arthur B., and Douglas A. McManus
  1994    Multiple imputation of the 1983 and 1989 waves of the SCF. In *1994 Proceedings of the
          Section on Survey Research Methods*. Alexandria, Va.: American Statistical Associa-
          tion.
Kennickell, Arthur B., and Janice Shack-Marquez
  1992    Changes in family finances from 1983 to 1989: Evidence from the Survey of Consumer
          Finances. *Federal Reserve Bulletin* (January):1-18.
Kennickell, Arthur B., and Martha Starr-McCluer
  1994    Changes in family finances from 1989 to 1992: Evidence from the Survey of Consumer
          Finances. *Federal Reserve Bulletin* (October):861-882.
  1995    Retrospective Reporting of Household Wealth: Evidence from the 1983-89 Survey of
          Consumer Finances. Federal Reserve Board, Washington, D.C.
Kotlikoff, Laurence J.
  1988    The relationship of productivity to age [including discussion by Edward P. Lazear]. Pp.
          100-131 in Rita Ricardo-Campbell and Edward P. Lazear, eds., *Issues in Contemporary
          Retirement*. Stanford, Calif.: Hoover Institute Press.
Kotlikoff, Laurence J., and Jagadeesh Gokhale
  1992    Estimating a firm's age-productivity profile using the present value of workers' earnings.
          *The Quarterly Journal of Economics* November:1215-1242.
KPMG Peat Marwick
  1995    *Retirement Benefits in the 1990s: 1995 Survey Data*. Washington, D.C.: KPMG Peat
          Marwick.
Kruse, Douglas L.
  1991    *Pension Substitution in the 1980s: Why the Shift Toward Defined Contribution Pension
          Plans?* NBER Working Paper No. 3882. Cambridge, Mass.: National Bureau of Eco-
          nomic Research.
  1993    *Profit Sharing: Does It Make a Difference?* Kalamazoo, Mich.: W.E. Upjohn Institute
          for Employment Research.
Lahiri, Kajal, Denton R. Vaughan, and Bernard Wixon
  1995    Modeling SSA's sequential disability determination process using matched SIPP data.
          *Social Security Bulletin* 56(4):3-42.
Lazear, Edward P.
  1988    Discussion [of Kotlikoff]. Pp. 126-129 in Rita Ricardo-Campbell and Edward P. Lazear,
          eds., *Issues in Contemporary Retirement*. Stanford, Calif.: Hoover Institute Press.
Lee, Ronald D.
  1993    Modeling and forecasting the time series of U.S. fertility: Age distribution, range and
          ultimate level. *International Journal of Forecasting* 9(2):187-202.
Lee, Ronald D., and Lawrence Carter
  1992    Modeling and forecasting the time series of U.S. mortality. *Journal of the American
          Statistical Association* 87(419):659-671.

Lee, Ronald D., and Jonathan Skinner
  1996    Assessing forecasts of mortality, health status, and health costs during baby-boomers'
          retirement. Pp. 195-243 in Eric A. Hanushek and Nancy L. Maritato, eds., *Assessing
          Knowledge of Retirement Behavior.* Panel on Retirement Income Modeling, Committee
          on National Statistics, National Research Council. Washington, D.C.: National Acad-
          emy Press.
Lee, Ronald., and Shripad Tuljapurkar
  1994    Stochastic population forecasts for the U.S.: Beyond high, medium, and low. *Journal of
          the American Statistical Association* 89(428):1175-1189.
Lewin-VHI
  1994    Labor Market Conditions, Socioeconomic Factors and the Growth of Applications and
          Awards for SSDI and SSI Disability Benefits: Background and Preliminary Findings.
          Prepared for U.S. Department of Health and Human Services. Lewin-VHI, Fairfax, Va.
Lindeman, David C., and Kathleen P. Utgoff
  1992    Pension taxes and the U.S. budget. Pp. 181-200 in Zvi Bodie and Alicia H. Munnell, eds.,
          *Pensions and the Economy—Sources, Uses, and Limitations of Data.* Pension Research
          Council, Wharton School, University of Pennsylvania. Philadelphia: University of Penn-
          sylvania Press.
LOGISIL
  1994    Canada Pension Plan Policy Model—Overview. Paper prepared for the Project Review
          Committee, Office of the Superintendent of Financial Institutions and Human Resources
          Development Canada, Ottawa.
Lohse, Deborah
  1993    Your money matters: Early retirees get healthy dose of reality. *Wall Street Journal*
          October 25:C1.
Lumsdaine, Robin L.
  1996    Factors affecting labor supply decisions and retirement income. Pp. 61-122 in Eric A.
          Hanushek and Nancy L. Maritato, eds., *Assessing Knowledge of Retirement Behavior.*
          Panel on Retirement Income Modeling, Committee on National Statistics, National Re-
          search Council. Washington, D.C.: National Academy Press.
Lumsdaine, Robin L., J.H. Stock, and David A. Wise
  1990    Efficient windows and labor force reduction. *Journal of Public Economics* 43:131-159.
Lumsdaine, Robin L., and David A. Wise
  1994    Aging and labor force participation: A review of trends and explanations. In David A.
          Wise, ed., *Aging in the United States and Japan: Economic Trends.* Chicago: University
          of Chicago Press.
MacDonald, Kathleen M.
  1995    Notes from the Conference of Members of the Academic Community on the BLS Em-
          ployment Cost Index and Employee Benefits Survey (September 16, 1994). Bureau of
          Labor Statistics, U.S. Department of Labor, Washington, D.C.
Mann, Thomas E., and Norman J. Ornstein, eds.
  1995    *Intensive Care—How Congress Shapes Health Policy.* Washington, D.C.: American
          Enterprise Institute and The Brookings Institution.
Manton, Kenneth G., Larry S. Corder, and Eric Stallard
  1993    Estimates of change in chronic disability and institutional incidence and prevalence rates
          in the U.S. elderly population from the 1982, 1984, and 1989 National Long Term Care
          Survey. *Journal of Gerontology: Social Sciences* 48:S153-S166.
Manton, Kenneth G., Eric Stallard, and Korbin Liu
  1993    Frailty and forecasts of active life expectancy in the United States. In K.G. Manton, B.H.
          Singer, and R.M. Suzman, eds., *Forecasting the Health of Elderly Populations.* New
          York: Springer-Verlag.

McLanahan, Sarah, and Lynne Casper
1995    Growing diversity and inequality in the American family. Pp. 1-46 in Reynolds Farley, ed., *State of the Union: America in the 1990's, Vol. 2, Social Trends*. New York: Russell Sage Foundation.

McNally, James, and Douglas A. Wolf
1996    Family Structure and Institutionalization: Results from Merged Microdata. Papers in Microsimulation Series No. 2. Center for Policy Research, Syracuse University.

Medoff, James L., and Katharine G. Abraham
1981    Are those paid more really more productive? The case of experience. *The Journal of Human Resources* 16(2):186-216.

Mitchell, Olivia S.
1988    Worker knowledge of pension provisions. *Journal of Labor Economics* 6(1):21-39.
1991    Evaluation of Pension Plan Survey Information. Memorandum to Terry Hoopes, Pension and Welfare Benefits Administration, U.S. Department of Labor, June 11. Department of Labor Economics, Cornell University, Ithaca, NY.

Mitchell, Olivia S., and Rebecca A. Luzadis
1988    Changes in pension incentives through time. *Industrial and Labor Relations Review* 41(1):100-108.

Mitchell, Olivia S., Thomas L. Steinmeier, and Jan Olson
1996    Construction of the Earnings and Benefits File (EBF) for Use with the Health and Retirement Survey. Working Paper. Wharton School, University of Pennsylvania, Philadelphia.

Mitchell, Olivia S., and Steven Zeldes
1996    A framework for analyzing Social Security privatization. *American Economic Review* 86(2):363-367.

Moon, Marilyn
1995    Projecting Health Care Costs for Older Americans. Paper prepared for the Panel on Retirement Income Modeling, Committee on National Statistics, National Research Council. Urban Institute, Washington, D.C.

National Center for Health Statistics
1992    *The Longitudinal Study of Aging: 1984-90*. Vital and Health Statistics Monographs, Programs and Collection Procedures, Series 1, No. 28. PHS 92-1304. Washington, D.C.: U.S. Department of Health and Human Services.

Nichols, Len
1996    Discussion [of Bilheimer and Reischauer]. Pp. 169 in Henry J. Aaron, ed., *The Problem that Won't Go Away*. Washington, D.C.: The Brookings Institution.

Office of Pension and Welfare Benefit Programs
1985    *Findings from the Survey of Private Pension Benefit Amounts*. Washington, D.C.: U.S. Department of Labor.

Office of Technology Assessment
1993    *An Inconsistent Picture: A Compilation of Analyses of Economic Impacts of Competing Approaches to Health Care Reform by Experts and Stakeholders*. OTA-H-540. Washington, D.C.: U.S. Government Printing Office.
1994    *Understanding Estimates of National Health Expenditures Under Health Reform*. OTA-H-594. Washington, D.C.: U.S. Government Printing Office.

Panis, Constantijn W.A., and Lee A. Lillard
1996    *Socioeconomic Differentials in the Returns to Social Security*. Labor and Population Program, Working Paper Series, No. 96-05. Santa Monica, Calif.: RAND.

Papke, Leslie E.
1995    Participation in and contributions to 401(k) pension plans: Evidence from plan data. *Journal of Human Resources* (Spring):311-325.

Parsons, Donald O.
   1996   Retirement age and retirement income: The role of the firm. Pp. 149-194 in Eric A.
          Hanushek and Nancy L. Maritato, eds., *Assessing Knowledge of Retirement Behavior*.
          Panel on Retirement Income Modeling, Committee on National Statistics, National Re-
          search Council. Washington, D.C.: National Academy Press.
Paxson, M. Chris, Don A. Dillman, and John Tarnai
   1995   Improving response to business mail surveys. Pp. 303-316 in Brenda G. Cox et al., eds.,
          *Business Survey Methods*. New York: John Wiley & Sons, Inc.
Pension and Welfare Benefits Administration
   1994   *Pension and Health Benefits of American Workers: New Findings from the April 1993
          Current Population Survey*. With the Social Security Administration, U.S. Small Busi-
          ness Administration, and Pension Benefit Guaranty Corporation. Washington, D.C.: U.S.
          Department of Labor.
   1995a  *Abstract of 1991 Form 5500 Annual Reports*. Number 4, Winter 1995. Washington,
          D.C.: U.S. Department of Labor.
   1995b  *Retirement Benefits of American Workers: New Findings from the September 1994 Cur-
          rent Population Survey*. Washington, D.C.: U.S. Department of Labor.
Peracchi, Franco, and Finis Welch
   1994   Trends in labor-force transitions of older men and women. *Journal of Labor Economics*
          12(2):210-242.
Polivka, Anne E., and Stephen M. Miller
   1995   The CPS After the Redesign: Refocusing the Economic Lens. Bureau of Labor Statis-
          tics, Washington, D.C.
Ponikowski, Chester H., Paul Scheible, and William Wiatrowski
   1994   The Survey of 1992 Health Expenditures: A Quick Response Survey. Paper prepared for
          the American Statistical Association Annual Meeting. Bureau of Labor Statistics, Wash-
          ington, D.C.
Poterba, James M.
   1996   Personal saving behavior and retirement income modeling: A research assessment. Pp.
          123-148 in Eric A. Hanushek and Nancy L. Maritato, eds., *Assessing Knowledge of Re-
          tirement Behavior*. Panel on Retirement Income Modeling, Committee on National Sta-
          tistics, National Research Council. Washington, D.C.: National Academy Press.
Preston, Samuel H., and Irma T. Elo
   1995   Are educational differentials in mortality increasing in the United States? *Journal of
          Aging and Health* 7(4):476-496.
Quinn, Joseph F., and Olivia S. Mitchell
   1996   Social Security on the table. *The American Prospect* 26(May-June):76-81.
Ransom, Roger L., Richard Sutch, and Gordon S. Streib
   1988   The decline of retirement in the years before Social Security: U.S. retirement patterns. In
          R. Ricardo Campbell and E. Lazear, eds., *Issues in Contemporary Retirement*. Stanford,
          Calif.: Hoover Institution.
Reimers, Cordelia, and Marjorie Honig
   1993   Responses to Social Security by Men and Women: Myopic and Far-Sighted Behavior.
          Paper prepared for the Association of Public Policy Analysis and Management meeting.
          Department of Economics, Hunter College.
Reno, Virginia P.
   1993   The role of pensions in retirement income. Pp. 19-32 in *Pensions in a Changing Economy*.
          Washington, D.C.: Employee Benefit Research Institute.
Rivlin, Alice M., and Joshua M. Wiener, with Raymond J. Hanley and Denise A. Spence
   1988   *Caring for the Disabled Elderly: Who Will Pay?* Washington, D.C.: The Brookings
          Institution.

Ross, Christine J.
  1991    DYNASIM2 and PRISM: Examples of dynamic modeling. Pp. 121-140 in Constance F.
          Citro and Eric A. Hanushek, eds., *Improving Information for Social Policy Decisions:
          The Uses of Microsimulation Modeling, Vol. 2, Technical Papers.* Panel to Evaluate
          Microsimulation Models for Social Welfare Programs, Committee on National Statistics,
          National Research Council. Washington, D.C.: National Academy Press.
Rust, John
  1993    Evaluation of the HRS and RHS from a Decision-Theoretic Perspective. Paper prepared
          for the Health and Retirement Survey Early Results Workshop, Survey Research Center,
          University of Michigan, Ann Arbor. Department of Economics, University of Wisconsin,
          Madison.
Rust, John, and Christopher Phelan
  1993    How Social Security and Medicare Affect Retirement in a World of Incomplete Markets.
          Unpublished paper. Department of Economics, University of Wisconsin, Madison.
Samwick, Andrew A., and Jonathan Skinner
  1993    How Will Defined Contribution Pension Plans Affect Retirement Income? Paper pre-
          pared for the Association of Private Pension and Welfare Plans and Center for Economic
          Policy Research, Stanford University, Conference on Public Policy Toward Pensions.
          National Bureau of Economic Research, and University of Virginia, Charlottesville.
Sandell, Steven H., and Howard M. Iams
  1996    Women's Future Social Security Benefits: Why Widows Will Still Be Poor. Paper
          prepared for the Population Association of America Annual Meeting. U.S. Social Secu-
          rity Administration, Washington, D.C.
Schieber, Sylvester J.
  1995    Why Are Pension Benefits So Small? Draft paper. Research and Information Center,
          The Wyatt Company, Washington, D.C.
Schieber, Sylvester J., and John B. Shoven
  1993    The Consequences of Population Aging on Private Pension Fund Saving and Asset Mar-
          kets. Paper prepared for the ACCF-CEPR Conference on Public Policy Toward Pen-
          sions. The Wyatt Company, Washington, D.C., and School of Humanities and Sciences,
          Stanford University.
Scott, Frank A., Mark C. Berger, and John E. Garen
  1995    Do health insurance and pension costs reduce the job opportunities of older workers?
          *Industrial and Labor Relations Review* 48(4):775-791.
Sheils, Jon
  1996    Discussion [of Bilheimer and Reischauer]. Pp. 165-169 in Henry J. Aaron, ed., *The
          Problem that Won't Go Away.* Washington, D.C.: The Brookings Institution.
Silverman, Celia
  1993    *Pension Evolution in a Changing Economy.* EBRI Special Report SR-17/Issue Brief No.
          141 (September). Washington, D.C.: Employee Benefit Research Institute.
Smith, James P.
  1988    *Recommendations to the NIA Extramural Program on Priorities for Data Collection in
          Health and Retirement Economics.* Report of the Ad Hoc Advisory Panel to the Behav-
          ioral and Social Research Program, National Institute on Aging. Washington, D.C.: U.S.
          Department of Health and Human Services.
  1993    *Racial and Ethnic Differences in Wealth Using the HRS.* Health and Retirement Study
          Working Paper Series, No. 94-022. Institute for Social Research. Ann Arbor: University
          of Michigan.
Sommers, John, David Chapman, and Christopher Moriarity
  1996    Sampling issues for the 1997 MEPS-IC. Paper prepared for the Joint Statistical Meeting,
          Chicago. Agency for Health Care Policy and Research, U.S. Department of Health and
          Human Services, Washington, D.C.

Statistics Canada
1995    Workplace and Employee Survey—An Integrated Approach to the Collection and Analysis of Data on Establishments and Their Employees. Business and Labour Market Analysis Division and Labour Division, Statistics Canada, Ottawa.

Sweet, James, and Larry Bumpass
1996    A National Survey of Family and Households. Background material prepared for the Workshop on Priorities for Data on the Aging Population, Committee on National Statistics and Committee on Population, National Research Council, Washington, D.C., March 4-5. University of Wisconsin, Madison.

Sze, Michael
1995    Stochastic simulation of the financial status of the Social Security trust funds in the next 75 years. Appendix B in 1994-95 Advisory Council on Social Security Technical Panel on Assumptions and Methods, *Final Report*. Population Aging Research Center Working Paper Series. Philadelphia: University of Pennsylvania.

Taylor, Amy K., and Jessica S. Banthin
1994    *Out-of-Pocket Expenditures for Personal Health Care Services: Changes in 1977 and 1987*. National Medical Expenditure Survey Research Findings 21, AHCPR Publication No. 94-0065. Agency for Health Care Policy and Research. Washington, D.C.: U.S. Department of Health and Human Services.

Troske, Kenneth R.
1995    *The Worker-Establishment Characteristics Database*. Discussion Paper. Center for Economic Studies, Bureau of the Census. Washington, D.C.: U.S. Department of Commerce.

U.S. General Accounting Office
1986    *Retirement Forecasting—Evaluation of Models Shows Need for Information on Forecast Accuracy*. Two volumes. Washington, D.C.: U.S. Government Printing Office.
1996a   *Public Pensions—State and Local Government Contributions to Underfunded Plans*. GAO/HEHS-96-56. Washington, D.C.: U.S. Government Printing Office.
1996b   *Social Security—Issues Involving Benefit Equity for Working Women*. GAO/HEHS-96-55. Washington, D.C.: U.S. Government Printing Office.

U.S. House of Representatives
1994    *Overview of Entitlement Programs: 1994 Green Book*. Background material and data on programs within the jurisdiction of the Committee on Ways and Means. Washington, D.C.: U.S. Government Printing Office.

U.S. Social Security Administration
1993    New Beneficiary Data System, Notes 1-5. *Social Security Bulletin* Fall.
1994    New Beneficiary Data System, Notes 6-11. *Social Security Bulletin* Spring.
no date SSA's Retirement History Study, Vol. 1, Compilation of Reports, and Vol. 2, Technical Description. Washington, D.C.: U.S. Department of Health and Human Services.

U.S. Treasury Department
1991    *Report to Congress on the Effect of the Full Funding Limit on Pension Benefit Security*. Washington, D.C.: U.S. Treasury Department.

Waidmann, Timothy, John Bound, and Michael Schoenbaum
1995    *The Illusion of Failure: Trends in the Self-Reported Health of the U.S. Elderly*. Population Studies Center Research Paper, No. 95-324. Ann Arbor: University of Michigan.

Wertheimer, Richard, II, Sheila R. Zedlewski, Joseph Anderson, and Kristen Moore
1986    DYNASIM in comparison with other microsimulation models. Pp. 187-206 in G.H. Orcutt, J. Merz, and H. Quinke, eds., *Microanalytic Simulation Models to Support Social and Financial Policy*. Amsterdam, Netherlands: Elsevier Science Publishers.

Wolf, Douglas A.
  1994    The elderly and their kin: Patterns of availability and access. Pp. 146-194 in Samuel H.
          Preston and Linda G. Martin, eds., *Demography of Aging*. Committee on Population,
          National Research Council. Washington, D.C.: National Academy Press.
Wolf, Douglas A., Jan Ondrich, Kenneth G. Manton, Eric Stallard, Max A. Woodbury, and Larry
          Corder
  1995    A Model for Simulating the Life Histories of the Elderly: Model Design and Implemen-
          tation Plans. Draft working paper. Center for Policy Research, Syracuse University.
The World Bank
  1994    *Averting the Old Age Crisis—Policies to Protect the Old and Promote Growth*. New
          York: Oxford University Press.
Zarkin, Gary A., Steven A. Garfinkel, Francis J. Potter, and Jennifer J. McNeill
  1995    Employment-based health insurance: Implications of the sampling unit for policy analy-
          sis. *Inquiry* 32(Fall):310-319.
Zedlewski, Sheila R.
  1990    The development of the Dynamic Simulation of Income Model (DYNASIM). Pp. 109-
          136 in Gordon H. Lewis and Richard C. Michel, eds., *Microsimulation Techniques for
          Tax and Transfer Analysis*. Washington, D.C.: The Urban Institute Press.

# Biographical Sketches of Panel Members and Staff

ERIC A. HANUSHEK *(Chair)* is professor of economics and public policy and director of the W. Allen Wallis Institute of Political Economy at the University of Rochester. He was formerly deputy director of the Congressional Budget Office and is a past president of the Association for Public Policy Analysis and Management. A member of the Committee on National Statistics, he previously held academic appointments at Yale University and the U.S. Air Force Academy and governmental appointments at the Cost of Living Council and the Council of Economic Advisers. His research has involved applied public finance and public policy analysis with special reference to schooling and aspects of income determination. He received a Ph.D. degree in economics from the Massachusetts Institute of Technology.

HENRY J. AARON is a senior fellow at The Brookings Institution. He previously was assistant secretary for planning and evaluation at the U.S. Department of Health and Human Services, as well as a professor at the University of Maryland. A former member of the Commission on Behavioral and Social Sciences and Education, he served on the Panel on Quality Control of Family Assistance Programs of the Committee on National Statistics. His research involves tax policy, health economics, and retirement policy. He received a Ph.D. in economics from Harvard University.

ALAN J. AUERBACH is Robert D. Burch professor of economics and law at the University of California, Berkeley. He previously taught at the University of Pennsylvania, where he was chair of the Economics Department. In 1992 he served as deputy chief of staff of the U.S. Joint Committee on Taxation. His research has addressed fiscal theory and policy, business finance and investment, the effects of tax provisions on firm behavior, and the impact of changing demographics on fiscal balance. He is a fellow of the Econometric Society and co-editor of the *Journal of Economic Perspectives*. He received a B.A. degree from Yale University and a Ph.D. degree from Harvard University.

CHRISTOPHER BONE is chief actuary at Actuarial Sciences Associates. He currently serves as chair of the Society of Actuaries' Committee on Retirement Systems Research and the ERISA Industry Committee (ERIC) Task Force on Fully Funded Plans. He previously was a member of the board of directors for the Association of Private Pension and Welfare Benefit Plans. He received a B.A. in mathematics from Michigan State University.

CONSTANCE F. CITRO *(Study Director)* is a member of the staff of the Committee on National Statistics. She is a former vice president and deputy director of Mathematica Policy Research, Inc., and was an American Statistical Association/National Science Foundation (NSF) research fellow at the Bureau of the Census. For the Committee on National Statistics, she has served as study director for the Panel on Poverty and Family Assistance, the Panel to Evaluate the Survey of Income and Program Participation, the Panel to Evaluate Microsimulation Models for Social Welfare Programs, and the Panel on Decennial Census Methodology. Her research has focused on the usefulness and accessibility of large, complex microdata files, as well as analysis related to income measurement and demographic change. She is a fellow of the American Statistical Association. She received a B.A. degree from the University of Rochester and M.A. and Ph.D. degrees in political science from Yale University.

PETER DIAMOND is the Paul A. Samuelson professor of economics at the Massachusetts Institute of Technology, where he has taught since 1966. He is currently serving as president of the National Academy of Social Insurance, and he has been president of the Econometric Society and vice president of the American Economic Association. He is a fellow of the American Academy of Arts and Sciences, a member of the National Academy of Sciences, and a founding member of the National Academy of Social Insurance. He was the recipient of the 1980 Mahalanobis Memorial Award and the 1994 Nemmers Prize. He has written on public finance, social insurance, uncertainty and search theories, and macroeconomics. He received a B.A. degree in mathematics from Yale University and a Ph.D. degree in economics from the Massachusetts Institute of Technology.

CANDICE S. EVANS is a project assistant with the Committee on National Statistics. In addition to her work for this panel, she works with the Panel on

Statistical Methods for Testing and Evaluating Defense Systems and the Panel on Integrated Environmental and Economic Accounting. Previously she helped steer the report of the Panel on International Capital Transactions, *Following the Money: U.S. Finance in the World Economy*, through the review process to final publication. She is continuing work toward a B.A. degree in political science at the University of Maryland.

MICHAEL D. HURD is professor of economics at the State University of New York at Stony Brook and a research associate at the National Bureau of Economic Research. He is a member of the National Academy of Social Insurance, the Steering Committee for the Health and Retirement Study, and he was a member of the Technical Panel for the Social Security Advisory Council in 1990-1991. His research involves income and wealth of the elderly and pension and retirement economics. He received a Ph.D. degree in economics from the University of California at Berkeley.

NANCY L. MARITATO has been a staff member of the Committee on National Statistics and the Committee on Population. She has also worked as an economist in the Office of the Assistant Secretary for Planning and Evaluation at the U.S. Department of Health and Human Services, at the Institute for Research on Poverty at the University of Wisconsin, and with the President's Council of Economic Advisers. Her interests focus on poverty and welfare policy analysis. She received B.A. and M.A. degrees in economics from the University of Wisconsin, where she is currently working on a Ph.D. degree in economics.

OLIVIA S. MITCHELL is the International Foundation of Employee Benefit Plans professor of insurance and risk management at the Wharton School at the University of Pennsylvania. She was previously a professor of labor economics at Cornell University. Her research focuses on the economics of private and public insurance, particularly employee benefits, pensions, and Social Security. She is a member of the National Bureau of Economic Research and the National Academy of Social Insurance and sits on the editorial boards of the *Industrial and Labor Relations Review* and the *Journal of Risk and Insurance*. She has consulted for several agencies on pension and retirement issues including the U.S. Department of Labor, the U.S. Department of Health and Human Services, the U.S. General Accounting Office, the U.S. Agency for International Development, the World Bank, and the International Monetary Fund. She received a B.S. degree from Harvard University and M.S. and Ph.D. degrees from the University of Wisconsin, all in economics.

SAMUEL H. PRESTON is Frederick J. Warren professor of demography and member of the Population Studies Center at the University of Pennsylvania. He is a member of the National Academy of Sciences and a member (and former chair) of the Committee on Population in the Commission on Behavioral and Social Sciences and Education. His research has been in mathematical demography, mortality, and family demography. He received a Ph.D. degree in economics from Princeton University.

JOHN P. RUST is professor of economics at Yale University. He was previously a professor of economics at the University of Wisconsin, Madison. His work focuses on methodology, and he has conducted econometric and time-series analyses of the decisions that determine labor force participation and income during retirement. He received a Ph.D. degree from the Massachusetts Institute of Technology.

TIMOTHY M. SMEEDING is professor of economics and public administration and the director of the Center for Policy Research at Syracuse University. He was a fellow at the Center for Advanced Studies in the Behavioral Sciences in 1994-1995. He also serves as project director for the Luxembourg Income Study, a multinational effort to build comparable databases for comparative analysis of income distribution, poverty, and other socioeconomic variables across countries. His research is in the areas of the economics of public policy, the economics of aging, and comparative international social policy. He received a Ph.D. degree in economics from the University of Wisconsin.

JAMES P. SMITH is director of the Labor and Population Studies Program at RAND Corporation in Santa Monica, California. He served as a member of the National Research Council's Committee on Research on the Urban Underclass and is currently a member of the Committee on Population, for which he chairs the Panel on the Demographic and Economic Impact of Immigration. His research has addressed labor market behavior of minorities and labor economics generally. He received a Ph.D. degree in economics from the University of Chicago.

# Index

## A

Academic centers, 170-172
Administrative costs, 34
Administrative records
  aggregate comparisons of surveys with, 128
  employer data, 123-124
  household survey reports compared with, 129-130
  individual data, 121-123
  linkage with other data collections, 6
  microlevel comparisons of surveys with, 128-129
  nonsampling errors in, 125
  recommendations for, 6, 124
  role of, 120-121
  trade-offs in data collection, 69-70
Age of retirement
  application for pension benefits, 49
  determinants, 50
  implications for retirement income security, 24
  mandatory, 43
  predictive modeling, 50
  Social Security system provisions, 26
  trends, 24
Agency for Health Care Policy and Research, 62

AHEAD. *See* Asset and Health Dynamics Among the Oldest Old
Analytical models
  consumption-saving motivations, 46
  data collection for, 70
  labor-leisure choices, 51
  need for, 41, 57
  research needs, 51
  role of, 15, 132
Asset and Health Dynamics Among the Oldest Old (AHEAD), 5, 7, 168
  contributions of, 48, 54, 88, 170-171
  cross-survey reviews, 95
  databases, 88-89
  design and management of, 170-171
  on expenditures, 94
  family asset surveys, 93
  future prospects, 91-92, 180-181
  goals, 48, 57, 88, 180
  incorporating employer survey in, 116-119
  linkage with administrative data, 5, 122-123
  matched SSA files, 122-123
  medical cost data, 57
  opportunities for validation studies, 130
  participants, 88, 180
  recommendations for, 5, 96, 120
  time horizons, 151-152

SSA models, 161-164
SSA validation techniques, 156-159
types of, 15, 133-135
uncertainty effects, 8, 38, 154-155
validation of databases for, 124, 153
Public Pension Coordinating Council, 103,
    111
Public policy
    cost-benefit analysis, 15-16
    current concerns, 1-2, 12-14
    current government agency
        responsibility, 12, 165-166
    data and research needs, 57-60, 61-62
    identifying uncertainty measures for, 8,
        38, 155
    near-term modeling strategies for, 159-160
    near-term options, 25-26
    options for health care, 30-31
    options for influencing personal savings,
        29-30
    options for pension plans, 27-29
    options for Social Security, 26-27
    outcome evaluation for, 31-34
    pension regulation issues, 13
    personal saving issues, 13, 23
    policy question formulation, 159
    program interactions, 34-35
    research needs, 3-4, 11
    Social Security system issues, 13-14
    structural models for, 51
    tools for, 2

## R

Reduced-form models, 50
Regulatory environment
    pension funds, 13
    retirement security issues, 12
Research
    current organizational structure for, 165-
        166
    need for, 3-4, 41
    priorities, 57-60
    role of, 2
Retirement Health Survey, 185
Retirement History Survey, 49, 72, 79, 81,
    84, 86, 87, 145, 185
Retirement income
    assessment of security of, 11-12
    current government policymaking
        structure, 12

current policy concerns, 1-2, 10, 12-14
current status, 17-19
determinants of security, 39
future challenges, 17, 19-20, 25
implications of health care cost trends,
    23-24
near-term policy options, 25-26
obstacles to modeling, 3
outcome criteria for policy evaluation,
    31-34
panel surveys, 72-89
personal savings for, 23
policy areas affecting, 12
sources of, 12
threats to, 12
trends, 17

## S

Savings behavior
    bequest motives, 46
    criteria for policy evaluation, 32, 33
    current practice, 23
    decision-making models, 46
    investment vehicles, 46
    life-cycle model, 46
    microsimulation modeling, 146-147
    near-term policy options, 29-30
    panel survey data, 72, 92, 93, 94
    policy issues, 23
    precautionary motives, 46
    projection modeling, 49
    proposals to stimulate, 26
    rate of return issues, 47-48
    research needs, 4, 46-47, 48, 58-59
    significance of, for policymaking, 26
    tax incentives, 13
    trends, 47
Schieber and Shoven Model, 196
Sensitivity analysis, 154-155, 156, 159, 164
Small businesses
    incentives for pension plan development,
        26
    obstacles to pension plan development in,
        42-43
    pension regulation, 13
Social Security Administration (SSA), 2, 10,
    152
    actuarial projections, 196-197
    administrative records, 121-123, 163
    model validation in, 156-159